THE WAY
MICROSOFT®
WORD
FOR
WINDOWS® 95
WORKS

WYSIWYG GUIDE

What You See Is   What You Get

THE WAY
MICROSOFT®
WORD
FOR
WINDOWS® 95
WORKS

Peter Gloster

***Microsoft* Press**

DK DIRECT

Series Editor: Robert Dinwiddie; **Series Art Editor:** Virginia Walter
Project Editors: John Watson, Maxine Lewis; **Editor:** Edda Bohnsack
Art Editors: Nigel Coath, Jenny Hobson
Designers: Stephen Cummiskey, Trond Wilhelmsen, Poppy Jenkins
Production Manager: Ian Paton
Editorial Director: Jonathan Reed; **Design Director:** Ed Day

MICROSOFT PRESS

Acquisitions Editor: Lucinda Rowley
Project Editor: Katherine A. Krause; **Technical Reviewer:** Marc Young

THE AUTHOR

Peter Gloster is the Deputy Editor of PC User magazine
in the UK and makes extensive use of Word for Windows 95. Previously,
he has edited a variety of computer and electronics publications.

ADDITIONAL CONTRIBUTORS

Illustrators: Anthony Bellue, Nigel Coath, Peter Serjeant, Andrew Green, Janos Marffy, Coral Mula
Airbrushing: Janos Marffy, Roy Flooks; **Model Making:** Sean Edwards; **Photography:** Tony Buckley, Andy Crawford, Mark Hill
Computer Support: Bijan Azari, Sam Segar, Andrew Shorrock; **Typing Assistance:** Margaret Little

Library of Congress Cataloging-in-Publication Data

Gloster, Peter.
    The way Microsoft Word for Windows 95 works / Peter Gloster.
       p.   cm.
    Includes index.
    ISBN 1-55615-820-3
    1. Microsoft Word for Windows. 2. Word processing. I. Title.
Z52.5.M523G54   1995
652.5 ' 5369—dc20   95-34355
                                             CIP

Color Reproduction by Mullis Morgan and Triffik Technology, UK

Flexibook

Printed and Bound in the USA

123456789 QEQE 98765

CONTENTS

INTRODUCTION

CHAPTER ONE

Getting Started

Welcome to Microsoft Word for Windows 95! In this introductory chapter you'll get to know the program and learn how to use it. You'll work with the mouse and learn about the Word application window with its toolbars, menus, dialog boxes, and other features. Then you'll take the plunge and create your first Word document — a simple letter.

CHAPTER TWO

Up & Running

Master the basic techniques for handling documents and text, and organizing your files efficiently.

CHAPTER THREE

Looking Good

Learn how to enhance the look of your documents by applying formatting and adding graphics, tables, and charts.

CHAPTER FOUR

Perfect Printing

Discover different printing techniques and find out how to use the printing options that are available in Word for Windows 95. Make use of the Print Preview Window, which shows you how your document will appear on the printed page. Learn how to use Word's Mail Merge feature to print personalized form letters.

CHAPTER FIVE

Timesavers

Practice using Word's timesaving features, such as templates, and macros, that can help you speed up the tasks you frequently have to perform. Learn how Word can work for you through its automatic features. Discover how to optimize Word's tools to suit your personal working style.

REFERENCE

Reference Section

About This Book

Welcome to *The Way Microsoft Word for Windows 95 Works*, an easy-to-follow guide containing all the basic information you'll need to create a variety of documents using Microsoft Word — and plenty more too!

This book is designed to make your introduction to Word as smooth as possible. It shows you how to use the most important features of Word and provides practical advice about many day-to-day word processing tasks. Throughout the book, you'll find step-by-step instructions for all the tasks you are asked to do; and you'll also find shortcuts, examples, and tips to make life even easier.

BUILDING YOUR CONFIDENCE

This book is organized so that you begin with the easiest tasks and move on to more advanced topics later. First you'll learn about the program itself and the elements you can see in the Word application window. Then you'll learn a few basic skills for creating your first Word document — a simple letter. As you move through the book, you'll perform a variety of more complex tasks, like designing images for your documents, performing a mail merge, and much more.

THE WYSIWYG CONCEPT

By the way, my name's the WYSIWYG wizard, and you'll find me popping up quite often, handing out a few tips on getting the most out of Word.

One of the first questions you may be asking is: What does the term WYSIWYG have to do with it? Well, WYSIWYG stands for "What You See Is What You Get." It was coined some years ago to describe programs with a special feature — namely that *what you see* on the screen is the same as *what you get* when you print it out. In this book we'll be turning the WYSIWYG concept around a little bit. Throughout the book, the practical instructions for learning about Word's features are accompanied by visual prompts showing exactly what is happening on your computer screen. In other words, *what you see* on the page is the same as *what you get* on the screen. Step by step, you'll find out how to get the most out of Word.

Creating Pictures
Find out how to create colorful images to enhance the appearance of a document on pages 72 to 77.

Character Shaping
Discover how to use Word's Formatting toolbar to create special typographical effects, such as making a word italic or bold, on pages 56 to 57.

SCREENS AND FRAGMENTS

Sometimes, an instruction will be accompanied by a screen "shot" (like the one at left) showing how your screen will look at a particular stage in an operation. Or you'll see a smaller box within the screen (like the one at right), called a dialog box, that allows you to specify a number of different options for the command you're performing. Alternatively, as you follow a set of step-by-step instructions, you might see an accompanying series of screen "fragments" (like those shown at right); these home in on where the action is taking place on screen.

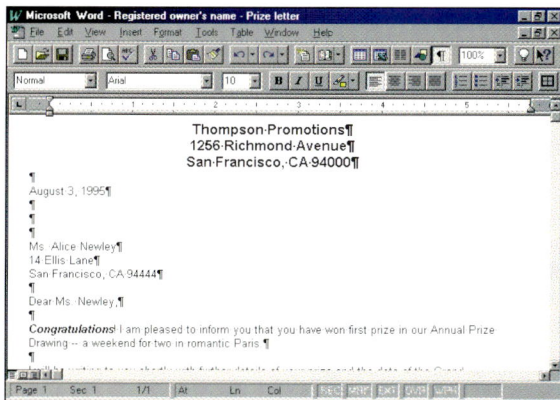

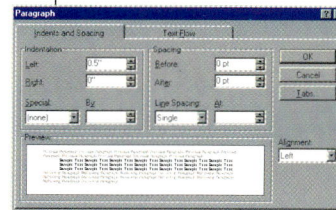

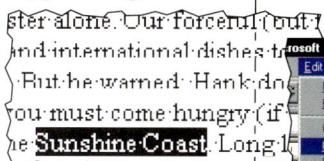

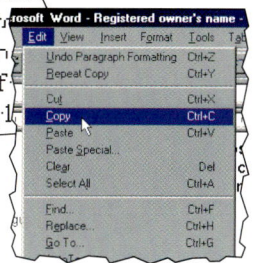

TIPS AND SHORTCUTS

In addition to the insights I'll provide, you'll see various tips in colored boxes scattered throughout the book. The *pink* boxes contain warnings about some common pitfalls you may run into when using your PC and Word. The *green* boxes offer advice on anything from troubleshooting common problems to useful shortcuts and tips.

REFERENCE SECTION

At the back of the book, there's a useful Reference Section. This includes essential information, such as how to install a printer; helpful advice, such as how to convert and manipulate files; and special entries on topics not covered in the rest of the book, such as Word's outlining feature, OLE, and customizing the program to suit your individual needs. At the end of the Reference Section, you'll find a comprehensive index to the whole volume.

EASY READING

The only way to become comfortable with any new program is to get hands-on experience. We believe that *The Way Microsoft Word for Windows 95 Works* will make the learning process as easy and enjoyable as possible. By the end of the book, you'll feel confident using the many features of Word, and you'll be able to create a wide variety of different types of documents — from impressive business reports to bright and colorful party invitations. Read on!

Forbidden Filenames!

When naming your file, never use any of the following characters:
| / \ ; * < > : ?
If you do, a message might appear telling you that it is not a valid file name. Otherwise you can use whatever combination of letters, numbers, and printable characters you wish. File names can be up to 255 characters long.

Missing Something?

If you can't see the Standard toolbar or the Formatting toolbar, open the *View* menu, and choose *Toolbars*. In the *Toolbars* dialog box, click in the boxes next to *Standard* and *Formatting*. Then click on *OK*. If you can't see the Ruler, choose *Ruler* from the *View* menu.

1

CHAPTER ONE

Getting Started

*This chapter introduces you to Microsoft
Word for Windows 95. In the first section you'll
learn how to start up the program and how to use
the menus, tools, and other elements that appear on
screen. You'll also learn how to obtain on-screen help
as you work on your Word documents and how to close a
document and exit Word. In the second section, you will
create, save, and print a simple letter. Here you'll
learn the essential steps involved producing
virtually any document using Word.*

WELCOME TO WORD FOR WINDOWS 95
YOUR FIRST LETTER

Welcome to Word For Windows 95 *10*

A quick rundown on some essential information, including what equipment you need, how to use the mouse, and how to start Word. You'll get acquainted with the *Microsoft Word* application window with its menus, toolbars, and other tools, and you'll find out how to get help and how to close a document and exit Word.

Your First Letter *18*

As a jumpstart to using Word, produce a short sample letter. Familiarize yourself with the basic steps for creating a new document — entering the text, editing and correcting it, formatting the text to improve the document's appearance, saving the document, and printing it.

Welcome to Word for Windows 95

W HEN WORD PROCESSING SOFTWARE was first introduced it was very simple and was used mainly to enter and store text and not much else. But times have changed. Microsoft Word provides a powerful, modern solution for integrating text and graphics. Unlike earlier word processing software, Word displays your document on screen exactly as it will appear on the printed page — producing the results you want.

Design to Impress

Word provides the tools so that, with a little practice, even the most inexperienced user can create all sorts of professional-looking, well-designed documents. You can experiment with a variety of typefaces, sizes, and styles; add pictures and charts; and draw rules and borders. You can also make sure your document reads well by using the program's spelling-check and grammar-check facilities. With Word, you have your very own desktop publishing system that is easy to learn and use.

Window Display

Rather than displaying a blank screen when you start up your program, Windows 95 *displays a "desktop" made up of the Taskbar and icons, allowing you to point to what you want rather than remember complex keyboard commands.*

? Do I Need a Special Printer?
The type of printer you choose for printing your Word documents depends on the quality of documents you want to produce. If you want to produce crisp, professional-looking documents, you'll probably need a laser printer.

What Equipment Do I Need?

In order to run Word version 7 you must have either the Windows 95 operating system or the Windows NT Workstation operating system, version 3.51 or later. The minimum hardware requirements include:

■ A computer with a 386DX or higher processor (486 recommended), and a hard disk drive with 16MB free for a typical installation, or 35 MB free for a custom installation.

■ Six MB of RAM for use on Windows 95, or 12MB of RAM for use on Windows NT Workstation. Additional memory will be needed for WordMail.

■ A VGA or higher resolution monitor and a 3.5" high-density disk drive.

■ We recommend a Microsoft or compatible mouse, and a CD-ROM drive.

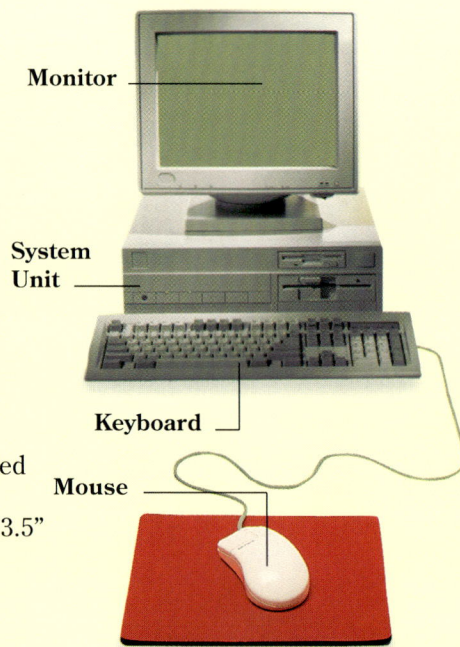

Monitor

System Unit

Keyboard

Mouse

Using Your Mouse

Word is specifically designed to be used in conjunction with a mouse. This hand-held device, which is connected to your PC's system unit, controls a pointer on the screen. The mouse has two buttons, you'll mainly use the left button. The four main actions you'll perform with your mouse are moving, clicking, double-clicking, and dragging.

■ *Moving* consists of gliding your mouse over a flat surface. As you do so, a pointer — which may be an arrow, an I-beam, or another shape — moves in unison on the screen. You can position the pointer over any on-screen item.

■ *Clicking* entails pressing and releasing the mouse button when the pointer is positioned over a particular on-screen item.

■ *Double-clicking* entails pointing to an item and then quickly pressing and releasing the mouse button twice.

■ *Dragging* consists of moving the mouse while holding down the mouse button.

Using one or a sequence of these mouse actions, you can open and close files, negotiate your way around your document, move blocks of text, and much more — all without having to type in any keyboard commands. Unless otherwise stated, all mouse actions in this book use the left mouse button.

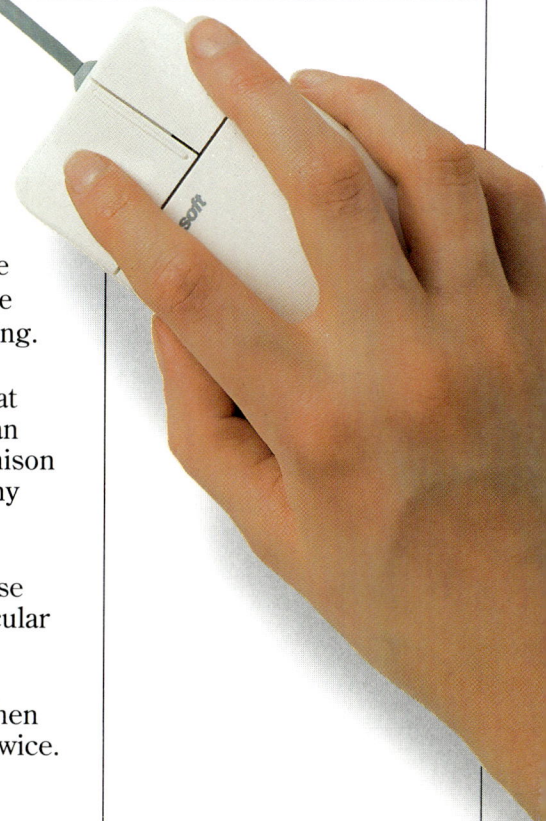

Pointer Problem?

If the pointer does not move on the screen when you move your mouse, check that the cable is correctly plugged into the back of your PC's system unit. Remember that the mouse must be plugged in before you start Windows 95.

What's New?

When you start Word for the first time, you might be greeted by a *What's New* box. To cancel this box and see the application window, click on the Close button in the top right corner of the box.

Running Microsoft Word

Once you have installed Word version 7, you are ready to start the program and begin working on a document. Simply follow the steps below.

How to Open Word for Windows 95

1 Click on the Start button and the Start menu appears. Move the mouse away from you. You'll see a blue bar (the *cursor)* move up the Start menu. When the cursor is over *Programs*, the Programs menu appears.

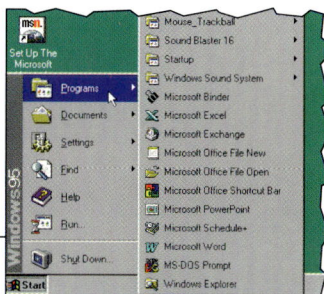

2 Move the cursor onto the Programs menu and then move the mouse towards you. Stop moving the mouse when the cursor is over *Microsoft Word*. Click once on the mouse button to open Word.

11

The Application Window

When you start Word, a new, empty document window, which is given the name **Document1**, opens. Below this name is a collection of menus, buttons, and tools. If you move your mouse pointer up to this area of the application window, the pointer becomes a white arrow. Pointing the arrow at a menu name, button, or tool and clicking the left mouse button chooses that item — in other words, it activates or allows you to use it. These are the features that you will be using as you work on your Word documents.

Here we briefly describe the elements you should see on your *Microsoft Word* application window when you start Word. If your screen does not look like the one shown, refer to "Let's Synchronize" at right.

Document Control Menu
If you click here, a drop-down list appears with commands for sizing, moving, and closing the document window, and for moving to another document window.

Ruler
The Ruler provides a simple, visual way to set margins and tabs in your active document.

Selection Bar
On the left-hand side of your screen, reaching from top to bottom, is an invisible "bar" called the selection bar. You click in this area of the screen when you want to select certain amounts of text (see page 30).

Formatting Toolbar
This displays buttons you can use to change the appearance of your text. Using the Formatting toolbar, you can specify different fonts, styles, point sizes, text alignments, and so on.

View Buttons
Clicking on these buttons gives you different views of your document (see page 66). Make sure you are in Normal View by clicking on the far left button.

Status Bar
This displays information about your position in the active document and about certain options that have been chosen. The status bar also displays information about selected commands.

Title Bar
The title bar, at the very top of the screen, contains the words Microsoft Word — [the name of the registered owner] — Document1. *This means that you are in* Microsoft Word *and that* Document1 *is the active document — the document you are currently working on. (Your installation of Word may not show the registered owner's name.)*

Menu Bar
This contains nine menu names. If you click on one of these, a drop-down list of commands appears. Choosing a command instructs the program to perform a certain action.

Standard Toolbar
This contains a collection of buttons that speed up the most frequently used operations in Word.

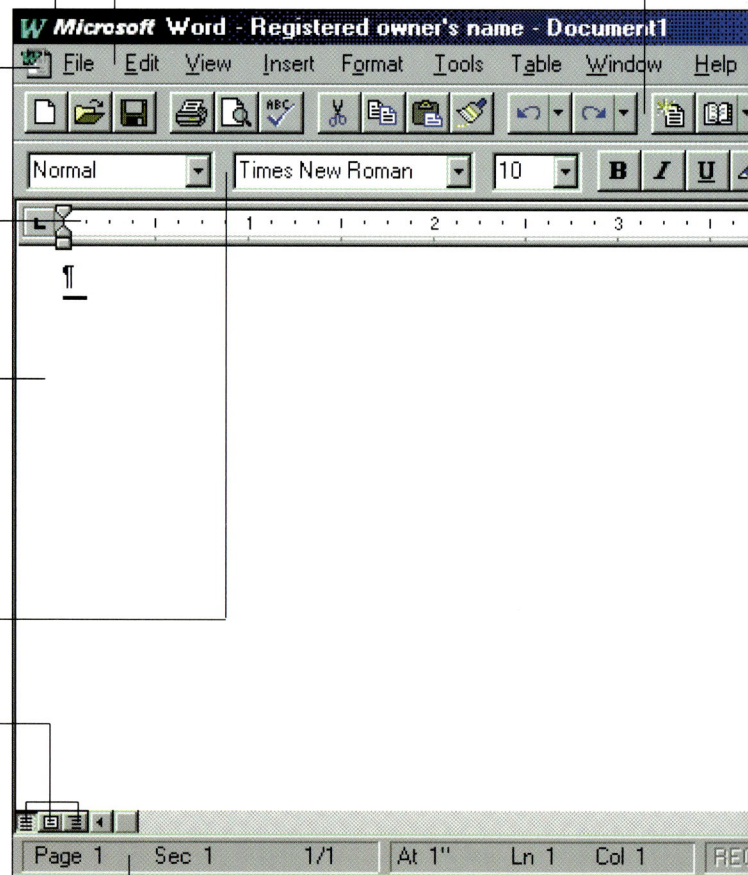

Office Shortcut Bar
Clicking on these buttons gives you access to other programs in the Microsoft Office suite of programs. If you want to close the Shortcut Bar, drag it into the text area and click on its Minimize button. When its icon appears on the Taskbar, click on it with the right mouse button and click on Close.

Minimize Button
Clicking on this button shrinks the Microsoft Word application window to an icon on the Taskbar, but leaves the program running and the document open.

Maximize/Restore Button
Clicking on this button switches the window between its maximum size and a smaller size, which will be the default size if it hasn't already been changed.

Close Button
The Close button will end the current session of Word. If you have made changes to your document since you last saved it, Word will ask you if you want to save the changes in the document.

Document Buttons
These buttons perform the same actions as the buttons above them, but only on the document and the document window. The Minimize button shrinks the document to a small title bar at the foot of the Word window; the Maximize/Restore button increases or decreases the size of the document window; and the Close button closes the document, but leaves the Word window active.

Text Area
This is the empty space where you enter text and create any graphical material. In the text area, the mouse pointer is an I-beam, a vertical bar that looks like a letter I.

Scroll Bars
If you click on the vertical or horizontal scroll bars or drag the box in the scroll bar in a particular direction, you will bring other parts of the document into view. You can also click on the arrows at the ends of the scroll bars to move the document vertically or horizontally.

Spelling check
This icon appears as soon as you begin to insert text into your document. Double-click on it to have your document spell-checked.

Let's Synchronize

■ If the Word window does not fill the whole screen, click on the Maximize/Restore button, which will be showing a single rectangle.

■ If your screen contains a separate *Document1* window within the *Microsoft Word* application window, click on the document Maximize/Restore button to merge the two windows.

■ If you have all the Microsoft Office programs, but the Office Shortcut Bar isn't displayed, click on the Start button. Select *Programs* and click on *Microsoft Office Shortcut Bar* in the *Programs* menu. When the Bar appears in the text area, place the mouse pointer over the Bar and hold down the mouse button. Drag the Bar to the top of the screen and release the mouse button to place the Bar in the Word title bar.

■ If you can't see the Standard toolbar or the Formatting toolbar, open the *View* menu, and choose *Toolbars*. In the *Toolbars* dialog box, click in the boxes next to *Standard* and *Formatting*. Then click on *OK*. If you can't see the Ruler, choose *Ruler* from the *View* menu.

If your screen still does not look like the one shown at left, you may have a version of Word other than version 7 installed.

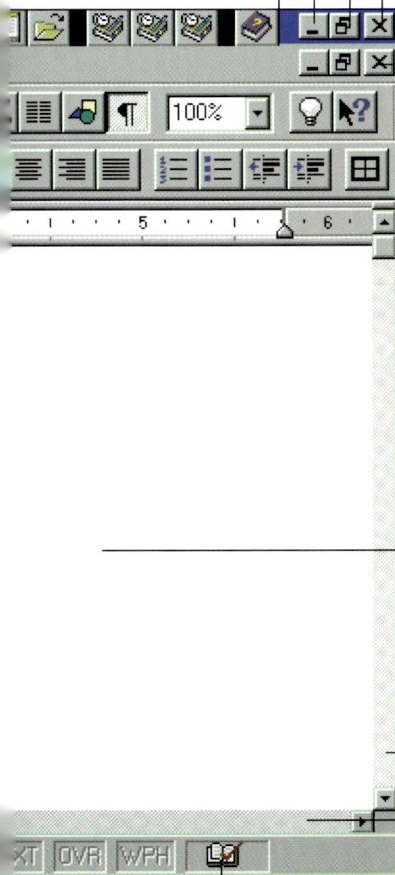

How to Use the Menu Bar

If you click on a menu name in the menu bar in Word, a drop-down list appears that displays a selection of commands. To choose a specific command with the mouse, you must click on its name. Word will carry out the action immediately unless the command is followed by an ellipsis (...). If you choose one of these commands, Word displays a dialog box in which you specify the options you want. Some commands in a menu list are followed by the name of a key or combination of keys. Pressing the specified keys achieves the same result as clicking on the command with the mouse. If you open a menu and don't find the command you want, you can close the menu by clicking again on the menu name.

Fingertip Control

If you prefer, you can use the keyboard to choose a menu command. Press the Alt key, then press the underlined letter in the menu item you want to select. For instance, to open the *File* menu press Alt and then F. Each command in the menu list also has an underlined character; you press the corresponding key to choose your command, or press Esc to close the menu.

No Response!

If a menu command is grayed out, you won't be able to select it — Word is telling you that the command is not relevant to your current activity and is therefore unavailable.

What Does That Hourglass Mean?

When you choose certain commands in Word, you may notice an hourglass symbol on the screen. This tells you that the program is in the process of performing some action; when it disappears, the action has been carried out.

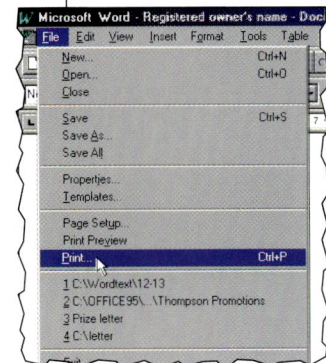

Choosing a Command

1 Click the mouse pointer on *File* in the menu bar.

2 The *File* menu drops down and displays the commands that you can choose. Click on *Print*.

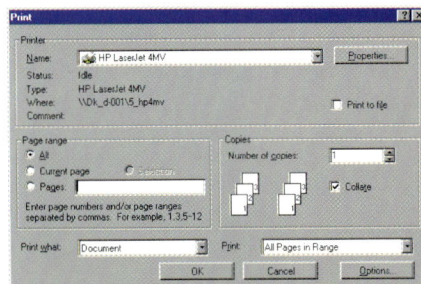

3 The *Print* dialog box appears. For now, simply click on the *Cancel* option, or the Close button in the dialog box to make it disappear.

Using a Toolbar

A toolbar is a selection of buttons displayed in a bar. Some buttons provide shortcuts to dialog boxes for commonly used commands; others are shortcuts around dialog boxes. With just a click on a button you can save a file, print, and much more. There may also be drop-down list boxes that give you a list of options.

The Standard and Formatting toolbars are normally displayed beneath the menu bar. Click the *right* mouse button anywhere on the Formatting or Standard toolbar to open a "pop-up" menu that displays other toolbars available (click the left or right mouse button outside the menu to close it).

At right we show the buttons on the Standard toolbar. The Formatting toolbar is shown on page 56. To determine a button's function, move the pointer over the button — after a pause, a small box with the button's name appears, and an explanation of its action appears on the status bar.

DIALOG BOXES

A dialog box appears when you choose a menu command that is followed by an ellipsis. It is a special window containing a variety of options that you choose in order to tell Word how to carry out the command. The dialog box displayed when you choose the *Print* command from the *File* menu illustrates some common features in dialog boxes.

Some dialog boxes have different sets of options, each on a separate "flipcard." For example, the *Symbol* dialog box (see page 28) has two flipcards — *Symbols* and *Special Characters*. To view the options in a particular flipcard, you simply click on the relevant tab.

Check Box

Clicking on a check box chooses that particular option, and a ✓ appears in the box. To switch the option off, simply click on the check box again; the ✓ disappears.

Drop-Down List

This contains a list of options that you can choose. To see the list, click on the drop-down arrow button at right of the box. Choosing an option, or clicking on the drop-down arrow button, closes the list.

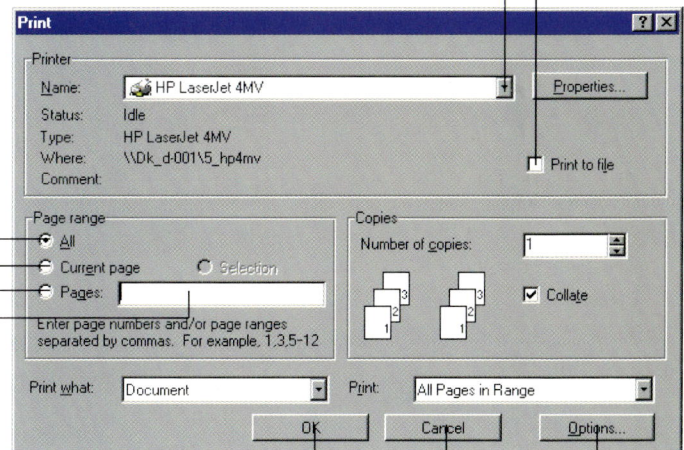

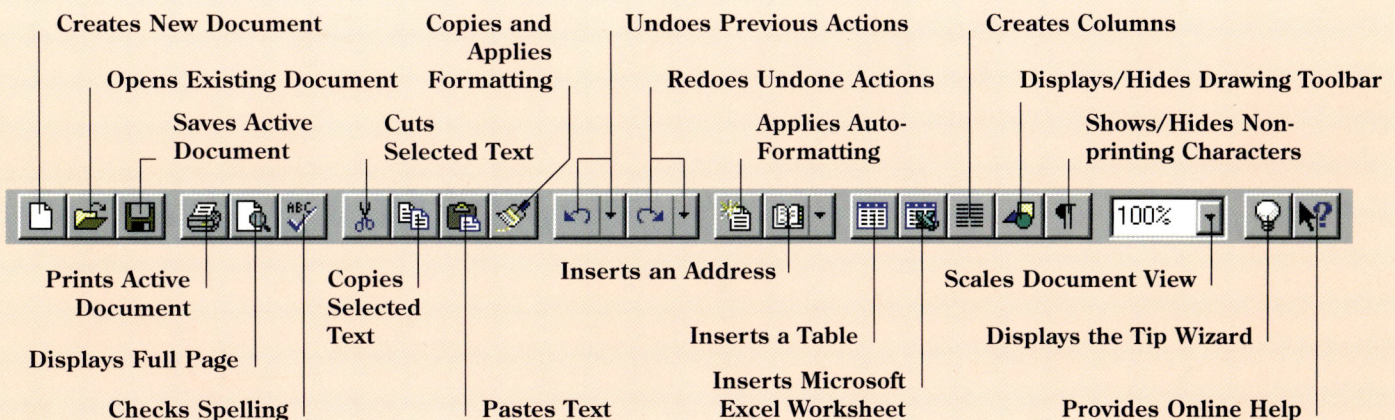

Option Buttons

These buttons represent mutually exclusive options. If you click on one of the options, the others are automatically switched off and the chosen button is filled with a round bullet.

Text Box

In a text box, you can type in information; clicking anywhere inside the text box causes a text insertion point to appear. In the Pages *box, for example, you can enter a range of pages that you want to print.*

Command Buttons

Clicking on a command button performs a particular action. Dimmed command buttons are unavailable. If you choose a command followed by an ellipsis, another dialog box appears.

Print dialog box

- Printer
  - Name: HP LaserJet 4MV
  - Status: Idle
  - Type: HP LaserJet 4MV
  - Where: \\Dk_d-001\5_hp4mv
  - Comment:
  - Properties...
  - Print to file
- Page range
  - All
  - Current page — Selection
  - Pages:
  - Enter page numbers and/or page ranges separated by commas. For example, 1,3,5-12
- Copies
  - Number of copies: 1
  - Collate
- Print what: Document
- Print: All Pages in Range
- OK — Cancel — Options...

Toolbar callouts:

- Creates New Document
- Opens Existing Document
- Saves Active Document
- Copies and Applies Formatting
- Cuts Selected Text
- Undoes Previous Actions
- Redoes Undone Actions
- Applies Auto-Formatting
- Creates Columns
- Displays/Hides Drawing Toolbar
- Shows/Hides Non-printing Characters
- Prints Active Document
- Displays Full Page
- Checks Spelling
- Copies Selected Text
- Pastes Text
- Inserts an Address
- Inserts a Table
- Inserts Microsoft Excel Worksheet
- Scales Document View
- Displays the Tip Wizard
- Provides Online Help

How to Obtain Help

If you need help at any time when working on a Word document, you simply have to ask for it! Word can supply instant on-screen help for a variety of tasks and in a variety of ways.

USING THE HELP POINTER

When you click on the Help button on the Standard toolbar, the mouse pointer becomes a help pointer — a question mark next to the white arrow. With this pointer, you can click on any menu command, or other tool to get an explanation of what it does. Follow these steps to obtain an explanation of the Save button:

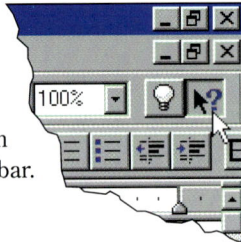

1 Click on the Help button on the Standard toolbar.

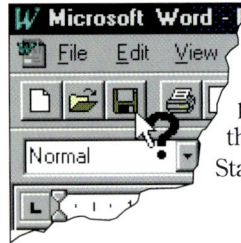

2 The mouse pointer changes to the Help pointer. Now click on the Save button on the Standard toolbar.

Save command (File menu)
Saves the active document with its current filename, location, and file format.

3 A Word Help window appears, displaying information about the *Save* command. You can click on any words that appear underlined and green to bring up more information on that topic. When you have finished reading the Help information, click anywhere on the screen to return to your Word document.

Help as You Work
To get context-sensitive help, press the F1 key. Word displays information about your current activity. For example, pressing the F1 key when a dialog box is on the screen displays information about the options in the box.

The Help Menu

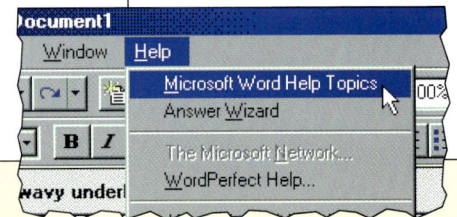

Using the Help Menu

You can also get help by clicking on *Help* in the menu bar. Click on *Microsoft Word Help Topics*.

■ *The Contents flipcard*. This flipcard contains related topics collected in several "volumes." Double-click on one of the volumes and it opens to display its contents. These can be either more volumes, or entries with the Help question mark alongside them. Double-clicking on one of these entries will display a Help window that you can read and then close by clicking on its Close button. Click on any green, underlined text with the hand pointer to get specific help.

■ *The Index flipcard*. Type the first letters of the topic on which you want help in the first box on this flipcard. In the second box, the index will show the entries beginning with those letters. Click on one of the entries, then click on

Display to open the Help window.

■ *The Find flipcard*. Find provides a complete database of words, topics, and characters contained in Word Help. The first time you use Find, it will offer to create the database, which only has to be carried out once.

■ *Answer Wizard*. Selecting this flipcard allows you to enter a query in plain English. Answer Wizard reads the words you've entered and displays a list of topics containing combinations of the words you've used. Click on one in the list and then click on *Display*.

■ *WordPerfect Help*. Specific help is offered by this option if you're more familiar with WordPerfect terms and key combinations. You will find translations from WordPerfect's to Word's shortcuts and descriptions for the most common word processing actions.

How to Close a Document and Exit Word

It is important to understand the difference between closing a document, minimizing a document or Word to an icon (see box at right), and exiting Word.

When you finish working on a document, it's a good idea to close it before opening another one. You can close a document without exiting Word.

When you exit Word, you also close all open documents. Whenever you close or exit, you are asked if you want to save any open documents.

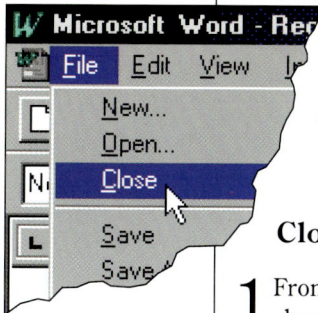

How Do I Minimize?
You minimize Word by clicking on the Minimize button (see page 13). To minimize a document, you click on the document Minimize button. Word is minimized to a button on the Taskbar. Documents are minimized to small title bars at the foot of the Word window.

Closing a Document

1 From the *File* menu, choose the *Close* command.

2 If you have entered anything in the document, a dialog box appears asking if you want to save the changes. In this instance click on *No*. (If you want to save the changes, see "Saving Your Document" on page 21.)

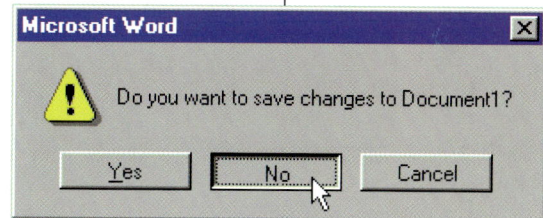

3 The document closes and the document window disappears, but the *Microsoft Word* application window remains on screen. The menu bar displays only the *File* and *Help* menu names.

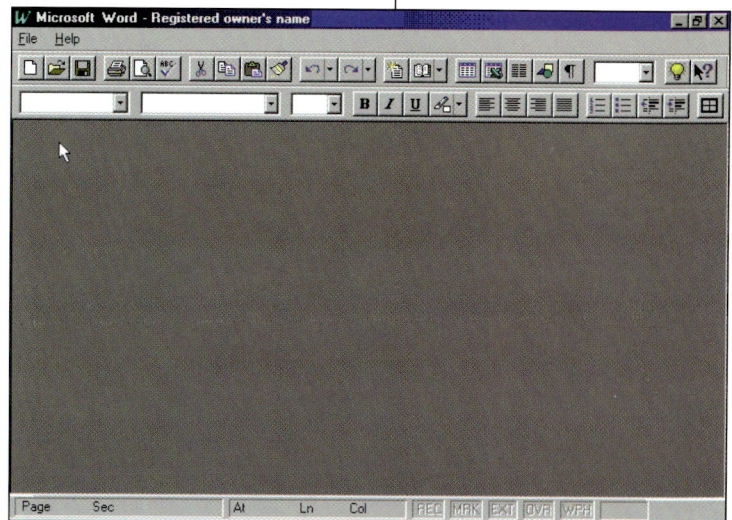

Application Window

Exiting from Word
To exit from Word, click on the Close button at top right of the application window. Normally, you are asked if you want to save changes to each open document. But in this instance, you have already closed the only document that was open. There is also an Exit option at the foot of the File menu.

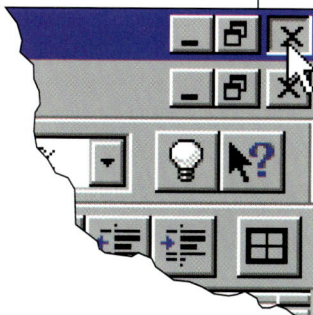

Your First Letter

A GOOD STARTING POINT for learning some basic Word techniques is to create a short sample letter. The steps involved in producing the letter — typing in, editing and correcting, formatting, and printing — are essential steps involved in producing virtually any document using a word processor. Each of these steps will be covered in greater detail later in the book, but here we take you briefly through the whole process. By the time you've finished the letter, you'll realize how easy using Word can be.

How to Create the Letter

Open Word (see page 11 if you've forgotten how to do this). An empty window, **Document1**, appears automatically on your screen. Don't worry about naming the document for now — you'll do this later when you save the document. In the **Document1** text area, you will enter the sample letter shown on the opposite page. As you work through your letter, you'll have the opportunity to use several special keys, such as the Tab key and direction keys, that perform specific operations during text entry.

Text Out of View?
If a document is long, you won't see all of it on the screen. Press the PgUp key to scroll up one screen, or press the PgDn key to scroll down. Word displays a few of the first or last lines of the previous screen so that you can keep track of where you are.

Steps to Creating a Document

Here are the basic steps you will follow to produce most Word documents.

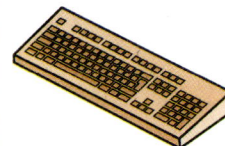

Typing In

Editing and Correcting

Formatting

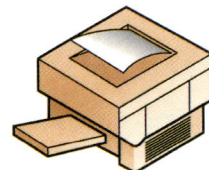

Printing

Want to Indent?
If you want to indent the first line of a paragraph, you can press the Tab key to move the insertion point a standard measure forward on the line. The standard (default) tab movement is equal to one-half inch. For more information on indentation, see page 61.

Moving Around Your Document

To move the insertion point (the flashing vertical bar) within a document, you can use the direction keys on your keyboard. If you press the Right or Left direction key, the insertion point moves one character to the right or left; if you press the Up or Down direction key, it moves up or down a line. If you hold down the direction key, the insertion point moves through the document continuously.

If you want to move the insertion point a long distance over an area of text, you'll find it easier to use your mouse. Simply move the mouse I-beam pointer to where you want the insertion point to appear and then click the mouse button. You'll find more information on the different ways to negotiate your way around a document in Chapter 2 (see "How to Move Around the Text Area" on page 29).

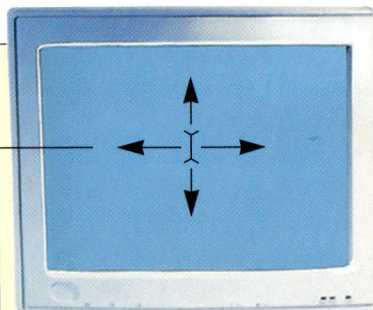

Insertion Point or I-Beam Pointer Movement

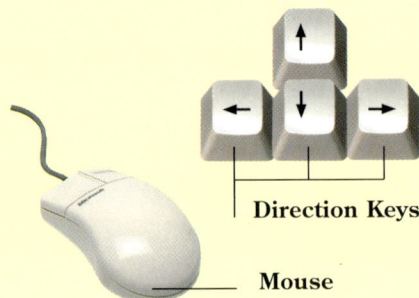

Direction Keys

Mouse

ENTERING YOUR TEXT

The first step in creating any Word document is to enter the text. In the empty **Document1** window, type the short letter shown below. The text will automatically begin at the insertion point, which you'll see flashing at the top left-hand corner of your screen. As you type, the automatic spell check places a red wavy line below some words, especially the names. The Tip Wizard box will also open above the Ruler. There's no need to do anything about this right now, but see Correcting Your Mistakes (page 20) for more information about the automatic spell check. Don't worry if the lines in your letter break in different places; simply follow these steps:

Key Positions
To create the letter shown below, you have to use the Enter key and the Tab key. Here is what they look like:

Enter Key

Tab Key

Typing In

1 Type the name of the sender, and then press Enter to move down to a new line.

2 Type the sender's street address, and then press Enter. Type the next line and then press Enter twice after the zip code to create a blank line.

3 Type the date, and then press Enter four times.

4 Type the addressee's name and press Enter. Follow this pattern for the next two lines of the address, pressing Enter twice after the zip code to create a blank line.

5 Type **Dear Ms. Newley,** and press Enter twice.

6 Press Tab once to indent the first main paragraph of the letter and begin typing. Don't press Enter at the end of lines. At the end of this paragraph press Enter twice to create a blank line between the paragraphs.

7 Press Tab and type the second paragraph. Now press Enter twice.

8 Type **Yours sincerely,** press Enter five times, and then type **Simon Swan**. Press Enter and then type **Promotions Manager**.

Thompson Promotions
1256 Richmond Avenue
San Francisco, CA 94000

August 3, 1995

Ms. Alice Newley
14 Ellis Lane
San Francisco, CA 94444

Dear Ms. Newley,

Congratulations! I am pleased to inform you that you have won first prize in our Annual Prize Drawing -- a weekend for two in romantic Paris.

I will be writing to you shortly with further details of your prize and the date of the Grand Presentation. In the meantime, I hope you have fun celebrating your good fortune!

Yours sincerely,

Simon Swan
Promotions Manager

Correcting Your Mistakes

Don't worry if your typing or spelling is not accurate when you work on your Word documents. Word automatically spell-checks the words as you type. If you enter a word that is not in Word's dictionary, a red wavy line appears under the word. Also, the Tip Wizard box opens above the Ruler telling you to click the right mouse button on the word to correct it. When you do this, a pop-up menu appears offering several options. The first offers alternative spellings from which you can select the correct one if it's shown. If the word you've typed has been spelled correctly, then simply click on *Ignore All* in this menu. The red line disappears and the word isn't queried again. If you want to add the word to the dictionary, click on *Add* in the pop-up menu. The Spelling dialog box can be displayed by clicking on *Spelling*. This shows more alternative spellings, (see pages 40-41 for more about the Spelling dialog box). The pop-up Tip Wizard spelling menu can also be displayed by double-clicking on the left mouse button when the pointer is on the Spelling button on the Status Bar.

The simplest way to correct a word yourself is to use either the Backspace key or the Delete Key.

Backspace Key
Using the mouse, place the I-beam pointer just after a mistyped character, click the mouse button to position the insertion point, and press the Backspace key to delete the character.

Delete Key
Using the mouse again, place the I-beam pointer just before a mistyped character, click the mouse button and press the Delete key to remove the incorrect character.

SHOWING NONPRINTING CHARACTERS
Your document includes certain nonprinting characters that do not normally appear on the screen. Nonprinting characters include tabs (→), paragraph marks (¶), and space marks (·). It is useful to see these characters so that you can easily locate them — for example, if you want to delete them or insert text between them.

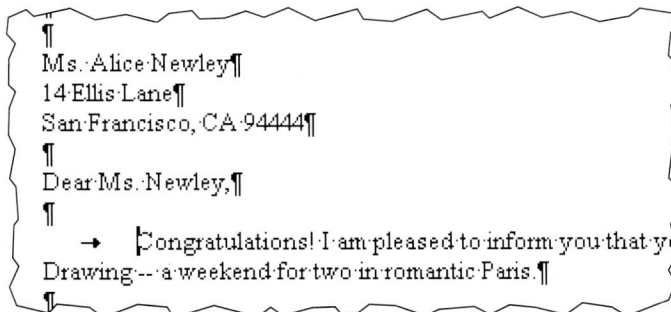

¶
Ms.·Alice·Newley¶
14·Ellis·Lane¶
San·Francisco,·CA·94444¶
¶
Dear·Ms.·Newley,¶
¶
→   Congratulations!·I·am·pleased·to·inform·you·that·yo
Drawing---a·weekend·for·two·in·romantic·Paris.¶
¶

1 Click on the Show/Hide ¶ button on the Standard toolbar to view nonprinting characters.

2 The nonprinting characters now appear on the screen. Move the insertion point just to the left of the word **Congratulations**. Press Backspace to delete the tab before the word.

3 The word **Congratulations** moves back to the left margin. Now delete the tab in front of the word **I** in the second paragraph.

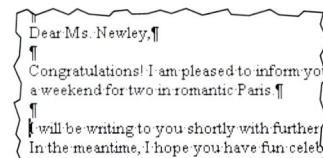

Dear·Ms.·Newley,¶
¶
Congratulations!·I·am·pleased·to·inform·you
a·weekend·for·two·in·romantic·Paris.¶
¶
I·will·be·writing·to·you·shortly·with·further
In·the·meantime,·I·hope·you·have·fun·celeb

4 Click on the Show/Hide ¶ button again to make the nonprinting characters disappear.

SAVING YOUR DOCUMENT

If you want to return to your document in the future, you need to give it a name and store it on disk. It's best to give it an obvious name that you'll remember easily.

Once you've given it a name, you need to save your document at regular intervals in order to keep any changes you've made. To save your document, you can use the *File* menu to access the *Save* command or you can click on the Save button on the Standard toolbar.

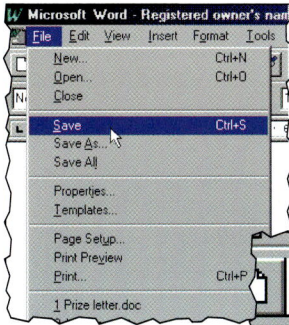

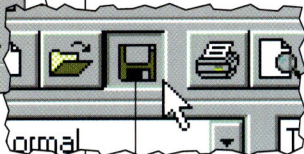

1 Choose *Save* from the *File* menu or click on the Save button on the Standard toolbar.

Save Button

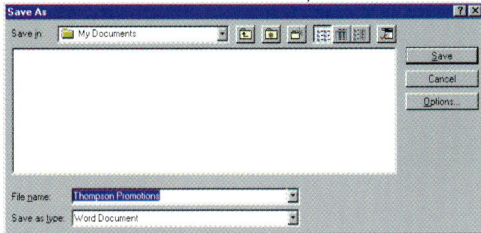

2 When you're saving a particular document for the first time, Word displays the *Save As* dialog box. In the *File name* textbox, the first few words of your document are highlighted as a suggestion for a file name. If there is no text in your document, then **Doc1** is suggested. As both these names are too general, it's better to think of a more identifiable name.

3 Type **Prize letter** in the *File name* box and then click on the *Save* button. The new name of your document appears in the title bar.

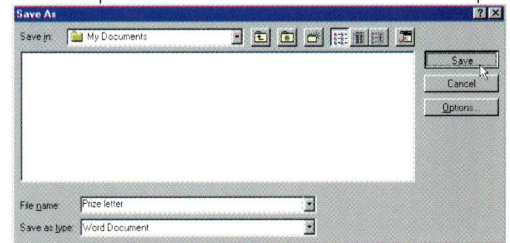

4 Now whenever you want to save any changes that you have made to your document, you either choose *Save* from the *File* menu or simply click on the Save button on the Standard toolbar.

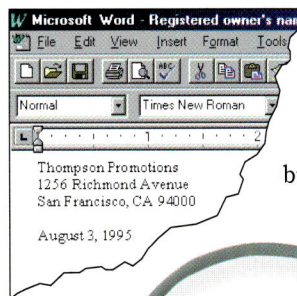

Different File Names?
If your file names look different from this example, you can change one the Windows 95 settings. In Windows Explorer, (see page 49), click on *View* and click on *Options*. Click on the *View* tab and you will find a check box for *Hide MS-DOS file extensions for file types that are registered*. Check this box to change the form of the file names in all Windows 95 programs.

Forbidden File Names
When you are naming your file, never use any of these characters:
| / \ ; * < > : ?
If you do, a message appears telling you that it is not a valid file name. Otherwise, you can use whatever combination of letters, numbers and printable characters you wish. File names can be up to 255 characters long.

Don't Forget to Save
No computer is completely immune to power failure. If the power fails, you will lose any changes that you have made since you last saved your document. To make sure you don't lose large amounts of work, devise a system to remind you to save at regular intervals. Also check that the Automatic Save feature is activated (see page 27).

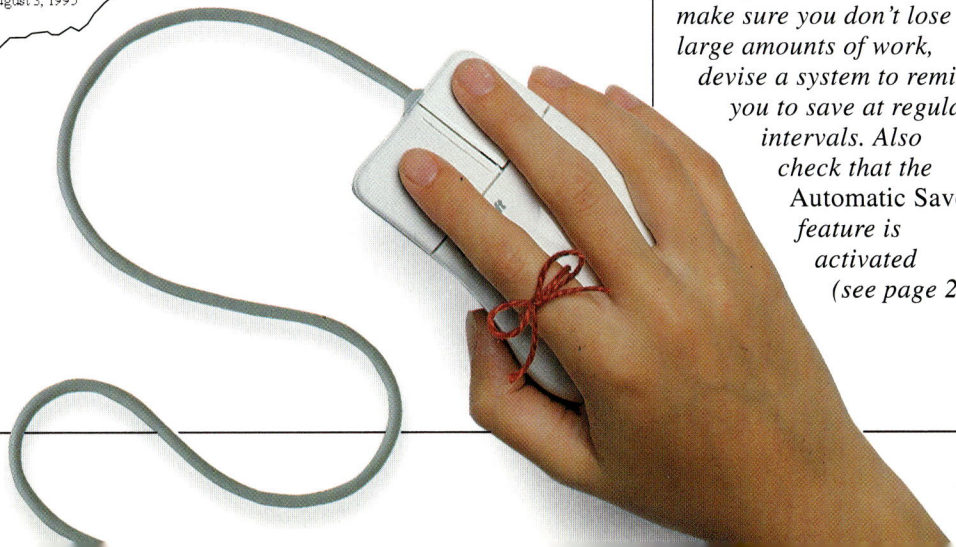

How to Format and Print Your Letter

When you have finished typing your letter, you may want to make it more interesting visually. Detailed information on the different ways in which you can style and format your documents is given in Chapter 2, but here you'll learn how to perform a few simple formatting tasks. When you are happy with the appearance of your document, you are then ready for the final stage of its production — printing.

FORMATTING

Using Word, you can improve the appearance of your letter in several ways. Before you can apply any formatting to an area of text, however, you must select it. You'll find it easier to format your document if the nonprinting characters are displayed. First click on the Show/Hide ¶ button, and then follow the steps below:

1 Select the whole letter by holding down the Ctrl key and clicking anywhere in the margin to the left of the text (this area of the screen is called the selection bar). The whole letter becomes highlighted.

2 Click on the down-arrow button to the right of the Font box on the Formatting toolbar. Use your mouse to scroll up and down the list to see the fonts that are available, and choose *Arial*. Word changes the highlighted text from the default font *Times New Roman* to the new font.

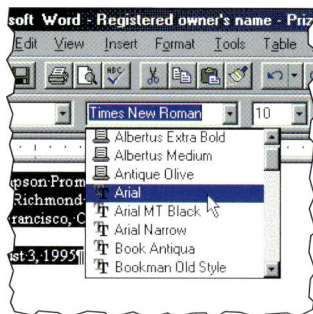

3 Select the return address by positioning the mouse pointer in the selection bar to the left of the word **Thompson**, holding down the mouse button, and dragging the pointer down until the whole address is highlighted. Then release the mouse button.

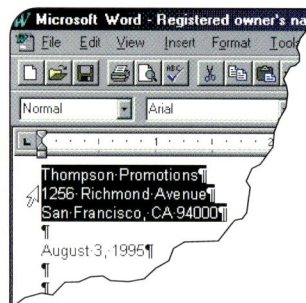

4 Center the selected text on the page by clicking on the Center button on the Formatting toolbar.

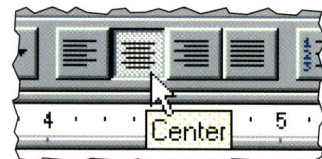

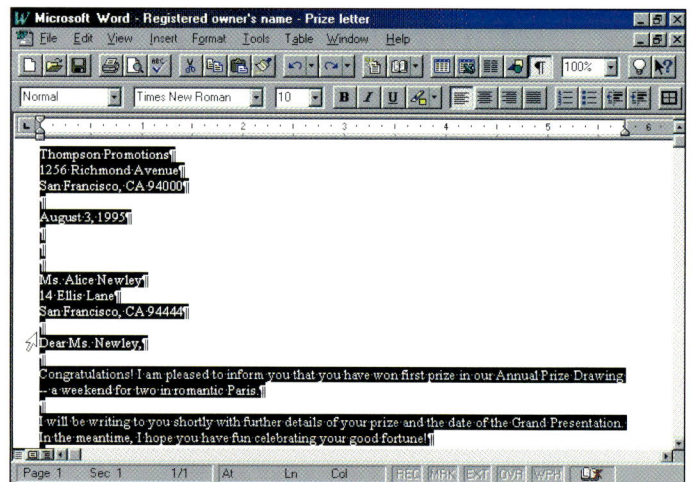

It Works Like Magic
Word can help format professional-looking documents at a touch of a button. Clicking on the AutoFormat button on the Standard toolbar prompts Word to analyze and polish your document for you.

5 While the return address is still selected, click on the down-arrow button to the right of the Font Size box on the Formatting toolbar and choose *12* as the new point size.

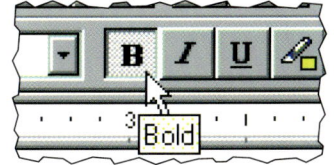

6 With the return address still highlighted, click on the Bold button on the Formatting toolbar.

7 Select the word **Congratulations** by double-clicking anywhere within the word. Click on the Bold button and then on the Italic button.

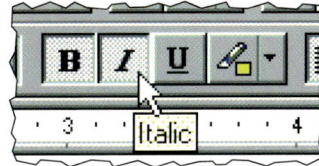

A Stylish Document
You now know how to use some of the tools that help improve the look of a document. The finished letter is shown at right.

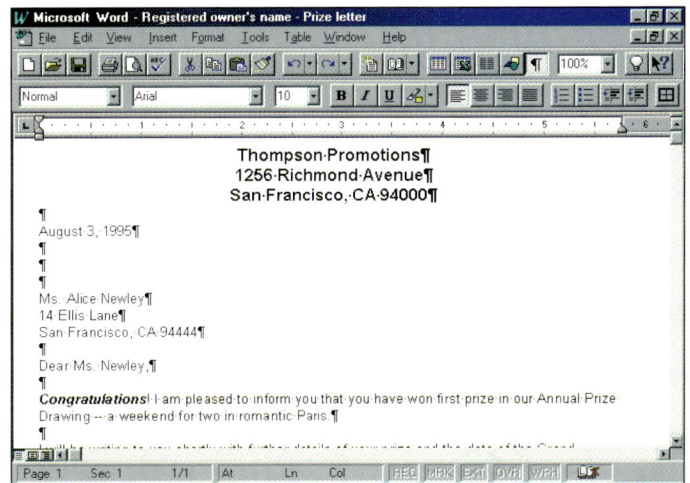

Thompson·Promotions¶
1256·Richmond·Avenue¶
San·Francisco,·CA·94000¶

¶
August·3,·1995¶
¶
¶
Ms.·Alice·Newley¶
14·Ellis·Lane¶
San·Francisco,·CA·94444¶
¶
Dear·Ms.·Newley,¶
¶
Congratulations!·I·am·pleased·to·inform·you·that·you·have·won·first·prize·in·our·Annual·Prize·Drawing·--·a·weekend·for·two·in·romantic·Paris.¶

PRINTING
When you are happy with the formatting changes you have made to your letter, you are ready to print and then close the document. Just follow these steps:

1 Click on the Save button on the Standard toolbar to save the changes you have made.

2 Click on the Print button on the Stan-dard toolbar to print your letter.

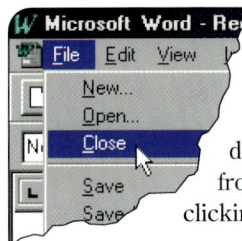

3 After you have printed your letter, close your document by choosing *Close* from the the *File* menu, or clicking on the Close button.

2

CHAPTER TWO

*U*p *& Running*

*In this chapter, you'll be
practicing a number of commonly
used word processing techniques by creating
and revising an example document — a restaurant
menu. You'll learn how to add special characters to
your document, move sections of text, find and replace
words, check spelling and grammar, and much
more. You'll also discover how to use split
screens and how to manage your
files efficiently.*

———————

TEXT ENTRY • TEXT SELECTION
TEXT REVISION • TEXT CHECKING
MANIPULATING WINDOWS
FILE MANAGEMENT

Text Entry

TYPING IN TEXT IS PROBABLY the first thing you'll do when creating any new document. In this section, you'll start entering the text of a restaurant menu. Later in the book, you'll format text and add other items to the menu. When you've finished, it will look like the menu at left. But before you begin, let's learn how to open new documents.

How to Open a New Document

When you first open Word, it displays a new empty document window, **Document1**, in which you can start typing. If you already have a document on your screen (or if you have just closed a document but have not exited Word) you can use the *New* command from the *File* menu to open a new document. It's a good idea to save the document with a name that reflects its content before you enter any text.

Opening a New Document

1 To create a new document, choose *New* from the *File* menu or click on the New button on the Standard toolbar.

New Button

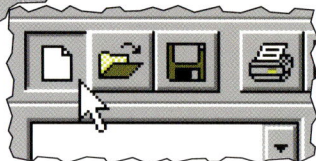

2 If you choose the command from the *File* menu, the *New* dialog box appears, and displays the available templates in the General flipcard. More templates are available in the other flipcards, but click on *OK* for now to select the *Blank Document* template. If you click on the New button on the Standard toolbar, Word will use the *Blank Document* template automatically.

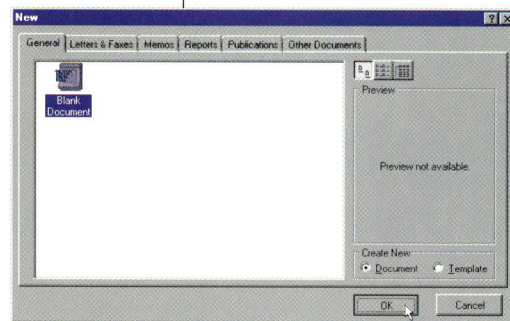

3 Word creates a new document window, **Document2**, in which you can start typing.

4 Before you enter any text in a new document, you should save the document. Click on the Save button on the Standard toolbar and the *Save As* dialog box appears (see page 21). Delete the suggested name **Doc2** or simply begin typing. Call this file **Menu** and click on *OK*.

How to Type in Text

Now start entering some text into the file **Menu** that you've created. Don't worry if your typing or spelling isn't accurate — you can ignore any errors for now because you'll use the spelling check to help you correct your mistakes later in this chapter.

Remember that Word automatically moves the insertion point to a new line when you reach the right margin, so you need to press Enter only when you reach the end of a paragraph. Pressing Enter more than once creates additional blank lines between paragraphs. Type the text below, pressing Enter only where you see <Enter> in the text. If they are not already displayed, click on the Show/Hide ¶ button to display the nonprinting characters (see page 20).

> Sunset Bay Grill <Enter> <Enter>
>
> TRADITIONAL FRESH SEAFOOD (AND PLENTY MORE BESIDES)
> <Enter> <Enter>
>
> Like many other restaurants, Sunset Bay Grill boasts a relaxed, anything-goes atmosphere. Open every day from noon to midnight, we will provide the type of service you need, whether you want a quiet meal for two or a fun-filled group night out. For the extra rowdy, we have a large back-room -- soundproofed! Unlike most seafood restaurants, however, Sunset Bay Grill does not dwell on fresh fish and lobster alone. Our forceful (but friendly) chef, Hank, insists that we serve a wide range of interesting and international dishes too! And all at very reasonable prices. We pride ourselves on good value. But be warned: Hank doesn't believe in small portions -- when you come to Sunset Bay Grill, you must come hungry (if you manage three whole courses, we'll be amazed). Long live the Sunshine Coast. Long live Sunset Bay Grill.

OPENING AN EXISTING DOCUMENT

You may need to close your **Menu** document at some point during these exercises. To do so, choose *Close* from the *File* menu and click on *Yes* to save the changes. When you want to open the restaurant menu again, simply follow these steps:

Automatic Save

Word automatically saves a temporary copy of the document you're working on at 10-minute intervals. After a power failure or other problem, Word will display the last-saved copy of that document on the screen. (You'll see *(Recovered)* in the document title.)

To change the time interval between saves, choose *Options* from the *Tools* menu. In the *Options* dialog box, click on the *Save* tab. Under *Save Options*, you'll see the checked *Automatic Save Every* box. Change the value in the *Minutes* box to the value you want, and then click on *OK*.

Open Button

1 Choose *Open* from the *File* menu or click on the Open button on the Standard toolbar.

2 The *Open* dialog box appears. From the list of files, choose **Menu** and click on *Open*. (See "File Management" on pages 48 to 51 for more information on how to store and find files.)

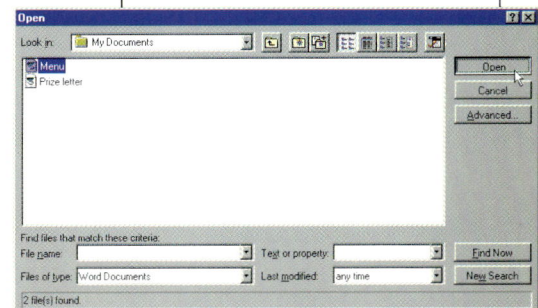

How to Insert Special Items

Some text items, such as accented characters and special symbols, cannot be typed in using the keyboard. To display and print such special items, you can use the *Symbol* dialog box from the *Insert* menu.

ADDING ACCENTED CHARACTERS

Before adding any accented characters, let's add some more text to your restaurant menu. Put your insertion point at the end of what you have typed so far, press Enter twice, and then type in the text shown at right. After you finish typing, perform the steps below:

September 15, 1995 <Enter>
TODAY'S SPECIAL <Enter>
Try our "hungry sailor" menu: <Enter> <Enter>

Crab soup <Enter>
All the fresh pasta you can eat <Enter>
Rum and raisin sundae (very large) <Enter> <Enter>
only $10.95 <Enter> <Enter> <Enter>

Starters <Enter> <Enter>

French onion soup $2.00 <Enter>
Garlic bread $2.00 <Enter>
Vegetable soup $2.95 <Enter>
Lobster pate with bread $3.50 <Enter>
Bay oysters (6) $4.00 <Enter>

1 Click the I-beam pointer just to the left of the **a** in **pate**. Hold down the left mouse button, drag the mouse one character to the right, and release the button to highlight just this letter.

French onion soup $2.00¶
Garlic bread $2.00¶
Vegetable soup £2.95¶
Lobster pate with bread $3.5(
Bay oysters (6) $4.00¶

2 Choose *Symbol* from the *Insert* menu.

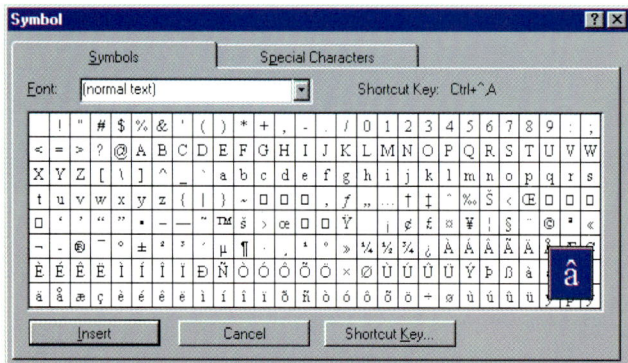

Registered owner's name
Insert Format Tools
Break...
Page Numbers...
Annotation
Date and Time...
Field...
Symbol...
Form Field...

3 The *Symbol* dialog box appears. Make sure the *Font* text box reads *(normal text)*. If it does not, click on the down arrow to the right of the box and select *(normal text)*. Then click on **â** and click on *Insert*, or simply double-click on **â**. You'll see the accented character replace **a** in your restaurant menu.

Symbol

| Symbols | Special Characters |

Font: [normal text]   Shortcut Key: Ctrl+^,A

Insert   Cancel   Shortcut Key...

4 The *Symbol* dialog box remains open until you click on *Cancel* or the Close button, so you can scroll to other locations in your document and insert as many symbols as you want. Click in your document and use the same method to insert **é** at the end of **pâte**.

Garlic bread $2.00¶
Vegetable soup £2.95¶
Lobster pâte with bread $3.5(
Bay oysters (6) $4.00¶
¶

ADDING OTHER SPECIAL CHARACTERS

Your text contains other characters such as double hyphens that you can now modify using the *Symbol* dialog box. To change the double hyphens to em dashes, follow the steps at the top of the next page:

Adding Today's Date
If you want to add the current date to your document, you may find it quickest to use the *Insert* menu. Position the insertion point where you want the date to appear, then choose *Date and Time* from the *Insert* menu. In the *Date and Time* dialog box, choose the date format you want and click on *OK*. To insert the current time, choose one of the time options in the same way.

How to Insert Special Characters

Sunset Bay Grill does not
...nk, insists that we serve a...
...asonable prices. We pride...
...mall portions ▪ when you...
...hole courses, we'll be am...

1 Click in your document and move upward in the text using the Up direction key. Drag the I-beam pointer across the two hyphens between **portions** and **when** to select them. You may find you need to move the *Symbol* dialog box to do this efficiently. To move the dialog box, point to its title bar, hold down the mouse button, and drag the box to a new position (see "Moving a Window" on page 47).

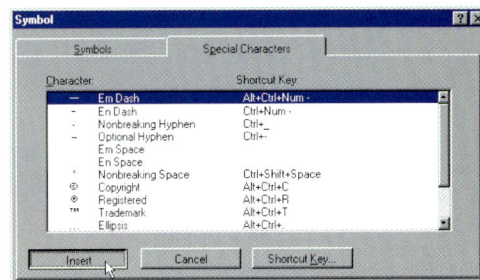

Symbol dialog box showing Special Characters tab with Em Dash, En Dash, Nonbreaking Hyphen, Optional Hyphen, Em Space, En Space, Nonbreaking Space, Copyright, Registered, Trademark, Ellipsis and their shortcut keys; Insert, Cancel, and Shortcut Key buttons.

2 In the *Symbol* dialog box, click on the *Special Characters* tab. A list appears showing you the special characters you can insert. Select the line representing the em dash (—) and click on *Insert*. Repeat the procedure to insert an em dash between **room** and **soundproofed**. Remember to click in your document before using the Up direction key.

every day from noon to mi...
a quiet meal for two or a fi...
room — soundproofed! U...
dwell on fresh fish and lob...
wide range of interesting s...

3 In the document, the double hyphens are replaced by em dashes. Click on *Cancel*, or the Close button, to close the *Symbol* dialog box.

Smart or Straight?
Word automatically inserts special "smart quotes" (curly quotation marks) when you type quotations marks with the keyboard. If you want to use straight quotes instead, choose *Options* from the *Tools* menu and click the *Autoformat* tab in the Options dialog box. Click on the check mark in the *Straight Quotes with 'Smart Quotes'* box to deselect this option, and then click on *OK*.

How to Move Around the Text Area

One way to move the insertion point within your document is to move the I-beam pointer to the new position using your mouse and then click on the mouse button (see page 18). But there are a number of other shortcuts to help you navigate around your text:

Moving Left and Right

■ To move to the left or right one character, press the Left or Right direction key on your keyboard. Hold the key down for continuous movement.

■ To move to the left or right one word, hold down Ctrl and press the Left or Right direction key.

■ To move to the beginning of the current line, press the Home key. To move to the end of a line, press the End key.

■ To move the entire document horizontally, drag the scroll box in the horizontal scroll bar to the left or right. Alternatively, click on the left or right arrow button at either end of the horizontal scroll bar. Hold down the mouse button with the mouse pointer positioned on one of these arrow buttons for continuous scrolling.

Moving Up and Down

■ To move up or down one line, press the Up or Down direction key. Hold the key down for continuous movement.

■ To move up or down one paragraph, hold down Ctrl and press the Up or Down direction key.

■ To scroll the document up or down one screen, press the PgUp or PgDn key.

■ To move to the top or bottom of your screen, hold down Ctrl and press PgUp or PgDn.

■ To move to the beginning of a document, hold down Ctrl and press Home. To move to the end of a document, hold down Ctrl and press End.

■ To move the entire document vertically, use the vertical scroll box or the up and down scroll arrow buttons.

Text Selection

BEFORE YOU CAN DO ANYTHING to a section of text — move it, copy it, delete it, or change its format — you must first select it. Word highlights any selection you make on the screen by displaying the text in white letters against a black background. Learning the most efficient way to select different amounts of text will speed up many of your operations in Word.

How Do I Deselect?
If you select an area of text and then decide that you don't want it selected, simply click anywhere outside the selection in the document window to deselect it.

How to Select Text

There are a variety of techniques for selecting text; the best method depends on the amount you want to highlight. For example, you might want to select a whole paragraph in order to move it, or you might want to select just one word in order to delete it. In many instances, you'll need to click on an area called the selection bar in the left margin of the screen. Use your restaurant menu to practice the following methods.

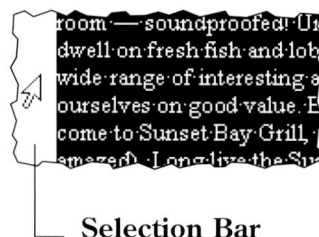

Selection Bar

Selecting a Single Word
To select a single word, you double-click on it with the mouse. Place the I-beam pointer over the word **other** *in the first sentence of the main paragraph, and double-click on it. The word and any spaces after it become highlighted.*

Selecting a Line
To select a line, you click in the selection bar next to the line you want. Select a line in the main paragraph by clicking in the selection bar next to it.

Like many other restaurants, Sunset Bay Grill boasts a relaxed, anything-goes atmosphere. Open every day from noon to midnight, we will provide the type of service you need, whether you want a quiet meal for two or a fun-filled group night out. For the extra rowdy, we have a large back-room — soundproofed! Unlike most seafood restaurants, however, Sunset Bay Grill does not dwell on fresh fish and lobster alone. Our forceful (but friendly) chef Hank, insists that we serve a wide range of interesting and international dishes too! And all at very reasonable prices. We pride ourselves on good value. But be warned: Hank doesn't believe in small portions — when you come to Sunset Bay Grill, you must come hungry (if you manage three whole courses, we'll be amazed). Long live the Sunshine Coast. Long live Sunset Bay Grill.¶

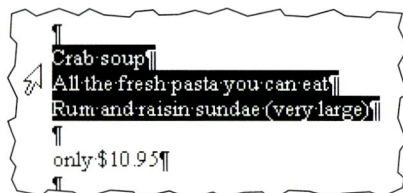

Selecting a Sequence of Lines
To select a sequence of lines, you click in the selection bar next to the first line you want to select and drag the mouse up or down. Hold down the mouse button when the pointer is in the selection bar next to **Crab soup**; *drag down to select the next two lines, and then release the mouse button.*

Crab soup¶
All the fresh pasta you can eat¶
Rum and raisin sundae (very large)¶
¶
only $10.95¶
¶

Selecting to the End of a Line
To select from the current position of the insertion point to the end of the line, you hold down Shift and press End. Holding down Shift and pressing Home selects from the current position to the beginning of a line. Click the I-beam pointer in front of (**AND PLENTY MORE BESIDES**), *hold down Shift and press End.*

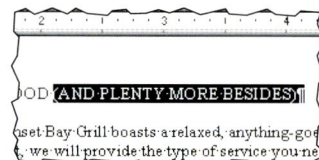

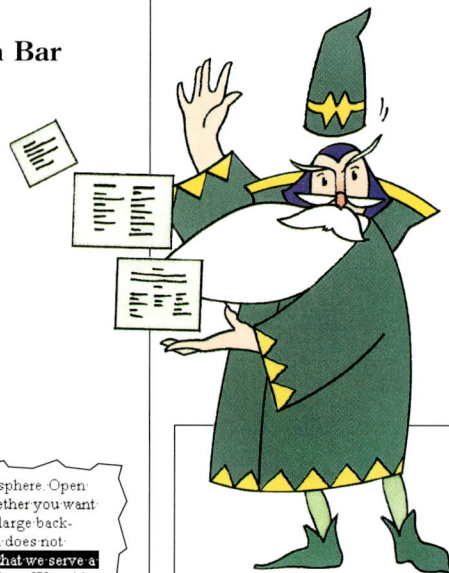

...OD (AND PLENTY MORE BESIDES)¶
...nset Bay Grill boasts a relaxed, anything-goe...
...we will provide the type of service you ne...

Rectangular Blocks
You can select a rectangular block of text of any size within your document. To do this, put your I-beam pointer at one corner of the block you want to select, hold down the Alt key, press down on the mouse button, and drag the mouse in a diagonal direction. Release the mouse button and the Alt key when the rectangular area of text you want is selected.

Selecting a Sentence

To select a whole sentence, you position the I-beam anywhere in the sentence, then hold down Ctrl and click the mouse button. Hold down Ctrl and click anywhere in the sentence beginning **But be warned**. *Any spaces at the end of the sentence are also selected.*

Selecting a Paragraph

To select a paragraph, you double-click anywhere in the selection bar next to the paragraph. Double-click in the selection bar next to the main paragraph that starts **Like many other**.

Selecting the Whole Document

To select the entire document, hold down Ctrl and click anywhere in the selection bar.

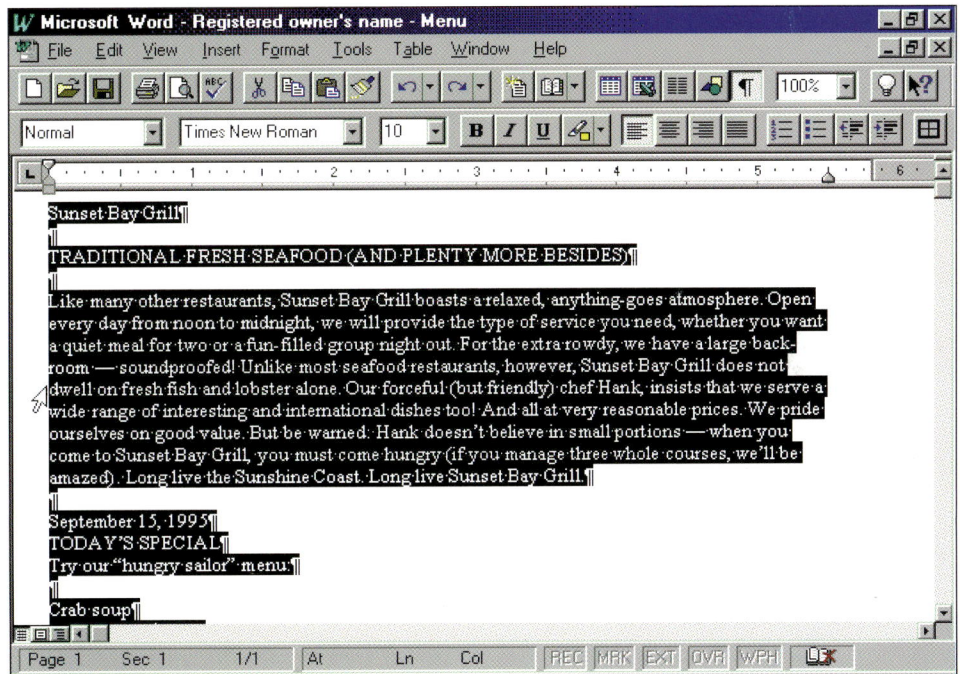

Clear That Box!

If you select by dragging over more than one word, and your selection includes a part or parts of words, Word automatically highlights the whole of each word, as well as any spaces after the words. If you don't want this automatic word selection, choose *Options* from the *Tools* menu, and then click on the *Edit* tab. Under *Editing Options*, clear the *Automatic Word Selection* check box, and then click on *OK*.

Selecting Any Amount of Text

To select just one character or any amount of text, you position the I-beam wherever you want the selection to start, hold down the mouse button, and drag the mouse pointer to the position where you want the selection to end. Then release the mouse button.

Text Revision

AFTER YOU HAVE TYPED IN SOME TEXT, you may decide to revise the text in a variety of ways. For example, you may want to insert or delete a sentence, change a word, or move or copy whole paragraphs from one place to another in the document. With Word you can even search for specific text and replace it with new text in one easy step. Let's find out how simple it is to perform these operations by revising some of the text you have entered so far for your restaurant menu.

How to Insert Text

To insert text in your document, all you need to do is position the insertion point at the place you want to insert the text, and then type. As you type, the existing text will be pushed along to the right. In your restaurant menu, carry out the following insertion:

September 15, 1995¶
TODAY'S SPECIAL¶
Try our "hungry sailor" menu:¶
¶
Crab soup¶
All the fresh pasta you can eat ¶

Adding Text

1 Position the insertion point just to the left of the words **"hungry sailor"** under **TODAY'S SPECIAL**.

2 Type **3-course** followed by a space. The text is inserted into your existing text.

September 15, 1995¶
TODAY'S SPECIAL¶
Try our 3-course "hungry sailor" menu:¶
¶
Crab soup¶
All the fresh pasta you can eat ¶

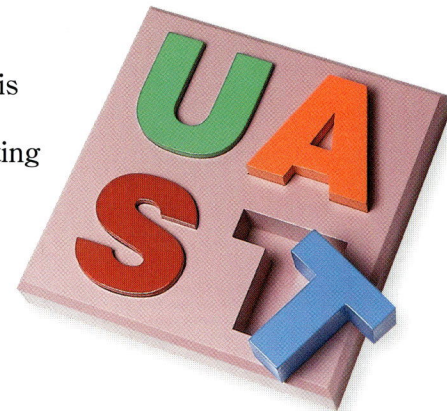

How to Delete Text

The simplest way to remove small amounts of incorrect text is to position the insertion point next to the text you want to remove and press either the Delete key or the Backspace key to remove one character at a time (see page 20). If you want to delete more than a few characters, however, Word provides a number of mouse and keyboard shortcuts to make text correction faster and easier.

DELETING ONE WORD AT A TIME
You can quickly remove a single word using Ctrl and Delete. In your document place the insertion point to the left of the word **fresh** in **All the fresh pasta**, and then press Ctrl and Delete together.

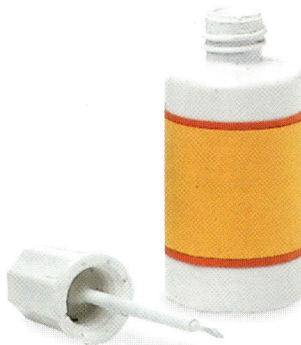

Lost Your Bearings?
Don't worry if you can't find the place where you were last editing, Word remembers the last three locations where you typed or revised text. Simply press Shift and F5 until you reach the location you want.

Wrong Word?
If you want to remove a word that you've just typed, press Ctrl and Backspace together. The insertion point must be positioned at the immediate right of the word.

DELETING SELECTED TEXT

The quickest way to delete whole sections of text, such as sentences and paragraphs, is to select the unwanted text (see pages 30 to 31) and then press the Delete or Backspace key. Follow these steps to practice this:

1 Select the line **French onion soup $2.00** under **Starters**. Make sure you also select the paragraph mark at the end of the line.

Starters¶
¶
French·onion·soup·$2.00¶
Garlic·bread·$2.00¶
Vegetable·soup·$2.95¶
Lobster·pâté·with·bread·$3.50¶

2 Press the Backspace key. All the lines below will move up.

Starters¶
¶
Garlic·bread·$2.00¶
Vegetable·soup·$2.95¶
Lobster·pâté·with·bread·$3.50¶
Bay·oysters·(6)·$4.00¶

OVERTYPING

You don't have to delete text in order to correct mistakes. Word lets you type over incorrect text with new text. There are two ways of doing this. If you select the incorrect text and then start typing in the replacement text, Word deletes the old text and inserts the new text. Alternatively, if you press the Insert key, Word switches to "Overtype" mode and anything you type will overwrite existing text, character for character. Let's practice these two methods in your document:

Typing Over Selected Text

Starters¶
¶
Garlic·bread·$2.00¶
Vegetable·soup·$2.95¶
Lobster·pâté·with·bread·$3.50¶
Bay·oysters·(6)·$4.00¶

1 Select the word **Vegetable** under **Starters**.

2 Type the word **Crab**. Word deletes the old text as you begin to type in the new text.

Starters¶
¶
Garlic·bread·$2.00¶
Crab soup·$2.95¶
Lobster·pâté·with·bread·$3.50¶
Bay·oysters·(6)·$4.00¶

Using the Overtype Mode

Starters¶
¶
Garlic·bread·$2.00¶
Crab·soup·$2.95¶
Lobster·pâté·with·bread·$3.50¶
Bay·oysters·(6)·$4.00¶

1 Press the Insert key to switch to Overtype mode and position the insertion point at the beginning of **bread** in the line **Lobster pâté with bread $3.50**.

2 Type **toast**.

Starters¶
¶
Garlic·bread·$2.00¶
Crab·soup·$2.95¶
Lobster·pâté·with·toast $3.50¶
Bay·oysters·(6)·$4.00¶

Because the new word contains the same number of characters, it simply overwrites the original word. Finally, press the Insert key again to turn off Overtype mode.

Unwanted Deletion?

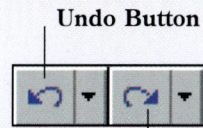

Undo Button

Redo Button

If you make a mistake when you are revising your text, don't panic. Word allows you to undo an action or command. For example, if you accidentally delete a selection of text, you can bring it back again. Simply click on the Undo button on the Standard toolbar; Word will undo the last action it performed. If you then decide to go through with the action after all, you can redo it by clicking on the Redo button.

ne - Menu
Table   Window   Help

Typing t
Typing s
Typing a
Typing o
Typing t
Typing "Crab"

Undo 5 Actions

A Multiple Undo

Multiple Actions

To undo or redo more than one action, click on the arrow next to the Undo or Redo button. A drop-down list shows the order in which the previous actions were performed. Click or drag to select the actions you want to undo or redo — they have to be undone or redone in order. Word remembers the last 100 actions that you carried out.

Check the Status Bar!
Be careful when you are using Overtype mode — if the text you are inserting is not the same length as the text you are replacing, you may type over text you want to keep. You must also remember to turn off Overtype mode when you have replaced the text. If the status bar displays the letters OVR, overtype mode is on. Press the Insert key again to turn off Overtype mode.

How to Move Text

Another way you may want to revise your document is to move text from one place to another, perhaps to reorder sentences or paragraphs. Word offers two main methods for moving text. Let's practice these different methods by moving some text around your restaurant menu.

DRAG AND DROP METHOD

If you want to move text over a short distance, the easiest technique is the drag and drop method. You can also use this method to move text or other items from one Word window to another (see "Multiple Windows" on page 46).

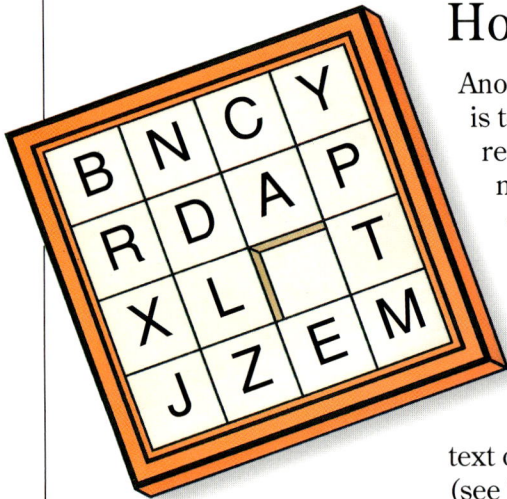

Dragging and Dropping

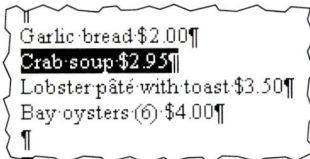

Garlic·bread·$2.00¶
Crab·soup·$2.95¶
Lobster·pâté·with·toast·$3.50¶
Bay·oysters·(6)·$4.00¶
¶

1 Select the line **Crab soup $2.95** in the **Starters** section of your restaurant menu. (Make sure you release the mouse button after selecting text.)

2 Place the mouse pointer over the highlighted text, and then hold down the mouse button. A dotted I-beam pointer and a small dotted box appear along with the pointer.

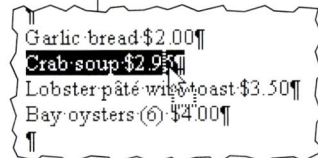

Garlic·bread·$2.00¶
Crab·soup·$2.95¶
Lobster·pâté·with·toast·$3.50¶
Bay·oysters·(6)·$4.00¶
¶

Garlic·bread·$2.00¶
Crab·soup·$2.95¶
Lobster·pâté·with·toast·$3.50¶
Bay·oysters·(6)·$4.00¶
¶

3 While holding down the mouse button, drag the text to its new position. Position the dotted I-beam pointer at the left margin directly below the line **Bay oysters (6) $4.00**.

4 Release the mouse button; the text drops into its new position.

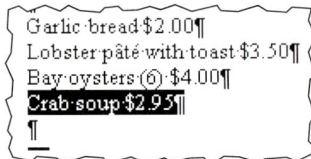

Garlic·bread·$2.00¶
Lobster·pâté·with·toast·$3.50¶
Bay·oysters·(6)·$4.00¶
Crab·soup·$2.95¶
¶

CUT AND PASTE METHOD

This method is better for longer moves over several pages within a document. Cutting erases the selected text and transfers a copy of it to the Clipboard, a temporary storage area. Pasting then copies the Clipboard contents to the new insertion point you choose. Let's practice this method on your restaurant menu.

?

What Can I Move?
Text is not the only thing you can move using the drag and drop and cut and paste techniques. You can move any item in your document including graphics, special screen symbols, and items you have inserted from other applications.

Cutting and Pasting

Garlic bread $2.00¶
Lobster pâté with toast $3.50¶
Bay oysters (6) $4.00¶
Crab soup $2.95¶
¶

1 Select the line **Crab soup $2.95** again.

2 Choose *Cut* from the *Edit* menu or click on the Cut button on the Standard toolbar. The selected text disappears from your document.

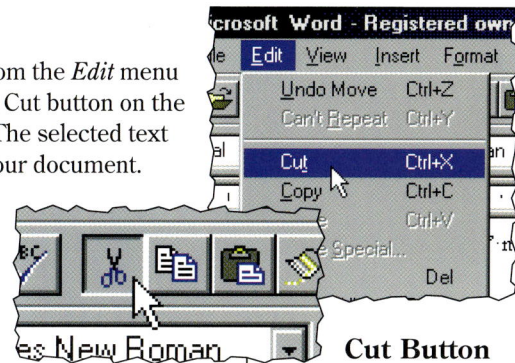

Cut Button

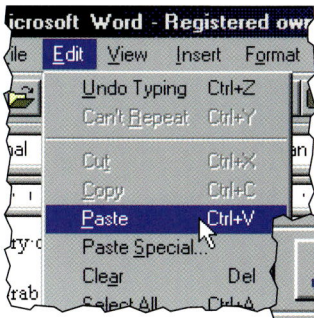

Paste Button

3 Move the insertion point to the beginning of the line **Garlic bread $2.00**, and then choose *Paste* from the *Edit* menu or click on the Paste button on the Standard toolbar.

4 The text reappears in its new position.

Crab soup $2.95¶
Garlic bread $2.00¶
Lobster pâté with toast $3.50¶
Bay oysters (6) $4.00¶
¶

How to Copy Text

When you are working on a document, you may want to copy sections of text that have to be repeated elsewhere. Copying text is similar to moving text in that you select the text and then use either the drag and drop method or the copy and paste method. Unlike moving text, however, copied text also remains at its original location.

DRAG AND DROP METHOD
To copy text, you use the same drag and drop technique you used for moving text, except you also hold down the Ctrl key.

1 Select the word **Sunset** at the top of your document. Place the mouse pointer over the selected text. Then hold down Ctrl and press the mouse button. You'll see a plus sign below the dotted box to show that you are copying text.

Sunset Bay Grill¶
¶
TRADITIONAL FRESH SEAF

Crab soup $2.95¶
Garlic bread $2.00¶
Lobster pâté with toast $3.50¶
Bay oysters (6) $4.00¶

2 Drag the dotted I-beam pointer in front of the word **Bay** in **Bay oysters**. Because **Bay** is not visible on the screen, you'll have to scroll while dragging. Drag the pointer to the bottom of the screen; the pointer will stay in place in this position but the screen will move upward to reveal the remaining text.

3 Release the mouse button and Ctrl to drop the copy of the text into position.

Crab soup $2.95¶
Garlic bread $2.00¶
Lobster pâté with toast $3.50¶
Sunset Bay oysters (6) $4.00¶
¶

? What's the Clipboard? Every time you cut or copy text, it is copied into the Clipboard, a temporary holding area. The item remains in the Clipboard until you choose *Cut* or *Copy* again, when it is replaced with the new item. One way of viewing the Clipboard's contents is to click on the Paste button, look at what's been pasted, and then click on the Undo button.

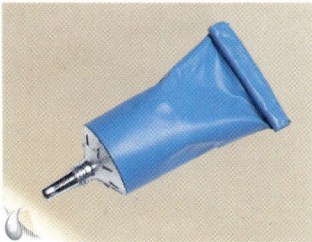

COPY AND PASTE METHOD

As with cutting and pasting, the following method is better if you want to copy text over several pages. For now, let's practice using the technique on your restaurant menu.

1 Select the words **Sunshine Coast** in the last line of the main paragraph.

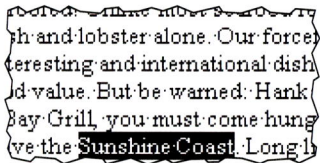

2 Choose *Copy* from the *Edit* menu or click on the Copy button on the Standard toolbar.

Copy Button

3 Place the insertion point at the beginning of the word **restaurants** in the first line of the main paragraph, and then choose *Paste* from the *Edit* menu or click on the Paste button on the Standard toolbar.

Paste Button

4 You'll see the copied text plus a space appear in its new position. Word automatically adds a space to make the text fit its surroundings. (If, for example, you select a word with a space and then paste it to the end of a sentence, Word will automatically remove the space in front of the period.)

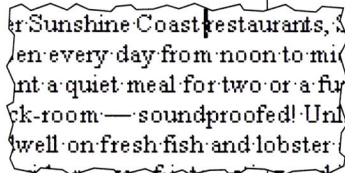

(?)

Want to Paste More Than Once?
Once you have copied a selection of text to the Clipboard, you can paste it into your document — or any other documents — as many times as you like. The text remains in the Clipboard until you replace it by copying or cutting a new item.

Spike It!
If you want to move (not copy) many pieces of text to the same place, use the Spike — a feature that is like the Clipboard but holds more than one entry at a time. To move text to the Spike, select the item you want to move and press Ctrl and F3 together. You can keep adding to the Spike in the same way. To paste the Spike contents, place the insertion point at the desired place and press Ctrl and Shift and F3 together.

Using Bookmarks

Like the name suggests, a bookmark is a "tag" that you can insert into a Word document to find a particular selection of text again. Bookmarks are helpful for navigating around long documents. To insert a bookmark, you have to assign a name to the location you want to tag. Word invisibly marks this location and leads you back to it when you call up its name. Bookmarks don't appear on the screen or when you print the document. You can assign as many as 450 bookmarks to one document.

Inserting a Bookmark

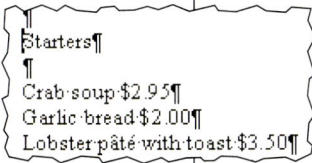

Starters¶
¶
Crab·soup·$2.95¶
Garlic·bread·$2.00¶
Lobster·pâté·with·toast·$3.50¶

1 Position the insertion point where you want to insert the bookmark. In your document, position the insertion point to the left of the word **Starters**.

2 Choose *Bookmark* from the *Edit* menu.

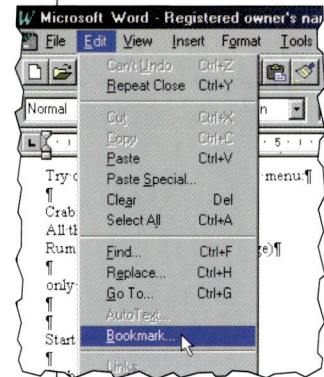

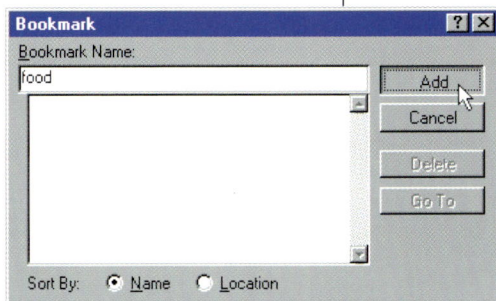

Bookmark
Bookmark Name:
food
Add
Cancel
Delete
Go To
Sort By: ● Name ○ Location

3 The *Bookmark* dialog box appears on the screen. In the *Bookmark Name* text box, type in the name **food** to define your bookmark and then click on *Add*. The location you chose is now named, and the name of your bookmark will appear in the *Bookmark Name* list box.

Jumping to a Bookmark

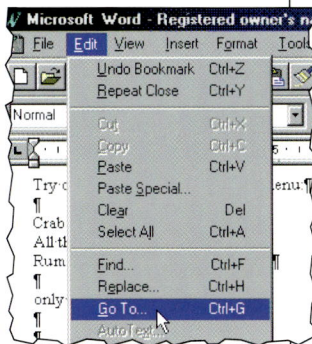

1 Position your insertion point somewhere else in the document, and then choose *Go To* from the *Edit* menu.

2 The *Go To* dialog box appears. Under *Go To What*, choose *Bookmark*. In the *Enter Bookmark Name* box, choose the bookmark you want to go to (in this case, **food**). Click on *Go To*, and then click on *Close* or the Close button.

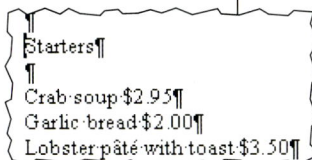

Starters¶
¶
Crab·soup·$2.95¶
Garlic·bread·$2.00¶
Lobster·pâté·with·toast·$3.50¶

3 Word jumps to the point in the text where your specified bookmark appears; in this case, in front of **Starters**.

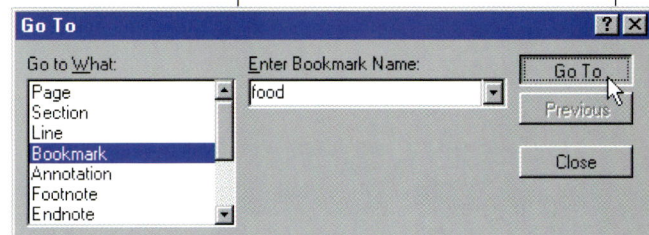

How to Find and Replace Text

Word lets you change the text in your document using the *Find* and *Replace* commands on the *Edit* menu. You can use the *Find* command to search a long document for specific words, characters, or other elements, such as graphics. To replace specific items, you can use the *Replace* command. The *Replace* command is most often used for changing text that occurs frequently throughout a document.

FINDING TEXT IN A DOCUMENT

The *Find* command is especially useful if you are looking for a section of text that contains a key word that easily identifies it. Let's use *Find* in your document.

Finding a Word

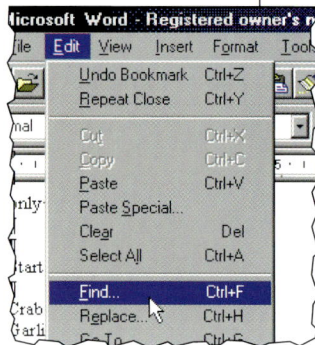

1 Position the insertion point anywhere in your restaurant menu, and then choose *Find* from the *Edit* menu.

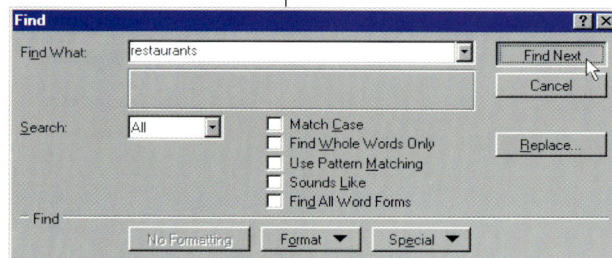

2 The *Find* dialog box appears. In the *Find What* text box, type the word **restaurants**. In the *Search* box, select *All*. Then click on the *Find Next* button to begin the search.

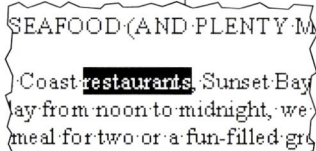

3 Because *All* is displayed in the *Search* box, Word will search the whole document. Word finds the word and highlights it. If you wanted to edit the word in your document without closing the *Find* dialog box, you could do so by simply clicking in your document and editing.

4 For now, click on the *Find Next* button to continue the search. When Word reaches the end of the document the message at left appears. Click on *OK*.

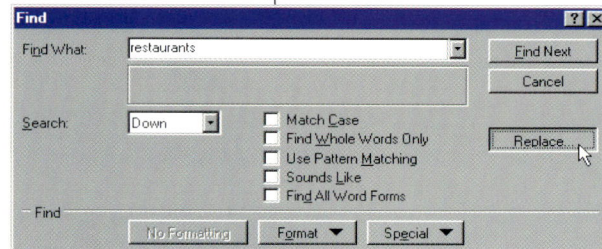

5 Click on the Close button to close the *Find* dialog box.

Want to Repeat a Search?
If you close the *Find* dialog box and then decide to repeat the search you've just completed, you don't have to open the dialog box again. Simply press Shift and F4 on your keyboard; Word will repeat the search.

Replaceable
If you want to change your search from finding text to replacing it, you can click on the Replace *button in the* Find *dialog box. The* Find *dialog box disappears and the* Replace *dialog appears in its place.*

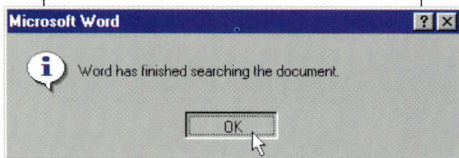

38

REPLACING TEXT IN A DOCUMENT

Word's *Replace* command is a useful timesaver when you want to change an item over and over again in your document. It can search for and replace all occurrences of a specified element in your document in one easy step. Practice using this command to replace a frequently occurring word in your restaurant menu.

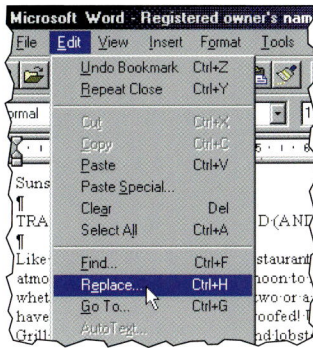

Replacing a Word

1 Place the insertion point at the beginning of your document, and then choose *Replace* from the *Edit* menu.

2 The *Replace* dialog box appears. Type **sunset** in the *Find What* text box and **sunrise** in the *Replace With* text box. Then click on the *Replace All* button to find and replace all occurrences of **Sunset** within your document.

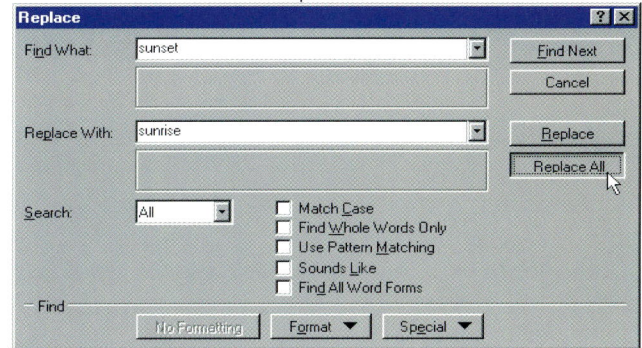

3 The message at right appears, telling you how many replacements were made. Click on *OK*. Then click on the Close button in the *Replace* dialog box.

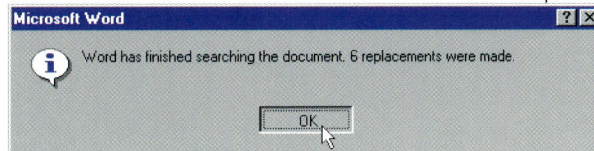

Perfect Matches

In both the *Find* and *Replace* dialog boxes, you'll find several options that make searching for an item more precise. By checking any of these options, you can control the way that Word searches through a document.

■ *Match Case* — If you check this option, Word will search through your document and find only those words with the specified pattern of uppercase and lowercase letters. For example, if you type **Sunrise** in the *Find What* text box, Word will find any instance of **Sunrise** but it won't find **sunrise.**

■ *Find Whole Words Only* — This option finds only separate words, not characters embedded in other words. This is useful if the word you are looking for could be part of a longer word.

■ *Use Pattern Matching* — This option can be used for special search operations. For example, you can type **r??d** to search for any four-letter string of characters that starts with **r** and ends with **d**.

■ *Sounds Like* — This option finds words that sound the same as the text you typed in the *Find What* box but are spelled differently, such as the words **pail** and **pale**.

■ *Find All Word Forms* — When this option is checked, Word will find all the forms of the word being searched for. If you search for the word **drink**, Word will also find **drank** and **drunk**.

■ *Search* — By default, the *Search* box is set on *All* and Word searches the whole of your document. You can limit a search by setting *Up* or *Down* in the *Search* box. This prompts Word to search your document from the insertion point to the beginning or end of your document only.

Not Just Words!
You can use the *Find* and *Replace* commands not only to find and replace text, but also to find and replace formats, such as bold and italic, and special characters, such as paragraph marks and tab characters. Click on the *Format* or *Special* buttons in the relevant dialog box to see the formats and special items you can find or replace.

Text Checking

WORD PROVIDES SEVERAL TOOLS to help you clean up your text. You can check spelling with the dictionary, look up synonyms with the thesaurus, and even check your writing style and grammar with the grammar checker. Before you use these tools, add some lines to the restaurant menu. First position the insertion point at the end of the current last line of text, press Enter twice, and then add the lines shown in the box below. Type the lines exactly as they appear, including the misspelling.

How Spelling is Checked

When you first use Word, the automatic spelling check is active. As you type, the spelling check compares the words you enter with the words stored in a dictionary file. If a word isn't in the dictionary, a red wavy line appears below the word, and a Tip Wizard box opens above the ruler telling you to place the I-beam pointer over the word and click the right mouse button.

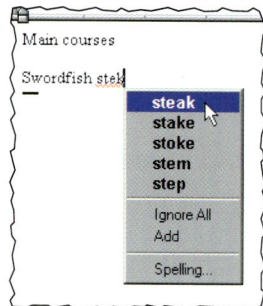

Main courses <Enter> <Enter>

Swordfish stek $13.95 <Enter>
Sunshine Coast lobster $15.95 <Enter>
Spaghetti carbonara (pasta with bacon, cream, egg, and parmesan) $7.95 <Enter>
Grilled halibut with lime and béarnaise sauce $14.95 <Enter> <Enter>

All dishes are served with a choice of vegetables of the day or side salad <Enter> <Enter>

Desserts <Enter> <Enter>

Rum and raisin sundae $2.95 <Enter>
Death by chocolate (a deep layer of chocolate mousse on a sponge base) $3.95 <Enter>
Cassata (layers of real Italian ice-cream) $2.95 <Enter> <Enter> <Enter>

why not try a delicious liqueur coffee for only $3.50? <Enter>

1 The red wavy line appears below the word **stek**. Right-click on the word and the spelling check pop-up menu appears. The correct word **steak** is the first alternative spelling offered, so click on it to replace **stek**.

2 Continue typing in the text, the next word to be underlined is **carbonara**. As this is correct, you can use the *Add* option in the spelling check menu. This will add the word to an empty custom dictionary that Word provides called **Custom.dic**. Word also consults this dictionary and prevents the word from being queried again.

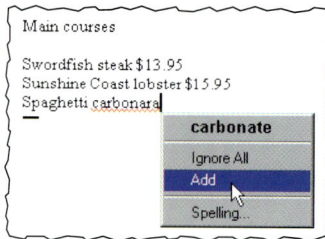

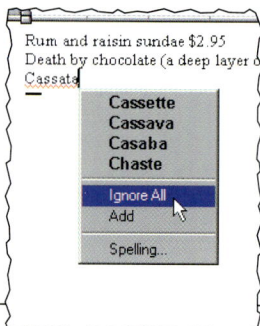

3 When the spelling check queries **cassata**, you can use *Ignore All* in the pop-up menu. This option is used for words that needn't be added to **Custom.dic** because you don't use them very often. Once you've clicked on this option, Word doesn't query the word again during the current session of Word. Finally, to close the Tip Wizard box, click on the Tip Wizard button on the Standard toolbar.

Don't Expect Miracles!
The spelling checker cannot identify an incorrectly spelled word that is a word in its own right and spelled correctly, for example, "form" when you wanted "from."

Want to Check Just One Word?
You might want to verify the spelling of a single word when the automatic spelling check is turned off. All you have to do is select the word by double-clicking on it, and then press F7.

Turning off Automatic Spelling Check

If you don't need to have your document spell-checked as you type, you can turn off the automatic spelling check. Select *Options* from the *Tools* menu and click on the Spelling tab in the *Options* dialog box. Click on the check box next to *Automatic Spell Checking* to deselect it. Finally click on *OK* to close the *Options* dialog box.

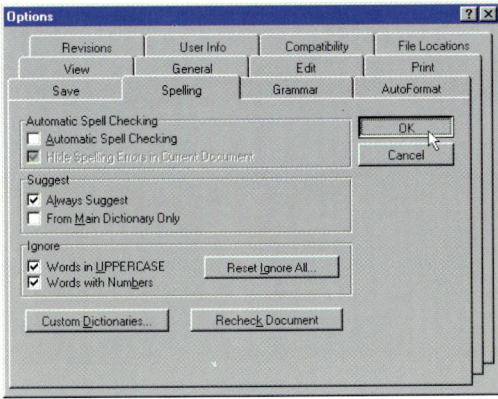

Running a Spelling Check

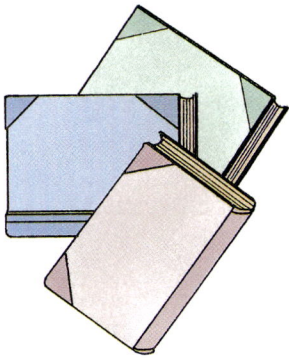

1 Even with the automatic spelling check turned off, you can still ask Word to spell-check your document at any time. Choose *Spelling* from the *Tools* menu or click on the Spelling button on the Standard toolbar.

Spelling Button

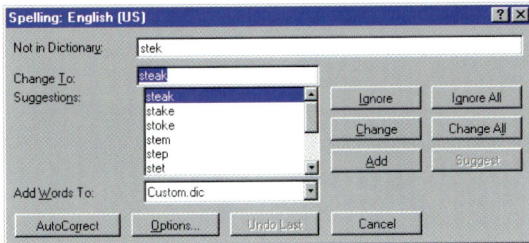

2 The *Spelling* dialog box appears when a potentially misspelled word is found. The *Not in Dictionary* text box displays **Stek**, and the *Change To* text box offers a likely alternative. The *Suggestions* list box displays a number of other possible spellings and you could click on any word that appears in this box to put it into the *Change To* text box. Sometimes none of the suggestions is appropriate, or no suggestions are made. In such instances, you must type the correct word in the *Change To* text box.

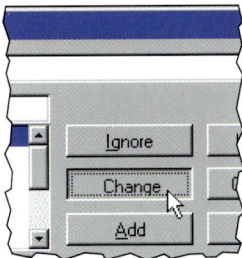

3 However, **steak** is the word you want, so simply click on *Change* to substitute **steak** for **stek**. If you don't want to change a word, just click on *Ignore*. Word then continues checking the rest of the document.

4 At the end of the document, the message at right tells you that Word has finished the spell-check. Simply click on *OK*.

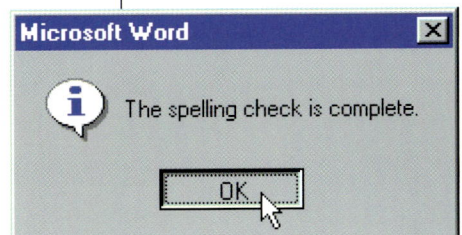

Common Errors

The AutoCorrect feature (see page 110) can automatically correct spelling errors you habitually make. When an error you frequently make is queried by the spelling check, click on the *AutoCorrect* button in the *Spelling* dialog box. This will add the error and its correct spelling to the AutoCorrect list, so when you make this error next time it will be automatically corrected as you type.

The spelling check is complete.

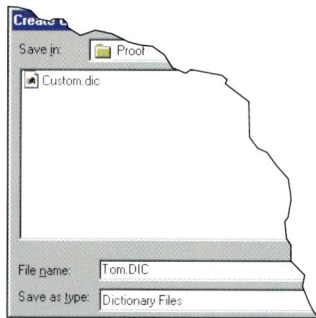

Additional Custom Dictionaries

To create an additional custom dictionary, choose *Options* from the *Tools* menu and click on the *Spelling* tab. (You can also reach this section of the *Options* dialog box while running a spelling check by clicking on the *Options* button in the *Spelling* dialog box.) Click on *Custom Dictionaries,* click on *New*. In the *Create Custom Dictionary* dialog box, type a name for the new dictionary in the *File name* box. Then click on *Save*.

You see the new custom dictionary and any other custom dictionaries listed in the *Custom Dictionaries* dialog box. If the box to the left of a custom dictionary is checked, the dictionary is open and can be consulted during a spell check. To close a custom dictionary, clear its check box. Click on *OK* to close the *Custom Dictionaries* dialog box and do the same in the *Options* dialog box.

To add a queried word to a specific custom dictionary during a spelling check, select the dictionary in the *Add Words To* list box (see left). Then click on *Add*.

Naming a Dictionary
It is a good idea to use your own name when naming a custom dictionary.

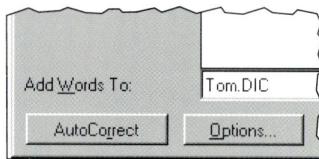

Adding a Word
Select the dictionary to which you want to add a word before clicking on Add. Double-check the spelling of a word before you add it. Be careful when adding uppercase words — the spelling checker will flag any occurrences that are not capitalized.

How to Use the Thesaurus

Word provides a thesaurus that helps you find synonyms for selected words. The thesaurus also lists related words and antonyms when appropriate.

No Thesaurus?
If you can't find the *Thesaurus* command in the *Tools* menu, the thesaurus probably was not installed with Word. To gain access to the thesaurus, reinstall Word and include the thesaurus. The same applies to the grammar checker and spelling check.

Substituting a Word

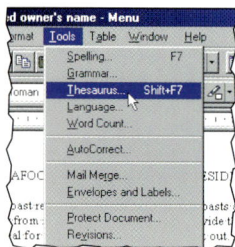

2 Choose *Thesaurus* from the *Tools* menu. The *Thesaurus* dialog box appears.

1 Select the word for which you want a synonym. Select **amazed** in the restaurant menu.

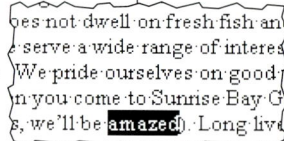

3 **Amazed** appears in the *Looked Up* text box, and the suggestion **blank** appears in the *Replace with Synonym* text box.

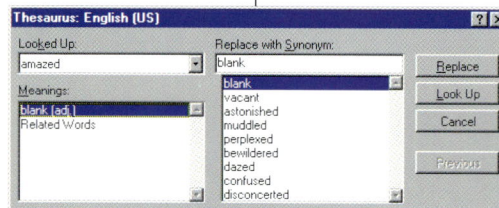

4 The word **blank** is unsuitable. Click on **astonished** in the *Replace with Synonym* list box. (You can also choose *Related Words* or *Antonyms,* if either appears, in the *Meanings* list box to display other choices.)

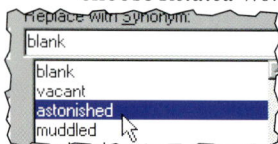

5 **Astonished** appears in the *Replace with Synonym* box. Click on the *Replace* button to substitute **astonished** for **amazed**.

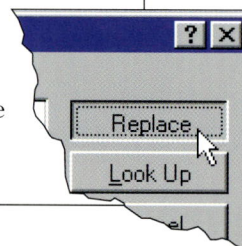

How to Use the Grammar Checker

If you want to check your document for grammatical errors, you can use Word's built-in grammar checker. The grammar checker offers advice about sentence structure and punctuation. It also performs a spelling check, so you don't need to run the spelling checker before doing a grammar check. Remember that the grammar checker is only a guide — you won't always want to use its suggestions.

Running a Grammar Check

1 Position the insertion point at the beginning of your restaurant menu. Choose *Grammar* from the *Tools* menu.

2 The grammar checker queries the second sentence. Click on the *Explain* button. After reading the explanation, click on the Close button of the *Grammar Explanation* window. Click on *Ignore* to disregard the grammar checker's advice.

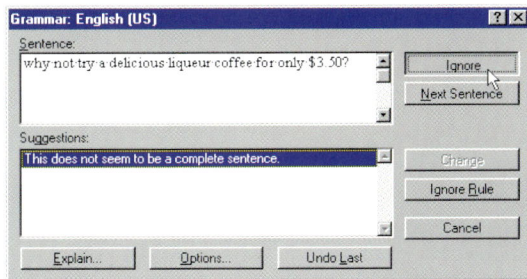

3 Continue checking the rest of your document. Ignore all the suggestions, including the two spelling suggestions. The grammar checker will query the last sentence as being incomplete — click on *Ignore*.

4 The grammar checker now advises you to substitute **Why** for **why**. Click on *Change* to accept this suggestion.

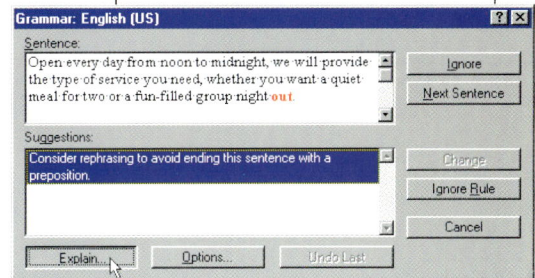

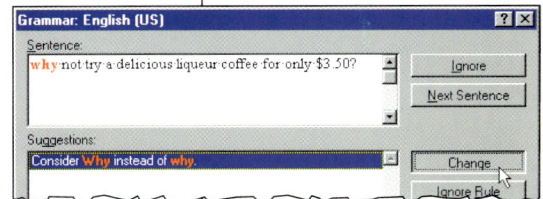

Checker Too Strict for You?
You can control how strictly Word examines your grammar. Choose *Options* from the *Tools* menu and click on the *Grammar* tab. Here you can choose from three rule groups — strict, business, and casual — all of which you can customize to observe or ignore specific rules.

Readability Statistics

When the grammar checker has finished, a dialog box containing document statistics appears. The statistics under the headings *Counts* and *Averages* and the *Passive Sentences* score are self-explanatory. The other statistics indicate how easy your document is to read — but use them only as a guide.

■ The *Flesch Reading Ease* and *Flesch-Kincaid Grade Level* scores are based on the average number of words per sentence and the average number of syllables per 100 words. A *Reading Ease* score of 60 to 70 is average; lower scores suggest that a document is harder to read. A *Grade Level* of 7 or 8 is average; higher scores suggest that the text is more difficult.

■ The *Coleman-Liau Grade Level* and the *Bormuth Grade Level* use both the word length in characters and the sentence length in words to determine a grade level.

After reading the assessment of your document, click on *OK* to close the *Readability Statistics* dialog box.

Manipulating Windows

YOU MAY SOMETIMES want to split the screen to see different parts of a document at the same time. This allows you to revise different parts of a document without scrolling back and forth continually. You may also want to change the size of a window or open a second document window to compare two documents and move or copy text between them.

Split Screens

You can split a window into two horizontal parts. Each part of the split window is called a pane; and each pane scrolls independently. A change made to the text in one pane automatically affects the text in another pane.

OPENING AND CLOSING A SPLIT SCREEN

The small bar just above the up scroll arrow on the right side of the screen is called the split box. You use the split box to split and unsplit the screen. Let's practice these procedures on your restaurant menu:

1 Point to the split box above the vertical scroll bar. The mouse pointer changes to two split lines with an arrow above and below.

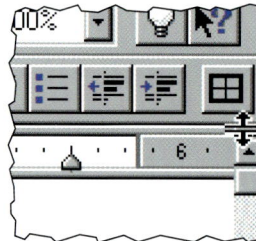

2 Hold down the mouse button and drag the pointer down the screen. You will see a horizontal guideline move downward along with the pointer as you drag the mouse.

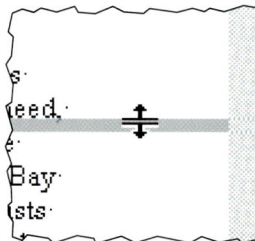

3 Release the mouse button when the guideline reaches the line just above the date. The screen splits into two panes.

4 There are two ways to close the split screen. Either position the pointer over the bar between the two vertical scroll bars and drag the split symbol to the top of the screen, or simply double-click on the split screen bar.

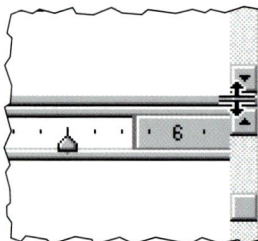

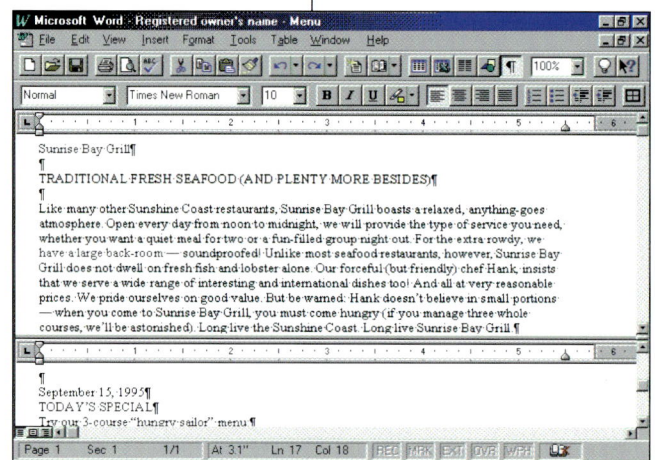

Across the Divide
Using a split screen makes it easy to cut or copy and paste sections of text in a long document. Split the screen into two panes and display the text you want to move or copy in one pane and the destination in the other; then perform the cut or copy and paste using the toolbar buttons.

Maximizing and Minimizing

So far you have only worked with the Word application window and the document window maximized and merged. However, you can change the size of your window with a click of a button. You might want to adjust your window size to view other documents.

Window Reduced to a Smaller Size

Word Maximize/Restore Button

When your Word application window is fully maximized, the Word Maximize/Restore button appears as two overlapping rectangles. When you click on the Word Maximize/Restore button, your window is reduced to a smaller size, as shown at the far right. The Maximize/Restore button now appears as a single rectangle. Click on it to restore the window to its full size.

Reducing the Window Size

Restoring the Window Size

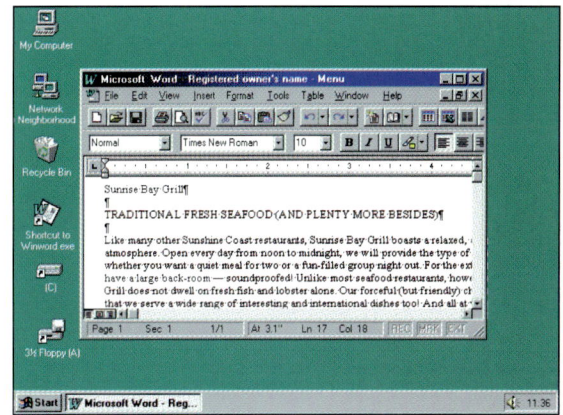

Document Maximize/Restore Button

The document Maximize/Restore button appears as two rectangles when the document window is merged with the application window. If you click on the button, the document window becomes separated from the application window, as shown at far right, and the document Maximize/Restore button changes to a single rectangle. Click on the button to merge the document with the Word application window again.

Separating the Document Window

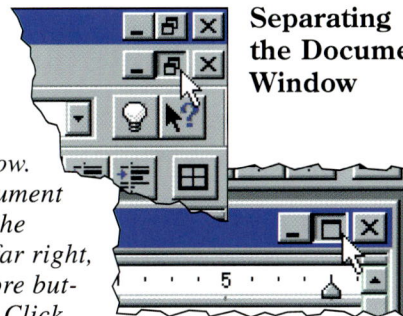

Merging the Document Window

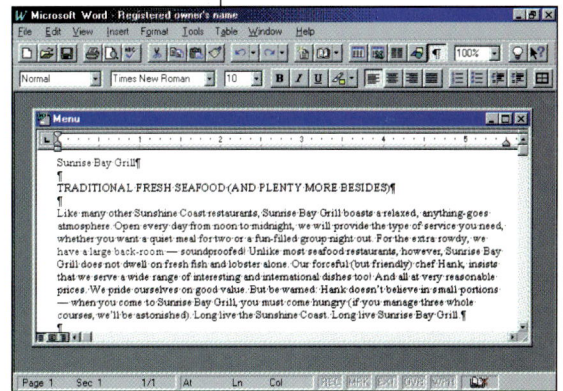

Document Window Separated from the Application Window

Word Minimize Button

If you click on the Word Minimize button, the whole application window shrinks to a button on the Taskbar, as shown at right. To display the window again, simply click on the icon.

Application Minimized

Document Minimize Button

You can minimize the document by clicking on its Minimize button. The document shrinks to a small title bar at the foot of the application window. Redisplay the document by clicking on either of the two Maximize/Restore buttons that appear in the icon's titlebar.

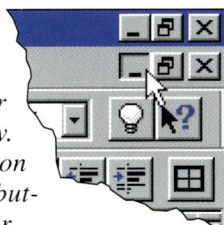

Minimizing the Document

Redisplaying the Document

Multiple Windows

Multiple windows are useful when you want to compare different documents or move text from one document to another document. With Word, you can have up to nine document windows open at one time. Multiple windows are different from a split screen in that they allow you to view several different documents rather than two different views of the same document.

OPENING A SECOND DOCUMENT

When you open another document, it automatically becomes active, which means it contains the insertion point, and any actions you carry out affect only this document. Here we show how to open a second document on screen. With your restaurant menu already open, choose *Open* from the *File* menu so that the *File Open* dialog box appears. Then follow these steps:

1 Choose **Prize letter** from the list of files, then click on *Open*. **Prize letter** will open on the screen, hiding the **Menu** window.

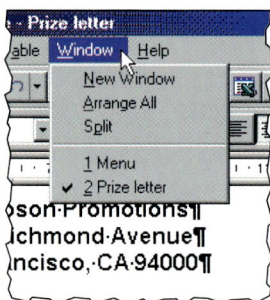

2 Each time you open a document, Word gives it a number that identifies it. To see the list of open documents, click on *Window* in the menu bar. A check next to a name indicates the active document. To bring a hidden window into view, simply click on its name.

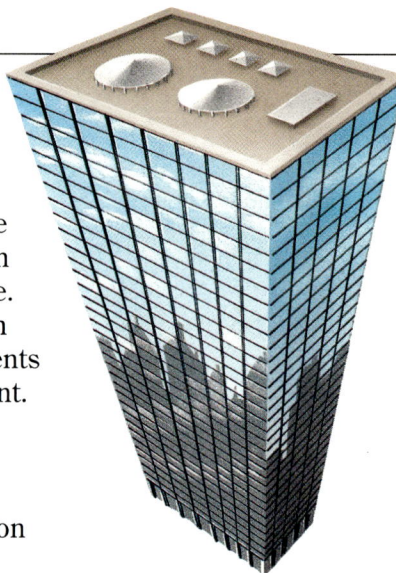

Opening a Recently Worked-On File?
To save time, Word displays the names of the four files you have worked on most recently at the bottom of the *File* menu. Simply drop down the *File* menu and click on the name of the file you want to open.

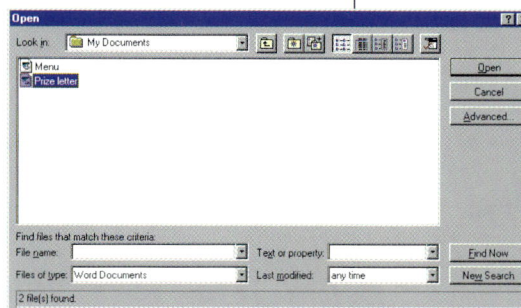

Switching Between Windows

If you want to see all your open windows on the screen at the same time, choose *Arrange All* from the *Window* menu (left). When all your windows are visible, it is easy to switch between them. Simply move the mouse pointer to the window you want to work on and click inside it to make it active. Then click again to place the insertion point where you want it to be in the document. A window must be active before you can do anything to it, such as enter text or move or resize the window.

Active Window

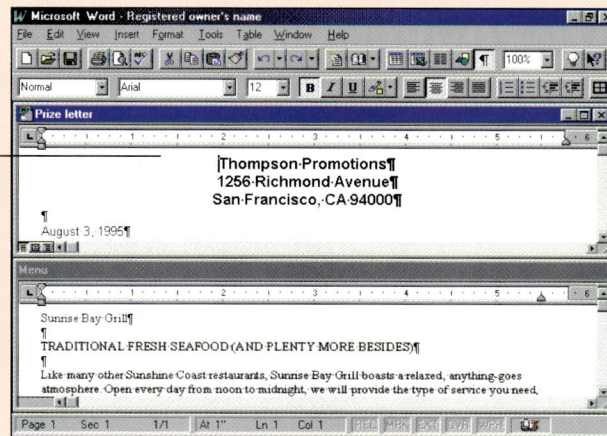

RESIZING A WINDOW

If you are working with several open documents, you may want to resize their windows so that you can see them all clearly. With Word, you can alter the size and shape of a window to suit your needs. Now that you have arranged your windows using the *Arrange All* command, let's resize them as follows:

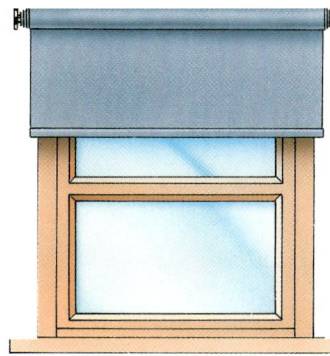

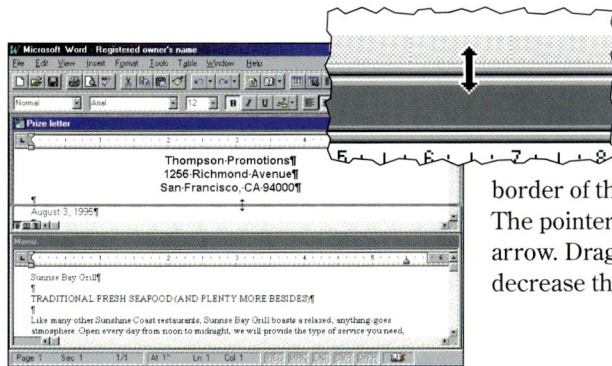

1 Position the mouse pointer at the bottom border of the upper document window. The pointer changes to a two-headed arrow. Drag the border upward to decrease the height of the window.

2 Point at the right-hand border and drag it inward to decrease the width of the window. Now click in the other document window to activate it, and follow the same procedure to resize it in the same way.

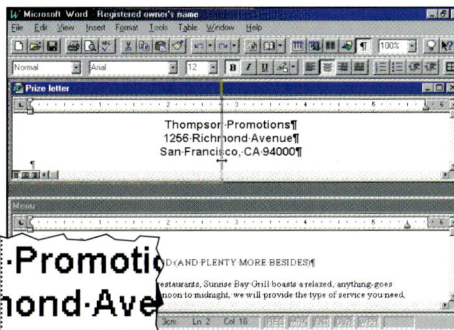

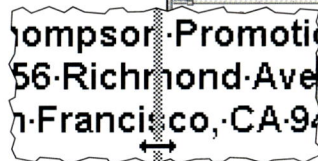

MOVING A WINDOW

You may want to move a window to see another window or an icon that is hidden behind it or to see several windows side by side. Your **Menu** document should still be active. Follow the steps below:

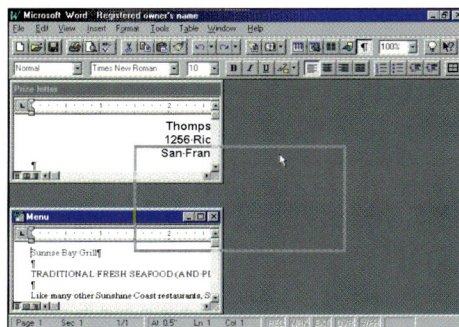

1 Point to the title bar of the **Menu** window, and then hold down the mouse button. Drag the window to a new position; you'll see its outline move on screen as you move the mouse.

2 Release the mouse button to place the window next to the **Prize letter** window. Then close both documents, saving any changes you made to **Menu**.

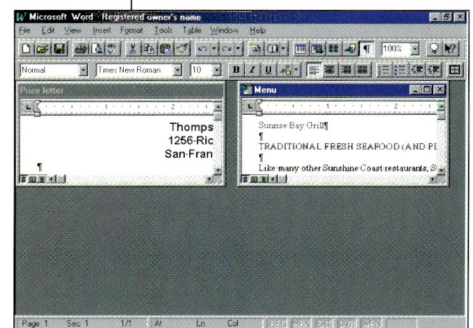

Restore to Resize!
You cannot resize either the Word application window or a document window if it is currently maximized. If the window you want to change has been enlarged to its maximum size, click on the appropriate Maximize/Restore button before trying to resize.

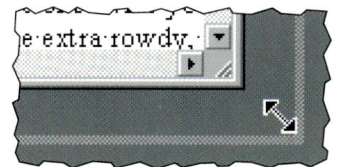

Drag Diagonally
If you want to change both the width and length of a window at the same time, position the pointer on the corner of the window. The pointer changes to a two-headed arrow. Drag it in a diagonal direction inward or outward. The window's width and length increase or decrease accordingly.

47

File Management

I F YOU ARE NEW TO A PC, the way in which the files are organized may seem a little intimidating. Just think of your computer as an electronic filing cabinet. A filing cabinet usually contains several drawers, which can each contain many folders; each folder in turn contains pieces of paper relevant to that folder. Inside your PC, the filing cabinet is the hard disk, the drawers and folders are all called folders, and the pieces of paper are individual files. Of course, folders can contain other folders as well as files.

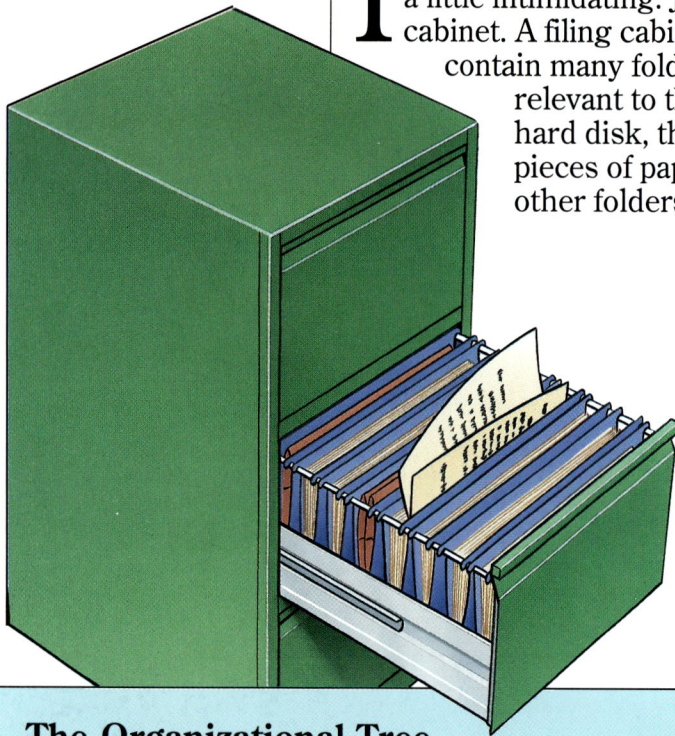

What's in a Name?

Every folder and every file you create with your PC must have a name that is easily recognizable. When you load Word, you'll find several folders and files already created and named on your hard disk. A folder's name usually indicates its contents — for example, the program files for Word are stored in a folder called Winword and your documents are initially stored in a folder called My Documents. File names are more specific — for example, **Menu** for your restaurant menu.

The Organizational Tree

Your PC's filing system has a structure similar to a business organizational chart, where each level of command is a branch of the one above it. The hard disk (usually C:) contains the files and folders that you usually work with. Sometimes folders are placed inside other folders alongside files, creating a clear hierarchy.

A Little History

Folders used to be called "directories," and they could contain either files or more directories. The main directory was called the "root" directory, directories within directories were called "subdirectories," and the location of any directory or file was called its "pathname." Windows 95 doesn't use these confusing expressions. Everything has been simplified into files and folders, which you can navigate by using Windows Explorer.

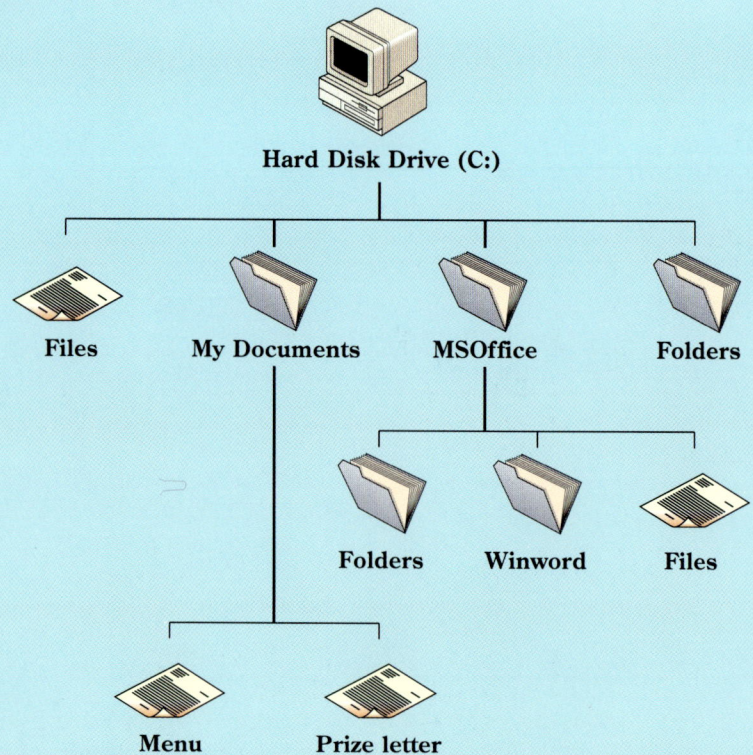

Hard Disk Drive (C:)

Files My Documents MSOffice Folders

Folders Winword Files

Menu Prize letter

How to Use Windows Explorer

To organize your folders and files in Word, you use the Windows Explorer. It is an invaluable tool for managing your documents — copying deleting, renaming and moving them whenever you need to. You can think of Windows Explorer as a guide through all the files and folders on your PC. In previous versions of Windows, most of the Windows Explorer functions were taken care of by the File Manager.

FINDING WINDOWS EXPLORER
Windows Explorer can be used at any time, there's no need to close Word or any other application that you might be using.

Closed Files!
Although you don't have to exit Word to use Windows Explorer, you can't copy, move, delete, or rename an open Word document — you must first close that document. For more information on using Windows Explorer, see page 121 in the Reference Section.

Opening Windows Explorer

1 Click on the Start button, select Programs, and click on *Windows Explorer.*

2 The Windows Explorer window opens showing you that you're *Exploring - (C:),* which is your hard disk drive. (Your files and folders may be different from this example.)

OPENING FOLDERS
On the left-hand side of the window, the folders are shown — these contain all your programs and data. If you click on the plus sign at the left of a folder, Windows Explorer opens the folder and lists the other folders it contains.

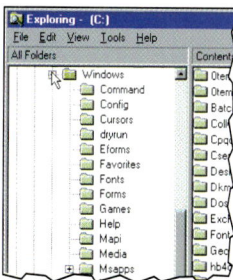

1 Click on the plus sign next to the **Windows** folder to see what other folders it contains. The plus signs next to the new folders show you that there are more folders inside. The dotted lines show how the folders are linked.

2 Now move down the list of folders and click on the **System** folder. Its files — shown as different icons depending on the kind of file — and folders are listed on the right-hand side of the window. You can experiment with the different ways of displaying the files and folders that are offered by the View menu.

Want to See More?
To move up and down in a long list of folders, you can use the vertical scroll bar in the left window. Move the mouse pointer over the arrow at the top or bottom of the scroll bar, and click on it to scroll up or down. To move through the list of files within a folder, use the scroll bar in the right window.

CREATING A NEW FOLDER

When you start using Word, it's a good idea to create one or more folders in **My Documents** for storing various types of documents — for example, for memos, reports, or personal letters. Now that you know your way around the folders, let's create an example folder in **My Documents**.

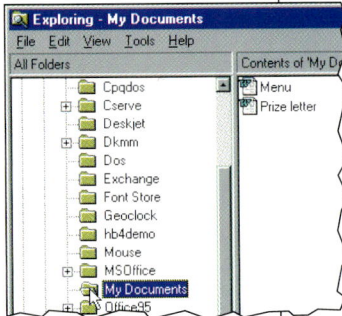

1 Click on the **My Documents** folder on the left-hand side of the Windows Explorer window to select it.

2 Choose *New* from the *File* menu and click on *Folder*.

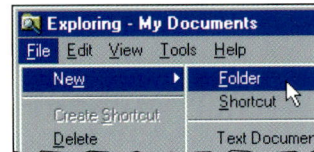

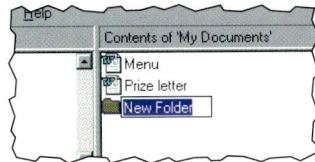

3 A new folder appears on the right-hand side of the window at the end of the list of files.

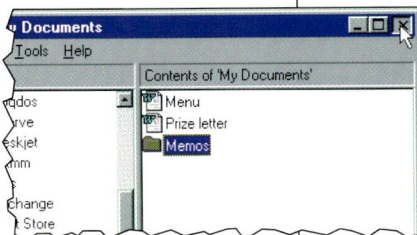

4 Rename the new folder **Memos** by typing the word while "New Folder" is highlighted, and then pressing Enter. You can use either uppercase or lowercase letters, and names can be up to 255 characters long. Close Windows Explorer by clicking on the Close button at top right.

5 The next time you open the **My Documents** folder in Windows Explorer, your new **Memos** folder will be listed in the alphabetic sequence.

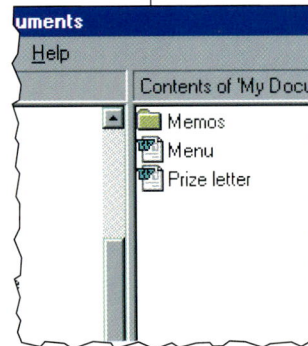

Not My Documents!
If Word is not automatically saving to the **My Documents** folder, first select *Options* from the *Tools* menu and click on the *File Locations* tab. Make sure that *Documents* is highlighted under *File Types* and click on the *Modify* button. Click on the Up One Level button, (a folder with an up-arrow), until (C:) is displayed in the *Look in* drop-down list box. Click on the **My Documents** folder, then click on *OK*. Finally, click on *Close* to close the Options dialog box.

Opening Time?
You can open any Word document listed in the right-hand side of the Windows Explorer window by double-clicking on its name. This will open Word (if it isn't already running) and the document.

Saving to a Specified Folder

Each time you open Word, the current folder is **My Documents**. If you want to save a file to a folder within **My Documents**, you can specify that folder by using the *Save As* dialog box. Let's practice saving a document to the **Memos** folder. Return to Word, open a new document, and then follow the steps at the top of the next page to save the document.

How to Save a File to the Memos Folder

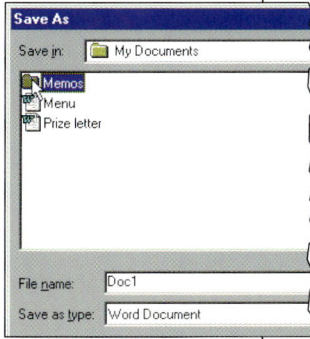

1 Choose *Save As* from the *File* menu to display the *Save As* dialog box. **My Documents** is shown in the *Save in* box, and its files and folders are listed in the panel below. Double-click on the **Memos** folder.

2 **Memos** appears in the *Save in* box. Type **Practice** in the *File name* box and click on *Save*. Having saved your document in the **Memos** folder, finally close the **Practice** document.

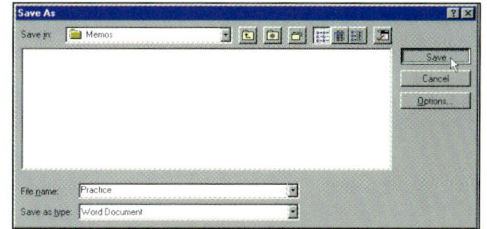

How to Use Find File

Over time you'll create many documents and may have trouble remembering what each file contains. The *Find Files or Folders* option on the Start menu allows you to view a file's contents without actually opening it.

Finding a File

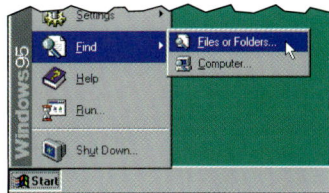

1 Click on the Start button, select *Find,* and click on *Files or Folders*.

2 The *Find: All Files* dialog box appears. Type **menu** in the *Named* text box and click on *Find Now*.

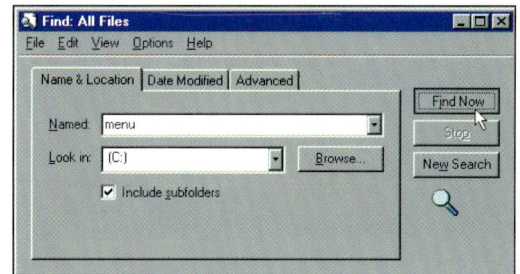

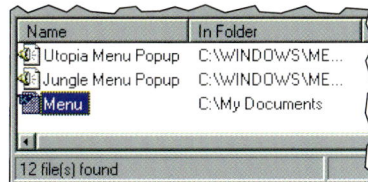

3 When the search has been completed, the list of files with names that match your request are listed at the foot of the dialog box.

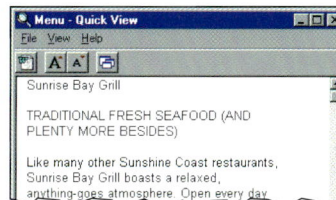

4 To check the contents of a file, click on it and then click on *Quick View* in the *File* menu. The *Quick View* window opens to show the first part of the file. If you don't have Quick View as an option, you will need to install it from your original disks.

Keep Tidy!
From time to time, you might want to use *Find Files or Folders* to browse through the files you've created in Word and clean up your folders. You can throw out any file you no longer need by clicking on the *File* menu when the file is selected and then choosing *Delete* from the menu that appears.

51

3

CHAPTER THREE

*L*ooking Good

*In this chapter you'll learn how to
improve the appearance and presentation of
your Word documents, using the restaurant menu
as an example. You'll find out how to format the text
in a variety of ways and how to add more advanced items
such as columns, frames, headers, and footers. You'll also
learn how to use the WordArt and Drawing toolbars
to create an attractive logo for your restaurant menu.
Later in the chapter, you'll start work on another
document that will allow you to practice
creating tables and charts.*

FORMATTING PRINCIPLES
FORMATTING A DOCUMENT • ADVANCED FORMATTING
ADDING A LOGO • TABLES AND SORTING
CHARTS • BE CREATIVE

Formatting Principles

O NCE YOU'VE ENTERED AND CHECKED THE TEXT of your Word document, the next step is to format it. Through formatting, you can emphasize the most important parts of your document and help make it more attractive and enjoyable to read. Every time you create a document, ask yourself: "Does this document look right for its purpose?"

A Good Start

In many cases, you'll find that the templates and document-creation "Wizards" provided with Word (see pages 104 to 107) are sufficient to create professional-looking documents. But if you want to produce attractive, well-designed documents to suit your specific needs, you may want to use a template as a starting point and then format the document yourself.

There is no set order in which to format your Word document — it depends on the type of document you are trying to create. One efficient way is to start with the most simple formatting procedures and then move on to more advanced techniques. The flow chart below gives you an idea of how to organize the formatting of documents. You'll follow the flow of this chart throughout the next pages as you format your restaurant menu.

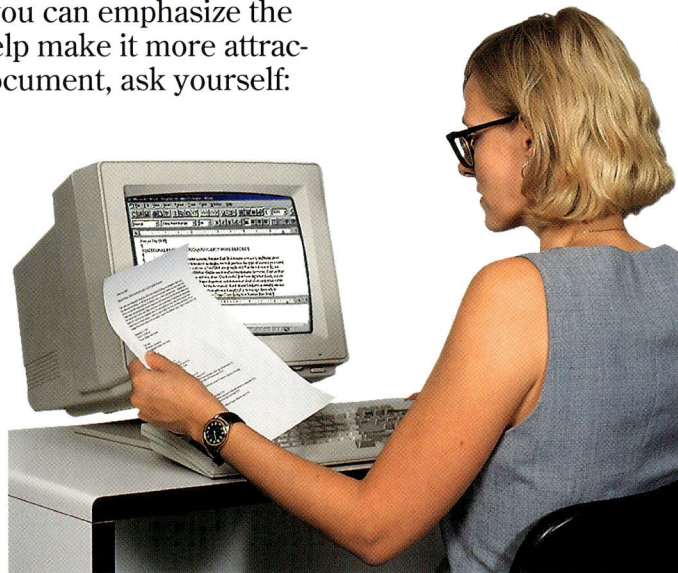

YOUR DOCUMENT'S LAYOUT

The layout of your document is an important part of formatting. For example, if a heading needs to begin at the top of a page, you can insert a manual page break into the text above it. A long document may also look more interesting if it is broken up into *sections,* which allow you to create special effects, such as multiple columns, for different parts of the document. For more information on sections, see pages 68 to 69.

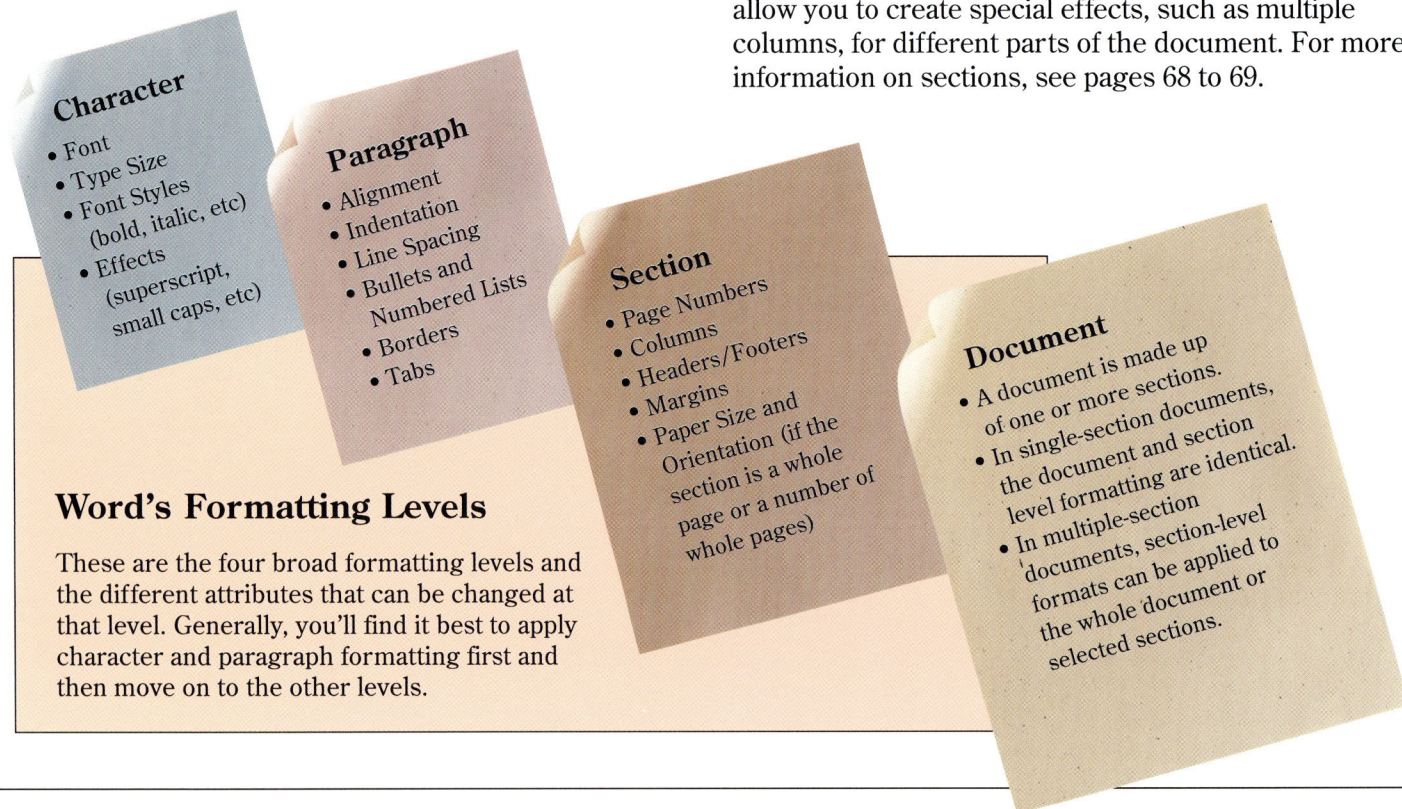

Character

- Font
- Type Size
- Font Styles (bold, italic, etc)
- Effects (superscript, small caps, etc)

Paragraph

- Alignment
- Indentation
- Line Spacing
- Bullets and Numbered Lists
- Borders
- Tabs

Section

- Page Numbers
- Columns
- Headers/Footers
- Margins
- Paper Size and Orientation (if the section is a whole page or a number of whole pages)

Document

- A document is made up of one or more sections.
- In single-section documents, the document and section level formatting are identical.
- In multiple-section documents, section-level formats can be applied to the whole document or selected sections.

Word's Formatting Levels

These are the four broad formatting levels and the different attributes that can be changed at that level. Generally, you'll find it best to apply character and paragraph formatting first and then move on to the other levels.

ELEMENTS IN FORMATTING A DOCUMENT

Each of the following items has a role in making your document look good. It is by no means a comprehensive list — the more documents you create, the more you'll get a "feel" for what looks right — but it is a good reference point for understanding some basic elements of formatting.

Paragraph Alignment

You should choose the alignment of your paragraphs according to the organization of your text. For example, the main bulk of the text is usually left aligned or justified (each line the same length) because it's easier to read, whereas a heading may look better centered.

Margin Settings

The margins set the overall shape of a document. By setting the margins, you determine how much space there is on either side and at the top and bottom of your text. You can give different sections of your document different margin settings.

Character Formatting

*With Word you can specify different fonts, type sizes, special effects (such as **bold**, italic, and underline), and even different colors for different areas of your document. Using these elements carefully, you can attract and keep a reader's attention.*

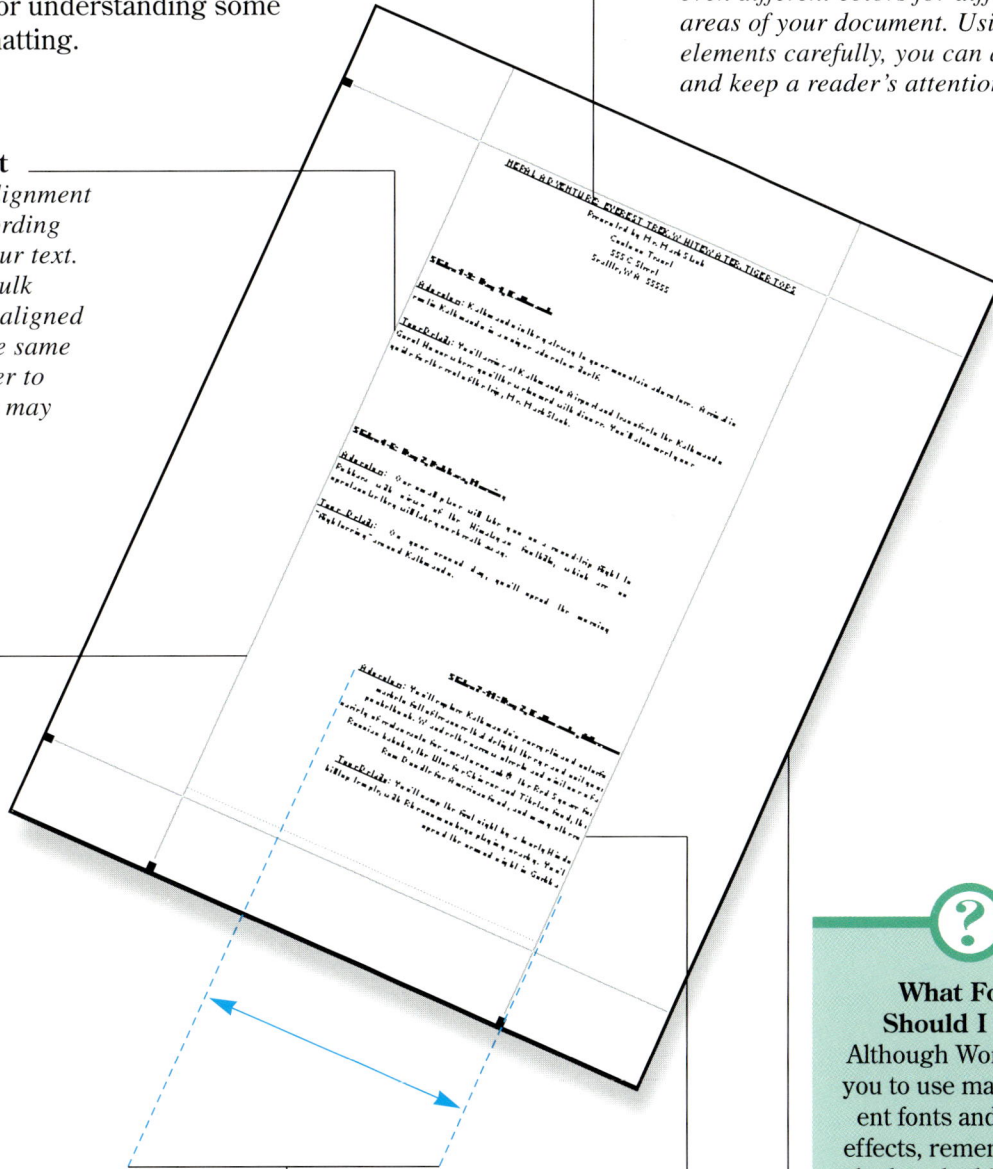

Paragraph Width

The width you choose for a paragraph depends on several factors, including the amount of text, its type size, and its font. One general rule of thumb is the smaller the type size, the narrower the text width should be.

Line Spacing

Word automatically selects the best line spacing for your text, based on the type size of the font you are using. But you can change the spacing in specific paragraphs or in your whole document — for example, bulleted lists often look better if they are double-spaced.

What Fonts Should I Use?

Although Word allows you to use many different fonts and special effects, remember that the best-looking documents are restrained in their use of these. For example, mixing lots of fonts together on one page can look clumsy. Bold and italic are meant to emphasize certain points, but they'll lose their impact if overused.

Formatting a Document

I N THE FIRST CHAPTER OF THIS BOOK you learned how to apply some basic formatting to a simple letter. This section shows you how to format a document of greater complexity. As you work with different formatting elements — font, type size, alignment, margins, and so on — you'll realize how easy it is to improve the appearance of a document.

Missing a Toolbar?
To make a particular toolbar appear on your screen, choose *Toolbars* from the *View* menu. In the *Toolbars* dialog box, check the box next to the toolbar name. If a toolbar is already visible on the screen, you'll see a check next to its name in the *Toolbars* dialog box.

Getting in Shape

You can apply formatting quickly and easily by using the Formatting toolbar, which provides the most commonly used formatting options. Alternatively, you can apply formatting by choosing commands from the *Format* menu and specifying options in the dialog boxes that appear. This is a slower method, but more formatting options are available. For our sample document, using the Formatting toolbar will usually suffice, so we'll concentrate mainly on this method.

Plain Text

Italicized Text

How to Format Characters

Letters, numerals, symbols, punctuation, and spaces are all characters. To change the appearance of characters — and the words, sentences, or paragraphs they make up — you select the text and then apply one or more attributes. You may, for example, want to emphasize a word by making it bold, by underlining it, or by changing its type size or font.

Bold Text

Underlined Text

Using the Formatting Toolbar

The Formatting toolbar contains three drop-down list boxes and several groups of buttons. After selecting the text you want to format, you choose the relevant item from the drop-down list or click on the button representing the desired format. A button appears depressed on the toolbar if the format it represents is already applied to selected text. Clicking on a button that appears depressed removes the formatting from selected text. Here are the names of the boxes and buttons that you'll find on the Formatting toolbar:

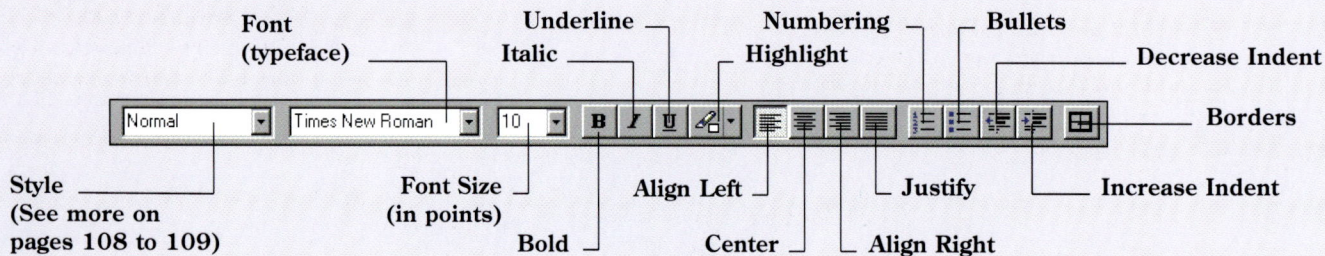

Font (typeface) — Underline — Numbering — Bullets — Decrease Indent — Borders

Italic — Highlight — Justify — Increase Indent

Style (See more on pages 108 to 109) — Font Size (in points) — Bold — Align Left — Center — Align Right

CHOOSING FONTS

When you change fonts, you alter the typeface that the text appears in. To change fonts you must first select the relevant text. Let's change the font in part of your restaurant menu. Open your **Menu** document and follow the steps below. Your PC may not have the same fonts in the Font list shown here. See page 119 for more information on fonts and their availability.

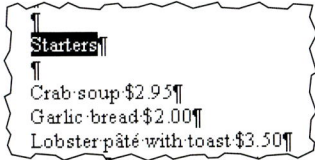

1 Select the heading **Starters** in your restaurant menu.

2 Click on the down-arrow button to the right of the Font list box on the Formatting toolbar. Choose *Arial*.

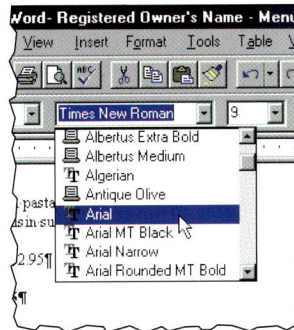

SETTING TYPE SIZE

You can alter the type size of any text using the Font Size list box on the Formatting toolbar. (The numbers in this list refer to points. A point is the fundamental unit of measure in typography — 72 points is exactly one inch.) Before you can change the type size, you must first select the text.

1 Select the heading **Starters** if it isn't still highlighted.

2 Click on the button to the right of the Font Size list box on the Formatting toolbar. Choose *14* point.

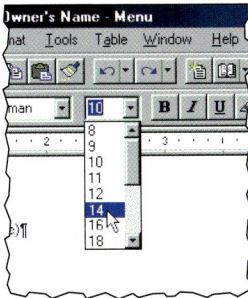

APPLYING FONT STYLES AND EFFECTS

Applying text attributes creates special typographical effects. To apply text attributes such as bold, italic, or underlining, first select the text you want to change.

1 The heading **Starters** should still be selected. Click on the Bold button on the Formatting toolbar.

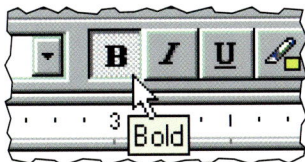

2 Click on the Under-line button on the Formatting toolbar.

Changing Size

You can change the type size of selected text quickly using your keyboard. To make selected text larger, hold down Ctrl and Shift and press >. Each time you press >, the type size is increased to the next available size. To make selected text smaller, press Ctrl and Shift and <. The type size is indicated in the Font Size drop-down list box on the Formatting toolbar.

The End Result

This is how your heading should appear after completing the formatting procedures.

ALTERNATIVE PATHS

If you want to apply several text attributes at once, you may find it easier to use the *Font* dialog box. Select the text you want to change and choose *Font* from the *Format* menu. In the *Font* dialog box, you'll see all the character formatting options, including several other options such as *Strikethrough*, *Small Caps*, and *All Caps* that do not appear on the Formatting toolbar. The *Preview* box in the *Font* dialog box displays how these choices will affect the text.

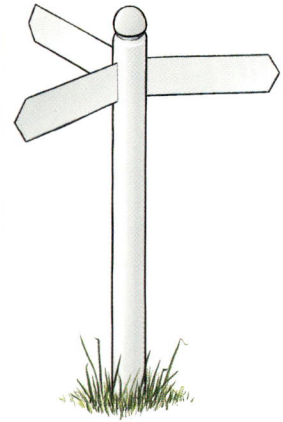

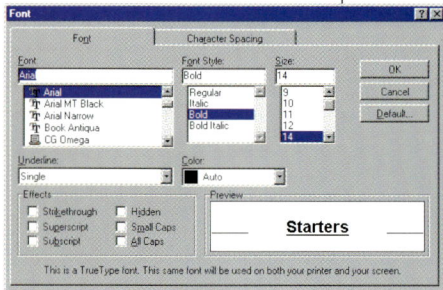

COPYING CHARACTER FORMATS

You can copy character formats from one part of your document to another using the Format Painter. To copy a format, first select the text containing the formats you want to copy, and then click on the Format Painter button on the Standard toolbar. The mouse pointer will change to a paintbrush with an I-beam pointer. You now select the text you want to format, and then release the mouse button. The new format is applied and the pointer returns to its normal shape. If you double-click on the Format Painter button after selecting text, you can continue to paste the copied format throughout your document. To return to the normal pointer, click on the Format Painter button again.

Font Dialog Box

Format Painter Button

Cut it Short

You can display a timesaving shortcut menu by selecting text you want to format and then clicking on the *right* mouse button. The shortcut menu contains a list of commonly used commands, such as the *Font* command, related to selected text. To close the shortcut menu without choosing a command, click outside the menu.

Working on Your Restaurant Menu

Now that you have practiced the basic character formatting techniques, you can apply them to other parts of your document. The standard (default) setting for your text is probably Times New Roman, 10 point.

- Select the heading **TRADITIONAL FRESH SEAFOOD....** Change the type size to 11 point and make it bold.

- Select the largest paragraph (**Like many other...Grill**) in your restaurant menu. Change the type size to 11 point.

- Select the heading **Main courses**. Change it to Arial, 14 point, bold, underlined. Repeat this for **Desserts** using the Format Painter.

- Select all the dishes — including the prices — under **Starters** (**Crab Soup ...$4.00**). Make them italic. Repeat this for the dish titles under **Main courses** (including the line **All dishes...**) and

the dish titles under **Desserts**.

- Now select only the prices of the dishes you have just formatted and make them bold.

- Select the entry for **TODAY'S SPECIAL**, beginning with **September 15, 1995** and ending with **only $10.95**. Make it 9 point.

- Select the date and the line **TODAY'S SPECIAL**. Make them bold. Repeat this for **only $10.95**.

- Select the last line of your restaurant menu — **Why not try....** Change it to 12 point and make it bold.

How to Set Paragraph Formats

Formatting a paragraph changes the way the whole paragraph is presented. Most paragraph formatting can be done quickly using the Formatting toolbar or the Ruler. You can also choose *Paragraph* from the *Format* menu and set options in the *Paragraph* dialog box. You can change text alignment, set degrees of indentation, determine spacing before and after the paragraph, and specify line spacing within the paragraph all at one time. The *Preview* box shows you how the paragraph will look with the options you've chosen.

Alignments

Text can be left aligned, right aligned, centered, or justified. Left aligned text has a flush left margin (straight and lined up against the left margin of the page) and a ragged right margin. Right aligned text has a flush right margin and a ragged left margin. Centered text lines up symmetrically down a center line and has ragged left and right margins. Justified text has both a flush left and a flush right margin and is often used for columnar text in magazines and newsletters. Let's practice changing the alignment of various parts of your **Menu** document.

Left Aligned Text

Centered Text

Right Aligned Text

Justified Text

TRADITIONAL·FRESH·SEAFOOD·(AND·PLENTY·MORE·BESIDES)¶

Like·many·other·Sunshine·Coast·restaurants,·Sunrise·Bay·Grill·boasts·a·relaxed,·anything·goes·atmosphere.·Open·every·day·from·noon·to·midnight,·we·will·provide·the·type·of·service·you·need,·whether·you·want·a·quiet·meal·for·two·or·a·fun-filled·group·night·out.·For·the·extra·rowdy,·we·have·a·large·back·room·—·soundproofed!·Unlike·most·seafood·restaurants,·however,·Sunrise·Bay·Grill·does·not·dwell·on·fresh·fish·and·lobster·alone.·Our·forceful·(but·friendly)·chef·Hank·insists·that·we·serve·a·wide·range·of·interesting·and·international·dishes·too!·And·all·at·very·reasonable·prices.·We·pride·ourselves·on·good·value.·But·be·warned·Hank·doesn't·believe·in·small·portions·—·when·you·come·to·Sunrise·Bay·Grill,·you·must·come·hungry·(if·you·manage·three·whole·courses,·we'll·be·astonished).·Long·live·the·Sunshine·Coast.·Long·live·Sunrise·Bay·Grill.¶

¶
September·15,·1995¶
TODAY'S·SPECIAL¶
Try·our·3-course·"hungry·sailor"·menu.¶
¶

Setting Alignments

1 In your restaurant menu, select the paragraph **Like many other...Bay Grill**.

2 Click on the Justify button on the Formatting toolbar. The last line may not be aligned at the right margin — this is an accepted typographic convention.

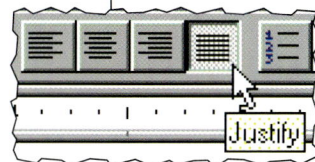

Justify Button

3 Select the line **TRADITIONAL FRESH SEAFOOD...** and click on the Center button on the Formatting toolbar. Follow the same procedure to center the line **Why not try...** at the bottom of the restaurant menu.

Center Button

Adding Bullets and Numbers

To make a document more readable, you can emphasize lists by adding bullets or by numbering sequential paragraphs. But doing so manually can take a lot of time. Word allows you to bullet or number paragraphs by clicking on buttons on the Formatting toolbar.

ADDING BULLETS

In a bulleted list, a bullet symbol is displayed at the beginning of each paragraph. To add bullets to a list you must first select the desired paragraphs.

1 In your restaurant menu select the dish titles below **Starters (Crab soup...$4.00)**.

2 Click on the Bullets button on the Formatting toolbar. You'll see bullets appear to the left of the dish titles in the **Starters** section.

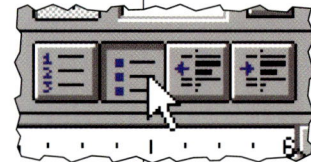

CHANGING THE BULLET CHARACTER

There are several different types of bullets available to you in Word. To change the appearance and the size of the bullets you have just created, follow these steps.

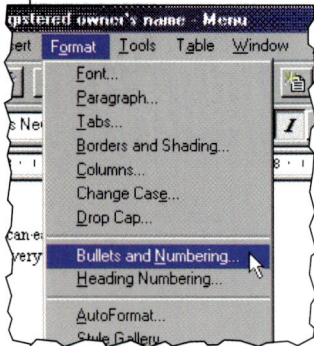

1 The dish titles below **Starters** should still be selected. Choose *Bullets and Numbering* from the *Format* menu.

2 The *Bullets and Numbering* dialog box appears. Under *Bulleted*, click on the bullet style shown with a blue border at right. Then click on *Modify*.

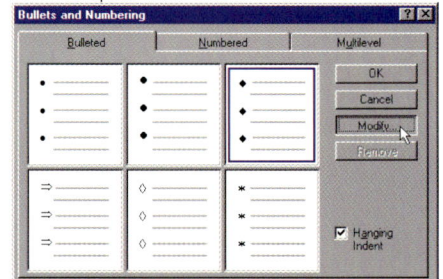

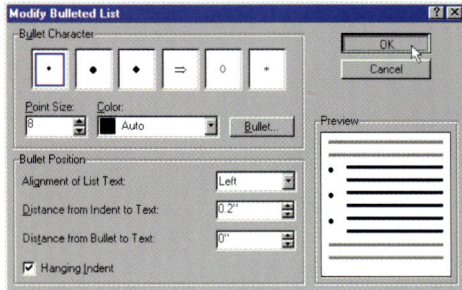

3 The *Modify Bulleted List* box appears. Under *Point Size*, change the value to *8*, and then click on *OK*.

4 The new bullets appear. Any more bullets you add will look like this until you change the bullet again. Use the Bullets button to add bullets to the dishes under **Main courses** and **Desserts**.

ADDING NUMBERS

In a numbered list, Word displays a number or letter at the beginning of each line or paragraph. To create a numbered list, select the relevant text and then click on the Numbering button on the Formatting toolbar.

Indentation

Indents determine the width of a paragraph. In Word, a quick way to change indents is to use the Ruler, the numbered strip below the Formatting toolbar.

Ruler Display
The Ruler displays the indent settings and tab stops of each paragraph.

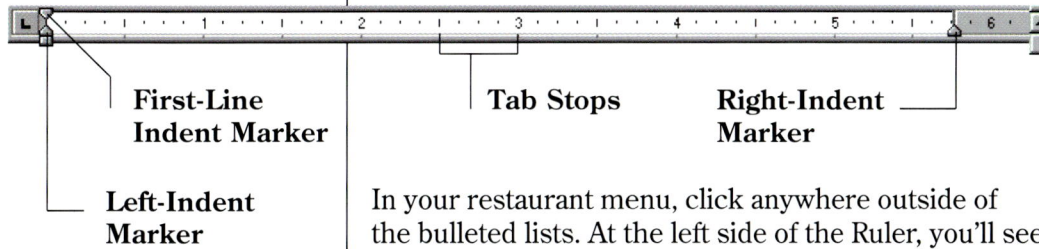

First-Line
Indent Marker

Tab Stops

Right-Indent
Marker

Left-Indent
Marker

In your restaurant menu, click anywhere outside of the bulleted lists. At the left side of the Ruler, you'll see two triangles; these are the left-indent markers. The position of the top triangle determines the indent of the paragraph's first line; the position of the lower triangle sets the overall left indent of the paragraph. The triangle on the right side of the Ruler is the right-indent marker; it determines the right indent. To move an indent marker, you point at it, and then hold down the mouse button and drag the marker along the Ruler (see box at left).

PRECISION INDENTING

Setting paragraph indents using the Ruler can be tricky; to set exact indents you should use the *Paragraph* dialog box. First you have to select the paragraph(s) you want to alter. Note that if you select text with different formats applied, some of the boxes in the Formatting toolbar and the *Paragraph* dialog box will be blank. Follow these steps to set indents for your restaurant menu.

Get to the Point
To change the formatting of a single paragraph, you can just position the insertion point anywhere within that paragraph. Only when formatting multiple paragraphs do you need to select at least a part of each paragraph you want to format.

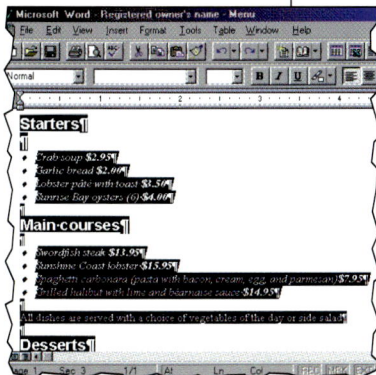

Setting Indents

To change the width of one or more paragraphs using the Ruler, select the paragraphs and then drag the relevant indent marker along the scale to the new location.

To set	Drag
First-line indent	
Left indent	
First-line and left indents	
Right indent	

1 Select the text beginning with the heading **Starters** down to the last dish in the **Desserts** list, **Cassata ... $2.95**.

2 Choose *Paragraph* from the *Format* menu to open the *Paragraph* dialog box.

3 Under *Indentation* on the *Indents and Spacing* flipcard, go to the *Left* box and click on the up arrow until you reach the value *0.7* inches. The highlighted text in the *Preview* window shifts to the right to indicate the result of your choice. Finally, click on *OK*. In your document, you'll see the selected text move to the right.

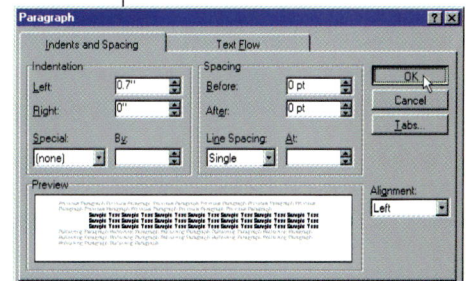

SPECIALIZED INDENTING

You can also use the *Indentation* section of the *Indents and Spacing* flipcard in the *Paragraph* dialog box to change indents from the left or right, specify an indent for the first line of each paragraph (*First Line*), or format a paragraph in which the first line begins farther to the left than the rest of the paragraph (*Hanging*). To avoid changing the **Menu** document, create a practice document if you want to practice these techniques. Clicking on the down arrow under *Special* in the *Paragraph* dialog box reveals the drop-down list from which you can choose the option you want. If you choose *Hanging* or *First Line*, Word sets the indent at 0.5 inches. To change this value, simply type or select the new value in the *By* box.

You can also use the Ruler to set a hanging indent. Select the paragraph that you want to format with a hanging indent. Then drag the bottom left-indent marker to the right to create the hanging indent. (You can see how a hanging indent is displayed on the Ruler by clicking in the bulleted list in your restaurant menu.)

Special Indents

First Line Indent

Hanging Indent

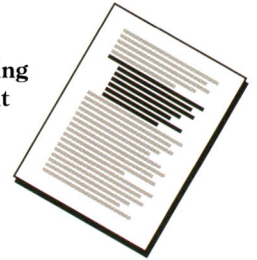

Creating a First Line Indent

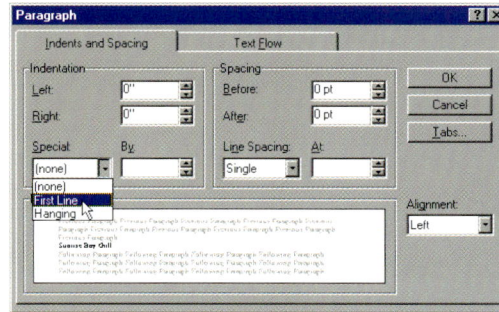

Setting Line Spacing

If you want to change the spacing between lines in a paragraph, you use the *Indents and Spacing* flipcard in the *Paragraph* dialog box. For the most part, the default spacing, *Single*, gives you perfect results for your documents because Word automatically adjusts the spacing according to the type size you use. But there are also other set spacings you can choose. Under *Spacing*, you can click on the down arrow next to the *Line Spacing* box to reveal a drop-down list. To select another spacing option, such as double-line spacing, simply choose *Double* and then click on *OK*. To set the line spacing manually, choose an option from the *At* box next to the *Line Spacing* box or type the measurement in points in the box (for example, **12 pt**).

You can also adjust the spacing between paragraphs. For example, you may want titles, lists, and pictures to have larger amounts of space before and after them than do paragraphs of text. To change the spacing between paragraphs, you highlight the relevant paragraphs, open the *Paragraph* dialog box, type or choose the measurements you want in the *Before* and *After* boxes in the *Spacing* section, and then click on *OK*.

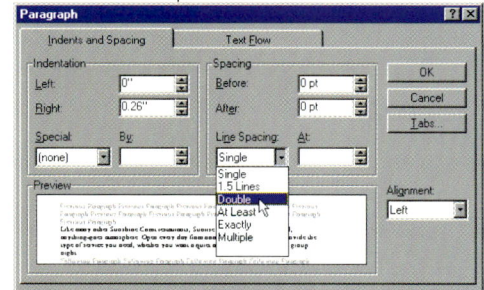

Examples of Different Line Spacings:

Line Spacing: *Single*

Line Spacing: *1.5 Lines*

Line Spacing: *Double*

Setting Double Line Spacing

? Quick Paragraph?
The quickest way to open the *Paragraph* dialog box is simply to double-click on the left- or right-indent markers.

Tab Stops

Tab stops are set positions marked on the Ruler at which you can align text or numbers in columns. Tabs are useful for presenting lists of information such as products and their prices. However, if you want to organize data in several rows and columns, you should create a table (see page 78).

Text or numbers can be aligned left or right against a tab stop, or centered across the tab stop. A decimal tab stop is used to align a column of decimal numbers such as the dish prices in your restaurant menu; the tab stop aligns the numbers on the decimal points.

Tabs are paragraph-level formats; to set them you must first select the paragraph or paragraphs you want to tab, and then set your tab stop(s). The button used to create tab stops, the Tab Alignment button, is on the left side of the Ruler. To set or change the tab stop, you must first click on this button until it displays the type of tab stop you want to create. The different appearances of the Tab Alignment button are shown at right.

Left-aligned Tab

Centered Tab

Right-aligned Tab

Decimal Tab

Want to Remove a Tab Stop?
To clear a tab stop quickly, simply select the paragraphs in which you want to remove the tab stop and drag the tab marker from its position on the Ruler to a position below the Ruler. The tab marker and tab stop position will then disappear.

SETTING TAB STOPS

Word provides preset left-aligned tab stops at every half-inch along the Ruler. You can add a tab stop by choosing the relevant Tab Alignment button (right, left, centered, or decimal) and then clicking on the Ruler at the position you want the new tab stop to appear. Word will clear the Ruler of the preset tab stops to the left of the new tab stop. The position of tab stops can also be altered by clicking on a tab-stop marker and dragging it to the left or right.

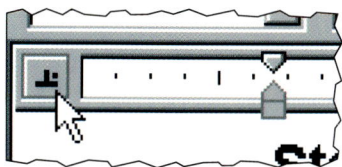

Tab Alignment Button

How to Set a Tab Stop

1 Before setting a tab, the text to be tabbed must be highlighted. Select the text beginning with **Crab soup** under **Starters** down to the last dessert dish, **Cassata ...$2.95**. Click on the Tab Alignment button until the decimal tab appears as shown here.

2 Click on the 5.25 inches mark on the Ruler.

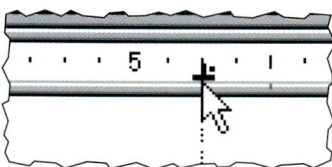

3 Place your insertion point to the left of the price (**$2.95**) for **Crab soup** in the **Starters** section and press the Tab key. Word aligns the decimal point at the 5.25-inch tab stop. Do this for all the dishes in all three courses as shown here.

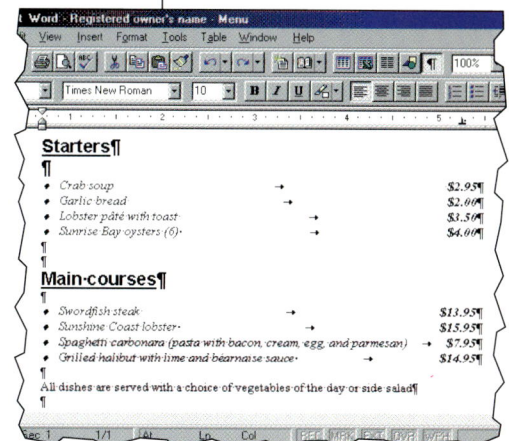

Word - Registered owner's name - Menu

View   Insert   Format   Tools   Table   Window   Help

Times New Roman   10

Starters¶
¶
• Crab soup $2.95¶
• Garlic bread $2.00¶
• Lobster pâté with toast $3.50¶
• Sunrise Bay oysters (6)· $4.00¶
¶
Main·courses¶
¶
• Swordfish steak $13.95¶
• Sunshine Coast lobster· $15.95¶
• Spaghetti carbonara (pasta with bacon, cream, egg, and parmesan) $7.95¶
• Grilled halibut with lime and bearnaise sauce· $14.95¶
¶
All dishes are served with a choice of vegetables of the day or side salad¶
¶

USING THE TAB DIALOG BOX

To set a tab stop with more precision, choose *Tabs* from the *Format* menu to open the *Tabs* dialog box. To set the tab, you type its value in the *Tab Stop Position* box, choose an option in the *Alignment* box, click on *Set,* and then click on *OK*. To remove tabs using the *Tabs* dialog box, select the relevant tabs in the *Tab Stop Position* box, click on *Clear*, and then click on *OK*.

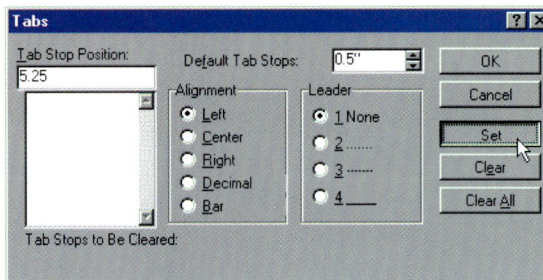

Tabs Dialog Box

How to Add Page Numbers

You don't need to add page numbers to your restaurant menu, but you may want to number the pages of other documents you create. You can number the pages of your document quickly and easily using the *Page Numbers* command from the *Insert* menu. Word inserts numbers on every page and automatically renumbers the pages for you if you move text. Note that you cannot see page numbers in Normal View; you have to change to Page Layout View (see page 66).

Page numbers are section-level formats; this means that you can apply different page number formats to different sections. Page numbers are inserted into either a header or footer that appears at the top or bottom of the page. See pages 67 to 69 for more information on headers, footers, and sections.

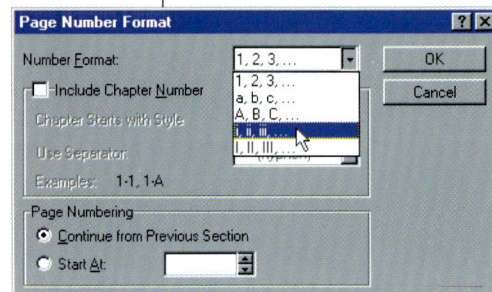

Adding Page Numbers
To number the pages of a document, choose Page Numbers *from the* Insert *menu to open the* Page Numbers *dialog box. Select a location in the* Position *box and an alignment in the* Alignment *box, and see the results in the* Preview *box. Click on* OK *to insert the numbers into the document.*

Your Format Options
If you want to change the format of your page numbers, click on Format *in the* Page Numbers *dialog box. The* Page Number Format *dialog box will appear showing the options that are available.*

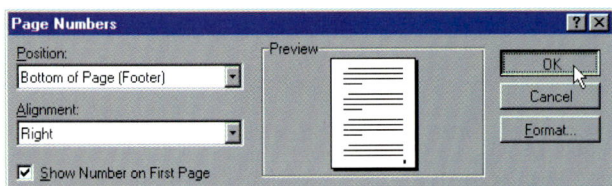

Using Your Margins

Top Margin
Right Margin

A margin can be defined as the distance between paper edge and text. Margins determine not only how much text you can fit on a page, but also how the layout looks overall. Word sets the left and right margins at 1.25 inches and the top and bottom margins at 1 inch by default. These margins are adequate for most documents, but you can easily change these settings. For example, for a short letter you may want to increase the margins so that the text sits more comfortably. On the other hand, you may want to gain space for text by decreasing the margins. Margins are usually considered document-level formats — if you change margin settings you usually change them for the whole document. But you can also change margin settings within different sections (see page 68).

Marginal Problems!
Most printers cannot print right to the edge of your paper — bear this in mind when you set your margins. A rough rule of thumb is to allow at least half an inch on either side and around one inch at top and bottom. Setting margins too narrow may also make a document look cramped.

Setting Margins Using the Rulers

With Word, you can simply drag your margins to different positions using the horizontal or vertical Ruler. If your document consists of only one section, the margins are changed for the whole document. To see the vertical Ruler, change to either Page Layout View (see page 66) or Print Preview. Print Preview is often easier to use because you can see the whole page on the screen, but the method you use for setting margins is the same in both cases.

If you click on the Print Preview button on the Standard toolbar, the Print Preview window will open, displaying the two different Rulers as shown here. If the Rulers are not displayed, click on the View Ruler button on the Print Preview toolbar. The gray areas on the Rulers indicate the current page margins. To change margins, place the mouse pointer over a margin boundary so that the pointer changes to a two-headed arrow, and then drag the boundary to its new position. The page display gets updated as you move the boundaries.

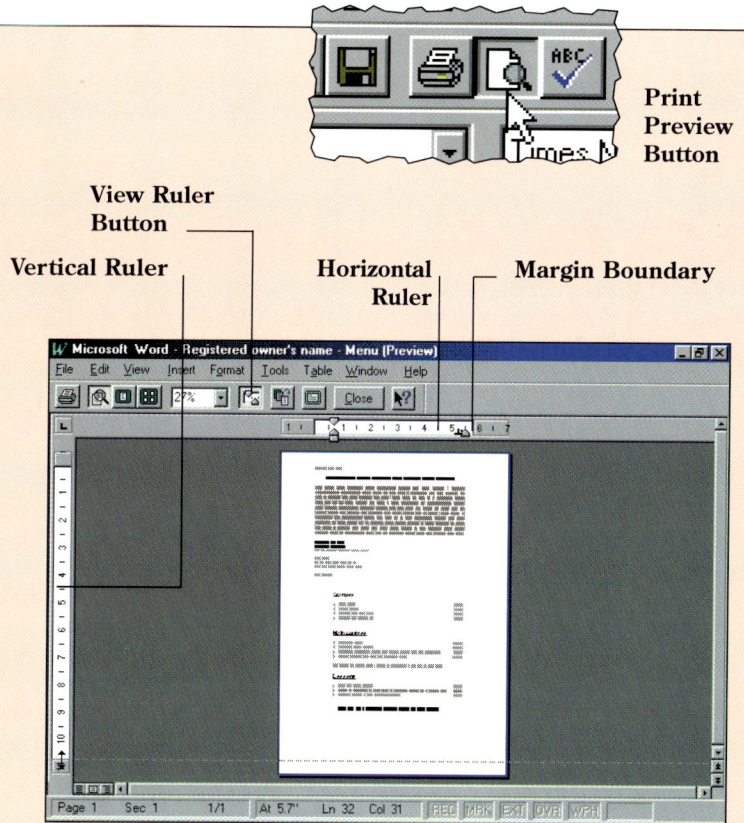

Print Preview Button

View Ruler Button

Vertical Ruler

Horizontal Ruler

Margin Boundary

ANOTHER WAY TO SET MARGINS

Alternatively, you can choose *Page Setup* from the *File* menu to change your margin settings. Let's practice using this method to narrow the margins of your restaurant menu. When you complete your document later in this chapter, you'll see that the narrower margins allow you to fit everything on one page.

Adjusting Your Margins

1 Choose *Page Setup* from the *File* menu to open the *Page Setup* dialog box.

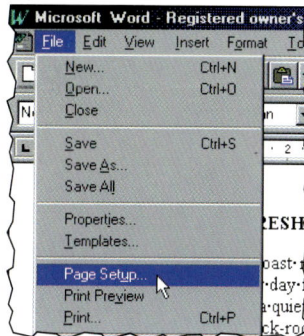

2 Click on the *Margins* tab if the *Margins* flipcard is not already displayed. In the *Top* and *Bottom* boxes, change the value to 0.5 inches. In the *Left* and *Right* boxes, change the value to 1.23 inches. Finally, click on *OK*.

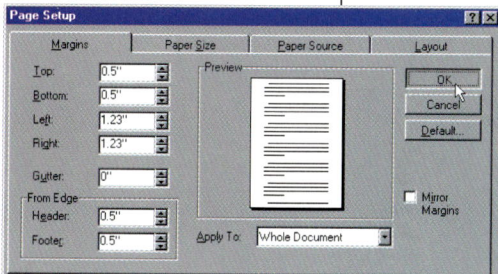

Advanced Formatting

WITH WORD YOU CAN MAKE your document look more attractive using some advanced formatting techniques. These include adding headers or footers, creating columns, and adding frames and borders. In this section, you will apply these advanced techniques to your restaurant menu. But before you perform these tasks, it's helpful to know how to change the view of your document.

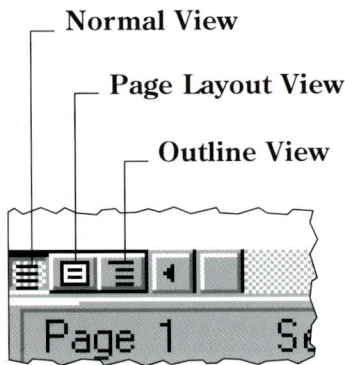

Normal View

Page Layout View

Outline View

View Buttons

Changing Your View

You can view a document on the screen in a number of ways. Each viewing option helps you focus on a different aspect of your work. The three options you are likely to use are Normal, Page Layout, and Outline. You can switch views by clicking on the relevant button above the status bar (see left) or by choosing an option from the *View* menu. The standard view, and the one that is convenient for most tasks, is Normal. It reveals all text formatting but doesn't show the full layout of the document. Page Layout View is best for viewing the document as it will appear when printed.

The Right Scale?
You can magnify or reduce the size of your document in any view. Click on the down arrow next to the Zoom Control box on the Standard toolbar (to the right of the Show/Hide ¶ button) and choose the scale you want or type the percentage you desire in the Zoom Control box. Bear in mind that zoomed views do not give accurate views of how the printed document will look.

Your Viewing Options

Later in this section, you will look at your restaurant menu using different views. Here are the three main views:

■ **Normal View** shows the document filling the entire document window. Although you see the correct fonts, the text appears in one continuous stream, with only dotted lines indicating page or section breaks. You can't see items such as columns (see page 69) or frames (see page 70) in Normal View.

■ **Page Layout View** is the closest to true WYSIWYG and shows your document as it will appear when it is printed. You can edit and format the text in this view and see the results on the screen. Page Layout View is useful for a final glance at your document to make sure any section breaks and page breaks you have made are in the right place.

■ **Outline View** helps you structure a document, using a hierarchy of headings in predetermined styles. Outlining allows you to collapse a document and view only the headings — the body text gets hidden temporarily. The overall structure of a document becomes more apparent and the outline tools make reorganizing your document very easy. For more information, see page 117.

A View from the Keyboard?
If you prefer, you can select a document view or switch between views by using the keyboard. Press down the Alt key, the Ctrl key, and N for Normal View, O for Outline View, or P for Page Layout View.

Headers and Footers

Different First Page?

To omit the header or footer on the first page of a document, click on the Page Setup button on the Header and Footer toolbar. Under *Headers and Footers* in the *Layout* flipcard of the *Page Setup* dialog box, check *Different First Page*. Click on *OK*.

A header or footer is text, such as a title or an explanatory note, that appears at the top or bottom of each page of a document section. Headers and footers are section-level formats. By default, a header or footer is printed 0.5 inches from the top or bottom paper edge. If you divide a document into sections, you can use different headers or footers for each section (see page 68). Because you can see a header or footer only in Page Layout view, begin by clicking on the Page Layout button on the status bar. Then follow these steps to insert a footer into your restaurant menu.

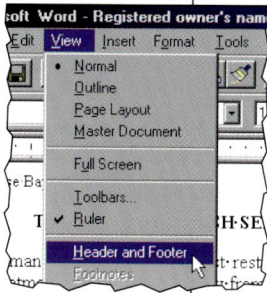

Inserting a Footer

1 Choose *Header and Footer* from the *View* menu. Your document appears dimmed, and the insertion point appears in the header area. The Header and Footer toolbar also appears.

2 Now click on the Switch Between Header and Footer button on the Header and Footer toolbar. This takes you to the footer area.

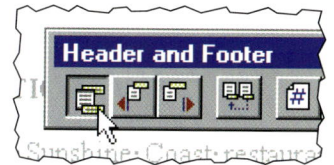

3 In the footer area, type **See our drinks menu for coffees, soft drinks, cocktails, wines, beers, and spirits**. Select the footer text and make it bold and italic with centered alignment. Do this in the same way you format other text. Don't close the Header and Footer toolbar just yet —you'll add a border to your footer on the next page.

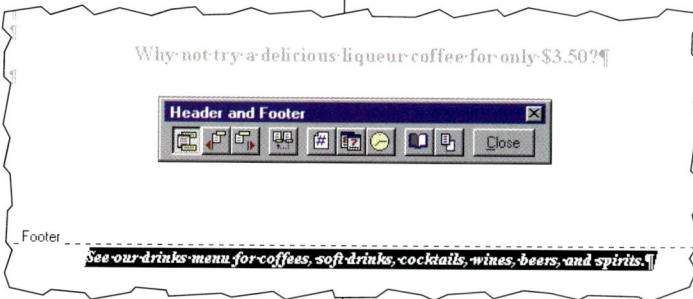

The Header and Footer Toolbar

Here is a brief explanation of the buttons you'll find on the Header and Footer toolbar.

Page Numbers
To insert page numbers automatically on each page.

Date
To insert the current date automatically .

Page Setup
To change the page setup of the document or selected sections.

Switch Between Header and Footer
To move between headers and footers.

Show Previous
To move to the previous header or footer, if there are different headers and footers in a document.

Show Next
To move to the next header or footer, if there are different headers and footers in a document.

Time
To insert the current time automatically.

Same as Previous
To apply a header or footer from a previous section to the current section.

Show/Hide Document Text
To show or hide the dimmed text in the main document.

Removing a Border?
To remove a border, select the item surrounded by the border, then click on the Borders button on the Formatting toolbar. On the Borders toolbar that appears, click on the No Border button. Click on the Borders button again to hide the toolbar.

ADDING A BORDER

A border is a box surrounding a block of text that makes it stand out from the main flow of text. You can add a border to any paragraph or group of paragraphs in your document. To add a simple border, you click on the Borders button on the Formatting toolbar to display the Borders toolbar. Then you can choose a border style and apply it. You can add more complex border effects by using the *Paragraph Borders and Shading* dialog box. Let's use this method to emphasize your footer by adding a border and a shadow.

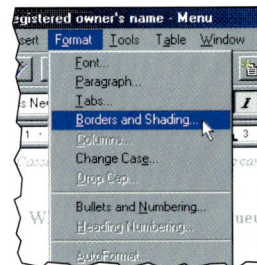

1 With your footer still selected, choose *Borders and Shading* from the *Format* menu.

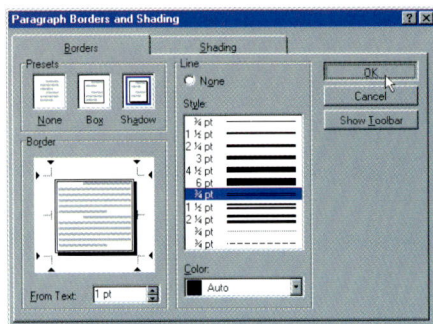

2 The *Paragraph Borders and Shading* dialog box appears. In the *Borders* flipcard under *Line*, select the ¾ pt double-line border in the *Style* box. Click on the *Shadow* icon in the *Presets* section. Finally, click on *OK*.

3 A double-line border with a shadow appears around the text of the footer. Now click on *Close* on the Header and Footer toolbar to return to your restaurant menu. Remember that you can see your footer only in Page Layout view.

See our drinks menu for coffees, soft drinks, cocktails, wines, beers, and spirits.

How to Create Sections

When you open a new document, there are no section breaks — the document consists of one section. With Word, it's easy to divide a document into different sections. You need to create sections if you want to apply certain formatting changes to a section that you don't want to apply to the rest of your document. If you simply want to format characters or format paragraphs — for example, making text bold and aligning it right — you don't need to create separate sections. But you do need to create sections if you want different parts of your document to have different margin settings or different numbers of columns. The importance of sections will become clear when you follow the steps on the opposite page to insert a separate section in the restaurant menu to create columns.

Different Margins?
If your document is broken up into sections, you can change the margin settings in one section without affecting the rest of the document. Position the insertion point in the relevant section, then choose *Page Setup* from the *File* menu. Type in the new margin values in the *Margins* flipcard and choose *This Section* in the *Apply To* box. To apply your changes, click on *OK*.

Creating Separate Sections

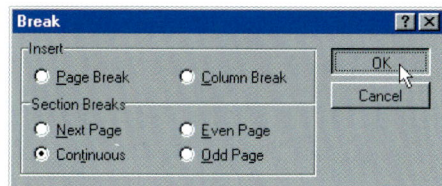

1 Position the insertion point at the beginning of the largest paragraph.

2 Now choose *Break* from the *Insert* menu.

3 The *Break* dialog box appears. Under *Section Breaks*, choose *Continuous* to create a section without starting a new page. Then click on *OK*. In your document the section break appears as a double dotted line. Position the insertion point at the end of the paragraph and press Enter. Then repeat steps 2 and 3 to mark the end of the section.

Breaking Point

You can use the Break *dialog box to insert a manual page break — to make sure, for example, that a particular heading is at the top of a page. Place the insertion point where you want the break to occur, then choose* Break *from the* Insert *menu. In the* Break *dialog box, choose* Page Break, *and then click on OK.*

How to Create Columns

With Word, you can format all or part of your document as newspaper-style columns in which text flows from the bottom of one column to the top of the next. You can specify however many columns you need, but as a general rule, two or three columns per page looks best. To create two columns for the largest paragraph of your restaurant menu, follow these steps:

Forming the Columns

1 Reposition the insertion point at the beginning of the largest paragraph.

2 Click on the Columns button on the Standard toolbar. Hold down the mouse button and drag to select two columns. Release the mouse button.

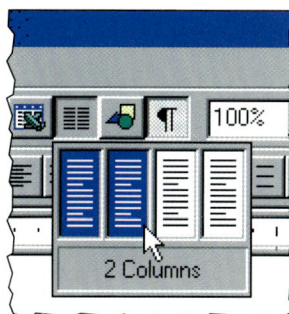

3 In your restaurant menu, the largest paragraph now appears as two columns.

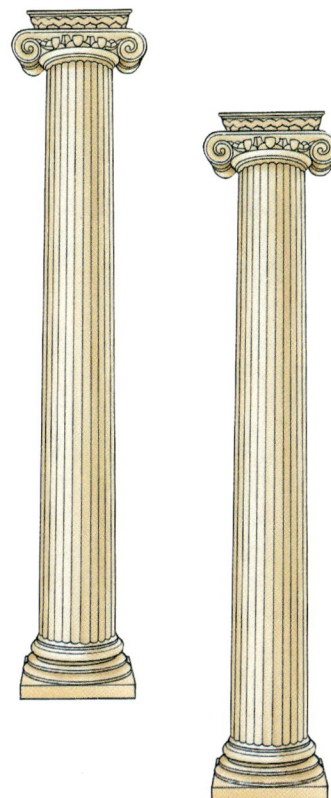

My Columns Are Missing!
Even if you have created separate columns, you will only see one column if you are in Normal View. To see your columns, you must make sure you are in Page Layout View.

Sunrise Bay Grill

TRADITIONAL FRESH SEAFOOD (AND PLENTY MORE BESIDES)

Like many other Sunshine Coast restaurants, Sunrise Bay Grill boasts a relaxed, anything-goes atmosphere. Open every day from noon to midnight, we will provide the type of service you need, whether you want a quiet meal for two or a fun-filled group night out. For the extra rowdy, we have a large back-room — soundproofed! Unlike most seafood restaurants, however, Sunrise Bay Grill alone. Our forceful (but friendly) chef Hank insists that we serve a wide range of interesting and international dishes too! And all at very reasonable prices. We pride ourselves on good value. But be warned! Hank doesn't believe in small portions — when you come to Sunrise Bay Grill, you must come hungry (if you manage three whole courses, we'll be astonished) Long live the Sunshine Coast

How to Create a Frame

A frame is a box of text, graphics, or a mixture of these elements that is separate from the body text and can be moved around the document independently. By default, any text outside the frame wraps around a frame. Placing items within a frame is a good way to separate them from the main text. To define a frame for your restaurant menu, make sure you are in Page Layout View, then follow these steps.

Adding a Frame

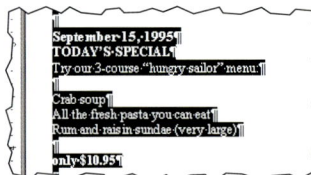

1 Position the insertion point on the blank line above the date. Select the blank line and the following lines of text down to and including the blank line after **only $10.95**.

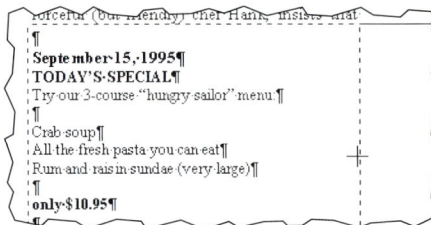

2 Choose *Frame* from the *Insert* menu. Word encloses the selected text in a box. This box is a frame. Because the frame is selected, you'll also see a shaded border with black handles.

On the Borderline
The standard border for a frame is a single-line box border. To change the border, click on the frame border to select the frame, choose *Borders and Shading* from the *Format* menu, and select the options you want in the dialog box.

3 To resize the frame so that it closely surrounds the text, move the mouse pointer to the handle at the center of the right hand border. The pointer changes to a two-headed arrow. Drag the border to the left to decrease the frame's width to just less than half its original width. As soon as you start dragging the border, the two-headed arrow changes to a cross hair.

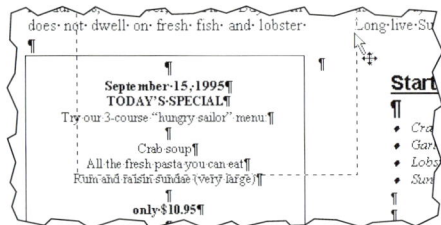

4 Click inside the frame and select all the text, including the two blank lines at the top and bottom. Then click on the Center button on the Formatting toolbar to center the text within the frame. Finally, deselect the text by clicking anywhere outside the frame.

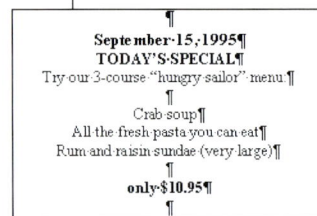

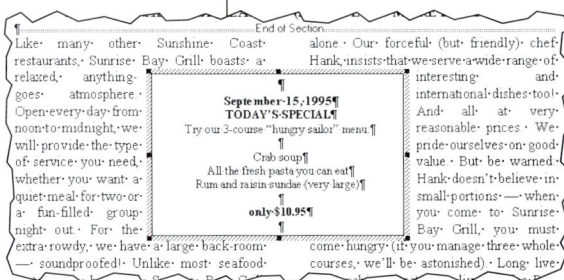

5 Click on the frame to select it. Move the mouse pointer over any part of the frame's border so that the pointer changes and has a four-headed arrow below it. Hold down the mouse button and drag the frame up and to the right.

6 Position the frame between the two columns so that its top border falls roughly in the space between the second and third lines, then release the mouse button. The frame should sit in the text roughly as shown at right. (It may take a moment for the new layout to appear on your screen.)

ADJUSTING YOUR FRAME

Now that you have inserted your frame, you may need to adjust its width and position so that the text flows neatly around it. You can adjust the frame's width by dragging the handles with the mouse and its position by dragging the whole frame. Use these methods on your frame so that the flow of the text around it is as close as possible to that shown at right.

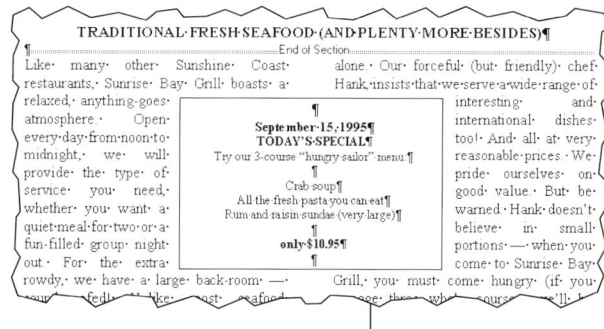

The Frame Dialog Box

For precise control over the adjustment of a frame, it's best to choose options in the *Frame* dialog box (right). To open the dialog box, you select your frame by clicking on its border, and then choose *Frame* from the *Format* menu. The various options you can choose are explained below.

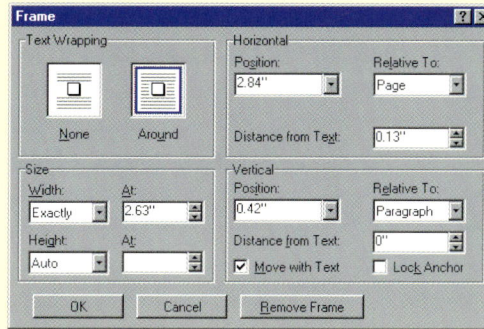

■ *Move With Text* — When this option is checked, Word will move the frame up or down the page automatically as you add or remove text above or below it.

■ *Distance From Text* — Type or select values in these boxes to set the spacing between the frame and the surrounding text.

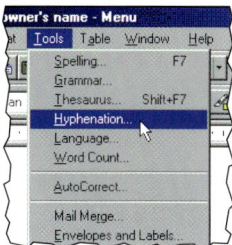

■ *Text Wrapping* — Choose whether you want the text to wrap around the frame or simply flow above and below it.

■ *Position* — In these boxes, type or select the horizontal and vertical positions you want for the frame.

■ *Relative To* — Select *Margin*, *Page*, *Column*, or *Paragraph* to indicate the item to which you want the positions in the *Position* boxes to relate.

■ *Lock Anchor* — Click on this option if you want your frame to remain locked in the specified position, regardless of any text changes you make.

■ *Size* — Use this section to choose a width and height for your frame. If you choose *Auto*, Word will size the frame according to the text inside it. If you want to specify your own measurements, simply type or select the required values in the *At* boxes.

How to Hyphenate Your Text

To avoid raggedness in left or right aligned text or to reduce gaps between words in justified text, you can hyphenate text. In the restaurant menu, highlight the justified text in columns, and then follow these steps:

1 Choose *Hyphenation* from the *Tools* menu. (If you don't have this option, you will need to install it from your original disks.)

2 In the *Hyphenation* dialog box, click on *Manual*.

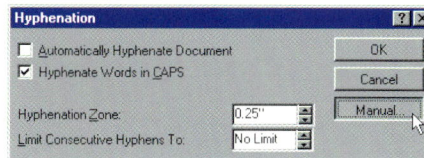

3 Word finds the first appropriate word, in our example **international**, and asks if you want it hyphenated. Click on *No*.

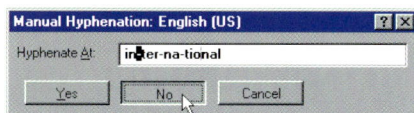

4 Word informs you when the hyphenation is complete. Click on *OK*.

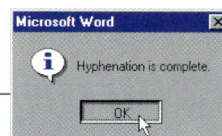

?

Auto Hyphenation? Word can hyphenate text as you type. In the *Hyphenation* dialog box, check the *Automatically Hyphenate Document* box. The smaller the measurement in the *Hyphenation Zone* box, the more words will be hyphenated.

Adding a Logo

GRAPHICS CAN BRIGHTEN up the appearance of any document. With Word it's easy to create such special effects — you can use WordArt for creating special typographical effects such as logos and the Drawing toolbar for designing your own pictures. In this section, you'll add the finishing touch — an attractive logo — to your restaurant menu. You'll also learn how to import ready-made pictures from Word's own "picture library."

Jazz Up Your Text

WordArt allows you to create special effects with words — for example, you can make words form a circle or an arch, make them slope diagonally, or even flip them upside down. Let's create a special effect for the name of the restaurant at the top of your document. In Page Layout View, follow the steps below.

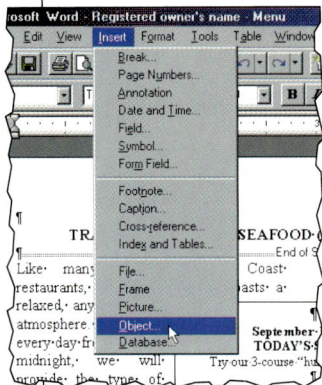

Styling the Name

1 Delete the name **Sunrise Bay Grill** at the top of the document. Press Enter and move the insertion point to the top left-hand corner of the window. Then choose *Object* from the *Insert* menu.

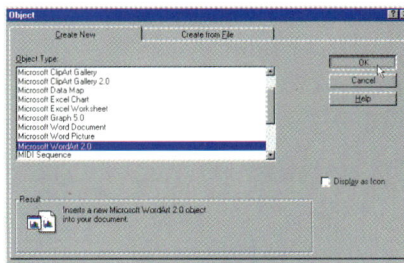

3 The WordArt toolbar appears and a text entry box opens. Type the words **Sunrise Bay Grill** in the *Enter Your Text Here* dialog box.

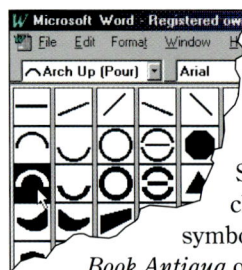

5 To return to Word, click outside the WordArt object — anywhere in your restaurant menu. The WordArt tools and the *Enter Your Text Here* dialog box disappear and the text is inserted into your document. Select the WordArt text by clicking on it, and then click on the Center button on the Formatting toolbar to center the name.

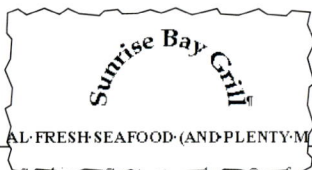

2 The *Object* dialog box appears. In the *Create New* flipcard, choose *Microsoft WordArt 2.0* in the *Object Type* box, and then click on *OK*.

4 On the WordArt toolbar, click on the down-arrow button next to the first drop-down list — the Shape list box — and click on the "arch-up" symbol to select it. Choose *Book Antiqua* or *Bookman Old Style* from the Font drop-down list (second drop-down list from the left) and *16* pt from the Font Size drop-down list (third list from the left).

WordArt Explorer
After selecting a shape for your text in WordArt, play with the buttons on the WordArt toolbar. For example, stretch or flip the letters by clicking on the Stretch Letters or Flip Letters button (seventh and eighth buttons from the right). Undo an effect by clicking on the same button again.

Changed Your Mind?
If you want to change WordArt text that you have already inserted into your document, simply double-click on the WordArt object to activate WordArt. Then change the text or change any of the formatting options.

A Budding Artist

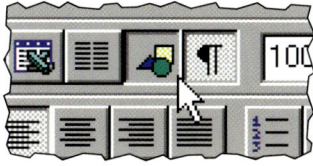

Using the Drawing toolbar, you can put together attractive pictures for your document. When you click on the Drawing button on the Standard toolbar, Word switches you to Page Layout View and the Drawing toolbar appears at the bottom of the screen. On the toolbar, you'll see a number of tools that you can use to create various shapes — lines, squares, rectangles, circles, ovals, and so on. You simply click on the relevant button to activate a particular drawing tool. You can also create text boxes and callouts, color single lines or the outline of an image, and fill your images with different colors. After drawing an image, you can manipulate it in several ways — for example, rotate the image or insert a frame around it. Over the next few pages, you'll assemble an image and add it to your restaurant menu. Below is a brief description of the buttons on the Drawing toolbar.

Drawing Button

Rise and Shine
The image you'll create for your logo will consist of the sun rising above the sea.

Calling Out?
A callout is a text box with a line extending from it that links text with a particular detail of an image. Click on the Format Callout button to open the *Format Callout* dialog box if you want to add a border around the text, change the type or angle of a callout line, or change the way the line is attached to the text box.

The Drawing Toolbar

By combining shapes formed with the drawing toolbar, you can create images such as logos, maps, flow charts, organization charts, and so on.

Line Tool
Draws a straight line; hold down Shift to constrain the line to a preset angle.

Rectangle Tool
Draws a rectangle; hold down Shift for a square.

Ellipse Tool
Draws an ellipse (oval); hold down Shift to produce a circle.

Arc Tool
Draws an arc; hold down Shift for a circular arc.

Freeform Tool
Draws any shape (polyline) you want to draw. Double-click to end the shape.

Text Box Tool
Creates a text box. You can format the text in the same way you format any other Word text.

Callout Tool
Draws a text box with an attached line.

Format Callout
Specifies the appearance of a callout.

Fill Color
Fills a drawing with a selected color.

Line Color
Outlines a drawing with a selected color.

Line Style
Specifies a line style.

Select Drawing Objects
Drag pointer to select one or several drawings at once.

Bring to Front
Brings a selected drawing in front of other drawings.

Send to Back
Sends a selected drawing behind other drawings.

Bring in Front of Text
Brings a selected drawing in front of a text layer.

Send Behind Text
Sends a selected drawing behind a text layer.

Group
Connects two or more drawings so they can be moved or sized as a group.

Ungroup
Ungroups drawings.

Flip Horizontal
Flips a selected drawing from right to left.

Flip Vertical
Flips a selected drawing from top to bottom.

Rotate Right
Rotates a selected drawing 90° to the right.

Reshape
Reshapes a selected Freeform drawing.

Snap to Grid
Sets up snapping grids to help position both text and drawings.

Align Drawing Objects
Aligns drawings to each other on the page.

Create Picture
Inserts an empty drawing container.

Insert Frame
Frames a selected drawing or text.

MAKING WAVES

The first part of the image you'll draw are the waves. To create them, you draw an arc, copy it, and overlap the arcs. If the Drawing toolbar isn't displayed, click on the Drawing button on the Standard toolbar. Position the insertion point immediately after **Sunrise Bay Grill** and press Enter six times to make space for the drawing. (You should have a total of seven "empty" lines.)

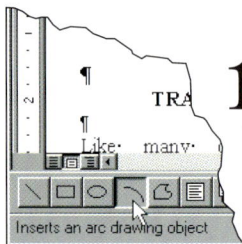

1 Click on the Arc tool on the Drawing toolbar. When moved into your document, the mouse pointer changes to a cross-hair shape.

2 Move the pointer to the area above **TRADITIONAL FRESH SEAFOOD....** Hold down the mouse button and drag the pointer up and to the right to create a "wave," and then release the mouse button. Roughly follow the position and proportions shown at right.

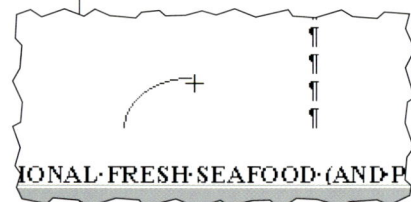

3 The wave you have drawn should be selected. (You can tell it's selected because black handles appear; if it isn't, click on the wave.) You can now copy this wave to produce several others of the same proportions.

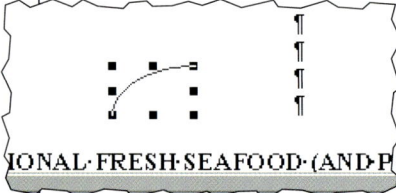

4 Place the mouse pointer over the wave so that it is accompanied by a four-headed arrow.

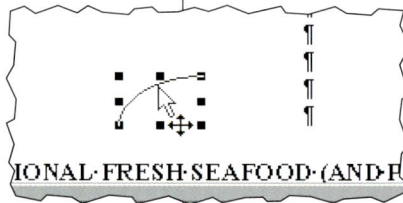

5 Hold down Ctrl — a plus sign appears — and drag the mouse pointer to the right as shown here. You'll see an outline of the wave move as you move the mouse. Release the mouse button and Ctrl to drop the copy of the wave into its new position.

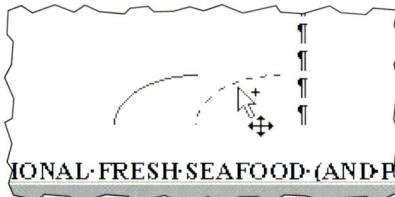

6 Repeat the procedure to produce two more waves, and then click outside the waves to deselect the last wave. You should now have four waves lined up in one row as shown at right.

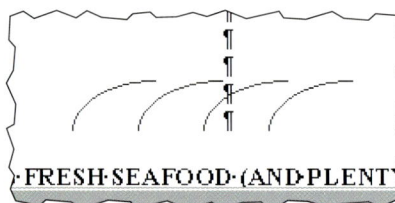

?

Drawn the Wrong Thing?
To delete a drawn object, first select the item by clicking on it. (If the object is not filled, click on one of the object's edges.) When an object is selected, a box with black handles appears around it. Now press Delete.

!

Wrong Size!
You can easily resize a drawn object. Simply click on the object to select it, and then drag any handle to resize it. To enlarge or shrink an object and keep its original proportions, hold down Shift and drag any corner handle.

LET THE SUN SHINE

Follow these steps to create the second part of your image — the sun and its rays. When you create an object, it appears in front of any text or other object in the document. (You'll be shown how to layer drawings in "Making the Final Adjustments" on page 76.)

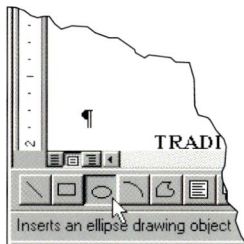

1 Click on the Ellipse tool.

Inserts an ellipse drawing object

2 Hold down Shift and position the pointer at the foot of and between the second and third waves. Hold down the mouse button and drag the pointer to the right to create a circle one inch in diameter. Then release the mouse button and Shift.

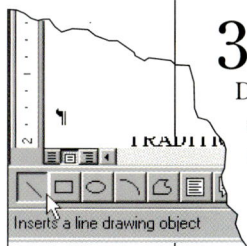

AL·FRESH·SEAFOOD·(AND·PLENTY·MO

3 Double-click on the Line button to select it. (Double-clicking on a Drawing button allows you to draw several objects of the same type without having to return to the toolbar.)

Inserts a line drawing object

4 Position the cross-hair at the left side of the sun, and then drag the cross-hair outward. Release the mouse button when the line is approximately the length as shown.

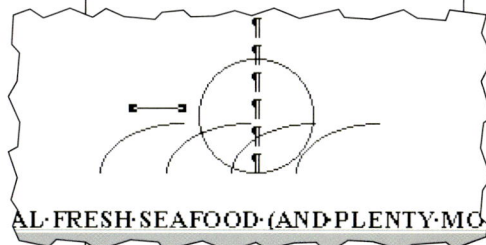

AL·FRESH·SEAFOOD·(AND·PLENTY·MO

5 Create four other rays around the top of the circle. Then hold down Shift and click the arrow pointer on each ray in turn to select all the rays.

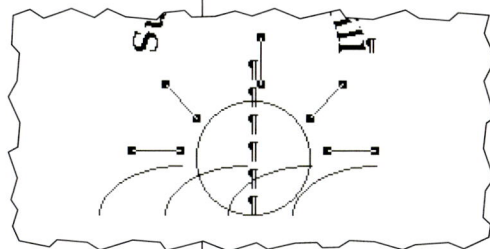

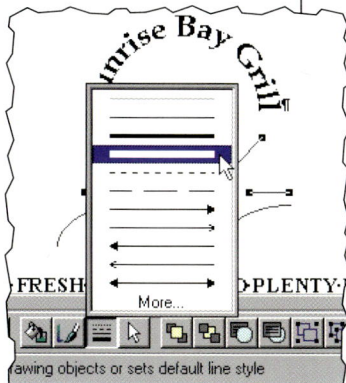

6 Click on the Line Style button and select the thickest line from the pop-up list. When you release the mouse button, the rays will be formatted with a thick line. Leave the five rays selected.

awing objects or sets default line style

Big Selection
To select several objects at the same time, you can either hold down Shift and then click on each object in turn, or you can click on the Select Drawings Object button (the arrow button) on the Drawing toolbar, and drag the pointer to create a rectangle that encloses the objects you want to select.

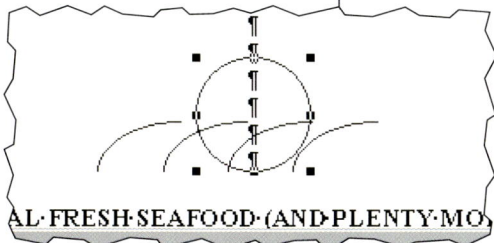

75

COLORING OBJECTS AND LINES

Now that you have drawn the separate parts of your image, you can color them. But bear in mind that unless you have a color printer, the colors show only on your screen — the image will be printed in black. Follow these steps to color your image.

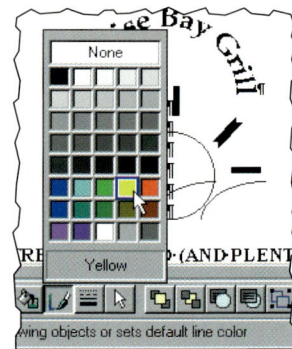

1 The rays should still be selected. Click on the Line Color button and select the yellow square from the pop-up palette — the rays turn yellow. Click in a blank spot to deselect the rays.

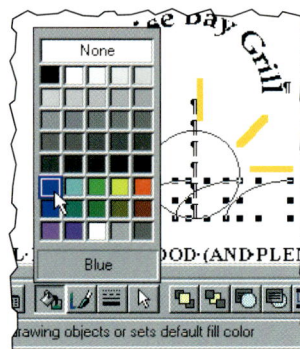

2 Hold down Shift and click on each wave to select them all. Click on the Fill Color button and select bright blue from the pop-up palette. While the waves are still selected, choose the same blue from the Line Color palette. Finally, deselect the waves.

3 Select the circle and choose yellow from both the Fill Color and the Line Color palettes.

MAKING THE FINAL ADJUSTMENTS

Your image is now complete except for its layering. For a better fit, you may also want to alter the size and shape of your WordArt text (see box at left).

1 Some of the waves are hidden behind the sun. With the sun still selected, click on the Send to Back button to move the sun behind the waves. Click in a blank spot to deselect the sun.

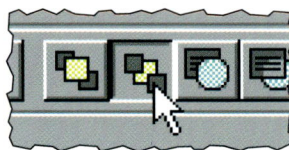

2 Your image is now complete and you've finished formatting your restaurant menu. Save your document and then print it. The printed version should look like the one shown here.

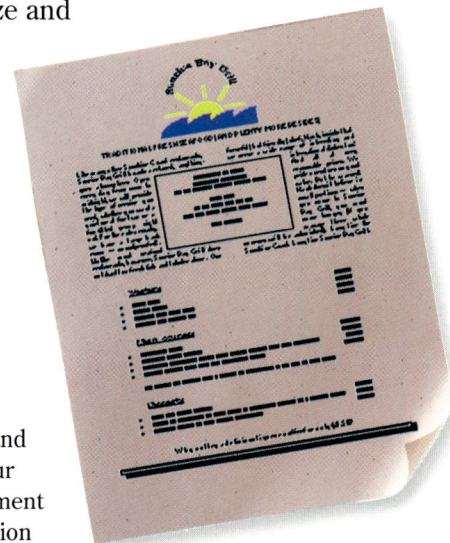

Cut It to Size

To resize the WordArt text, first double-click on the WordArt object to display the WordArt menu bar. Click on *Stretch To Frame* in the *Format* menu then click outside the object. Now you can drag any of the corner handles to enlarge or shrink the image without distorting it. Dragging a center handle will distort the image slightly.

Ready-Made Pictures

You can also include pictures from the Clipart folder. All the files in Clipart contain images that have already been created — you just choose the image you want and then import it into the document. After you have imported an image you can select and resize it in your Word document. Let's add an image to the **Prize letter** document that you created earlier in Chapter One. Make sure you have closed your **Menu** document, and then open **Prize letter**.

Not enough Clipart?
To find more Clipart images, insert your installation disk into the disk drive and click on *Run* in the Start menu then click on *OK* in the *Run* dialog box. Click on the Custom button when this option is offered after Setup has completed its second search for installed components. Select *Office Tools* and click on *Change Option*. Scroll down to Clipart and click on *Change Option* again. Here you'll find a large number of clipart packages on subjects ranging from animals to energy to transport.

Inserting the Picture

1 Place the insertion point in front of the word **Thompson** in the return address, and then choose *Picture* from the *Insert* menu.

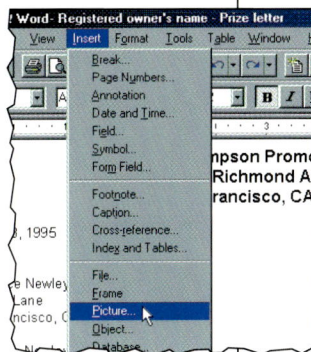

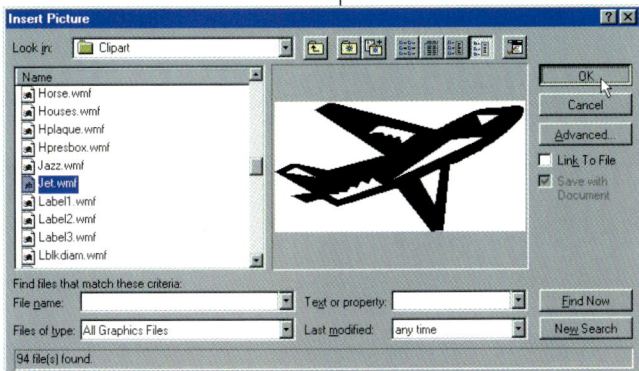

2 The *Insert Picture* dialog box appears. The Clipart folder should be shown in the *Look in* textbox. In the main panel you'll see a list of names for different Clipart images. Scroll through the list and choose the file **Jet.wmf**. Then click on *OK* to import the image into your document.

3 The picture appears at the top of the document, in front of the line **Thompson Promotions**, where the insertion point was placed. Press Enter once to insert a new line so that the picture is above the return address as shown here. Then save the document and close it.

Want to Modify Your Image?
To modify a picture, begin by double-clicking on it. This opens the picture as a separate document in Page Layout View and displays the Drawing toolbar. You can use the tools or buttons on the Drawing toolbar (see page 73) to modify the image. For example, you can select the jet you've just imported and color it by selecting a color from the Fill Color and Line Color palettes. When you've finished, click on *Close Picture* in the *Picture* dialog box.

Tables and Sorting

YOU MAY SOMETIMES want to organize and present text or data in a table. Word has several features that make working with tables easy. You can apply character and paragraph formatting to the items in a table; you can produce a chart directly from a table without entering any of the figures again; and you can instruct Word to sort data in various ways, such as alphabetically or chronologically. Word can even add up data in a table for you.

How to Create a Table

In a table, you enter text, data, or graphics into boxes, called cells, which are arranged in columns and rows. On the screen, nonprinting gridlines show the boundaries of individual cells and of the table. The gridlines are guides that make it easier to work with a table. If they don't appear, choose *Gridlines* from the *Table* menu. For gridlines that will print, click in the table, choose *Borders and Shading* from the *Format* menu, click on *Grid* under *Presets*, and then click on *OK*.

Before you build a table, decide how many columns and rows you'll need. Remember to add a row or column for the headings. You can also add extra rows and columns after you have created a table, if necessary.

AN ELECTION IN SMALLTOWN
In this section, you'll create an example table within a letter from a polling organization. Click on the New button on the Standard toolbar. Save the document as **Poll** in the My Documents folder, then type in the text below. Make the first line after the date, **Precision Polls Inc.**, 18 point, bold, and centered.

? **Want to Change Your Table Manners?**
In this section, you'll learn how to insert a table using the Standard toolbar, but you can also create a table by choosing *Insert Table* from the *Table* menu. In the *Insert Table* dialog box, type the number of rows and columns you want in the relevant text boxes, and then click on *OK*.

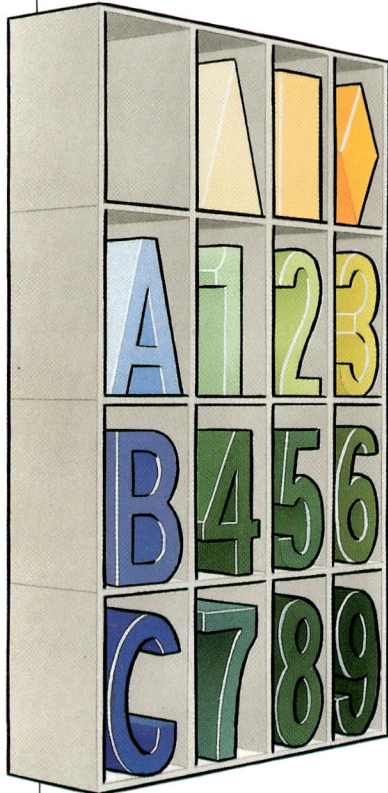

Wrapping Around
A table also provides a convenient way to present side-by-side paragraphs. Within each cell in a table, text wraps just as it does between the margins of a document; the cell expands vertically to fit the amount of text you type.

November 20, 1995 <Enter> <Enter>

Precision Polls Inc. <Enter> <Enter>

The Editor <Enter>

Smalltown Gazette <Enter>

Smalltown <Enter> <Enter>

Dear Sir, <Enter> <Enter>

Please find below the results of our latest survey (mid-November) of voting intentions for the forthcoming (December 10) election for Mayor of Smalltown. As before, we contacted the same sample of 835 Smalltown residents by telephone and asked them "Which candidate do you expect to vote for on December 10?" The answers were as follows (the results from our two previous surveys also appear): <Enter> <Enter>

SETTING UP THE TABLE

Position the insertion point two lines beneath the last paragraph. This is where you'll insert the table. Now follow these steps:

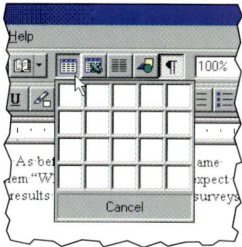

1 Click on the Insert Table button on the Standard toolbar. A small grid drops down.

2 Hold down the mouse button and drag over the grid to select five rows and four columns. The line at the bottom of the table displays how many rows and columns you have selected. Then release the mouse button.

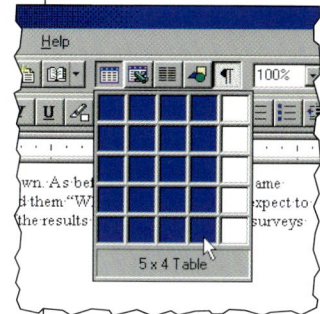

3 A blank table is inserted into your document. The small squares are end-of-cell and end-of-row marks. You can hide or display them by clicking on the Show/Hide ¶ button. Display them for now to make the table easier to work with.

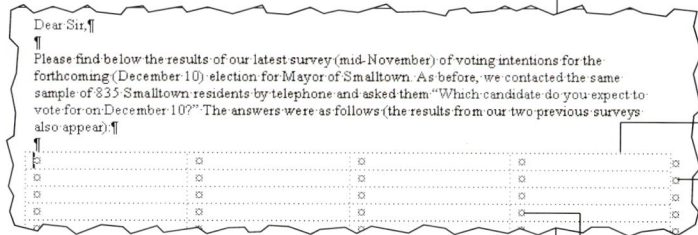

Dear Sir,¶
¶
Please find below the results of our latest survey (mid-November) of voting intentions for the forthcoming (December 10) election for Mayor of Smalltown. As before, we contacted the same sample of 835 Smalltown residents by telephone and asked them "Which candidate do you expect to vote for on December 10?" The answers were as follows (the results from our two previous surveys also appear).¶
¶

Gridline

End-of-Row Mark

End-of-Cell Mark

ENTERING AND FORMATTING DATA

Now type the following poll results into the table, row by row. Begin by positioning your insertion point in the second cell in the top row. After typing the contents of a cell, press Tab to move to the next cell in a row. At the end of a row, press Tab to move the insertion point to the first cell in the next row. Alternatively, use the direction keys.

	Sept.	Oct.	Nov.
John Red	267	287	265
Edith Blue	150	262	321
Matt Yellow	356	228	227
Undecided	62	58	22

Formatting Data in a Table

1 Select the column of candidates' names by clicking on the top gridline of the column — where the pointer changes to a black arrow.

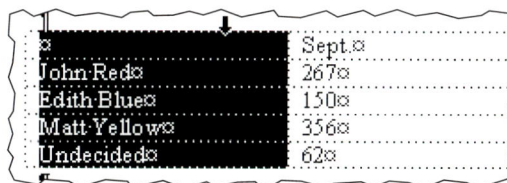

	Sept.
John Red	267
Edith Blue	150
Matt Yellow	356
Undecided	62

2 Click on the Bold button on the Formatting toolbar to make the candidates' names bold.

	Sept.
John Red	267
Edith Blue	150
Matt Yellow	356
Undecided	62

3 Select the top row of the table by clicking in the selection bar next to it, then click on the Bold button to emphasize the months.

How Can I Select Table Entries?
To select a single cell, position the I-beam pointer between the left edge of the cell and the first character in the cell, where the pointer changes to an arrow. Then click the mouse button. To select any rectangular block of cells, simply hold down the mouse button and drag over the area you want to select.

ADDING ROWS AND COLUMNS

If you want to include more data in a table, you'll need to add extra columns or rows. The quickest method is to select in your existing table the number of columns or rows that you want to add, and then click on the Insert Table button on the Standard toolbar. The button's name changes to "Insert Columns," "Insert Rows," or "Insert Cells" depending on what you have highlighted at the time. Word inserts new columns to the left of selected columns and new rows above selected rows.

To insert a new row at the bottom of a table, follow the procedure described at the bottom of this page. To add a new column at the right of a table, position the insertion point just to the right of the last column, choose *Select Column* from the *Table* menu so that the end-of-row marks are selected, and then choose *Insert Columns* from the *Table* menu.

INSERTING AND DELETING CELLS

To insert one or more new, blank cells (but not a whole row or column) in a table, select the cell or cells where you want the new cells to appear. On the Standard toolbar, click on the Insert Table button, which changes to Insert Cells. In the *Insert Cells* dialog box, choose *Shift Cells Right* or *Shift Cells Down* to specify whether the existing cells move to the right or down when the new cells are added. Click on *OK*.

To delete cells in a table, select the cell or cells you want to delete, and then choose *Delete Cells* from the *Table* menu. Choose one of the four options displayed in the *Delete Cells* dialog box, and then click on *OK*.

What a Drag!

You can easily change the order of columns or rows. Just like text, you can drag selected cells, columns, or rows to different positions within a table to re-organize your data.

Keep Tabs on It!

Make sure you press the Tab key when you want to add a new row. Pressing Enter by mistake adds a new line to the last row.

A Tight Fit?

If you want to change the width of a column in a table, first select the column and then position the mouse pointer over the column's right gridline, where it changes to a double-headed arrow. Drag the gridline to the right or left until the column is the desired width.

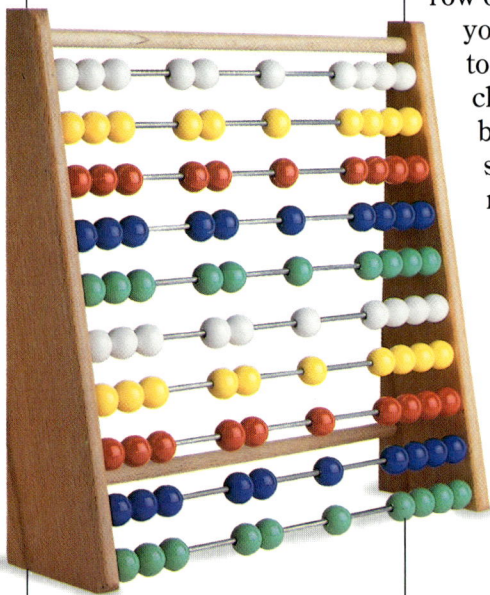

The Delete Cells Dialog Box

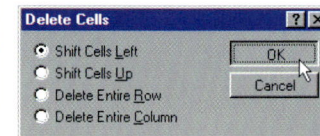

Delete Cells
- Shift Cells Left
- Shift Cells Up
- Delete Entire Row
- Delete Entire Column

OK
Cancel

Adding a New Row to Your Table

1 Position the insertion point in the rightmost cell of the last row of your table. Then press the Tab key.

	Nov	
	265	
	321	
	227	
	22	

2 A new row of blank cells appears at the bottom of your table. Type **Total** in the first column of the new row.

	Sept	Oct	Nov	
John Red	267	287	265	
Edith Blue	150	262	321	
Matt Yellow	356	228	227	
Undecided	62	58	22	
Total				

HOW TO TOTAL NUMBERS IN A TABLE

When you have set up a table, you can easily add up numbers in a column or a row. Let's total the contents of each column in your table.

Sept.¤		Oct.¤
267¤		287¤
150¤		262¤
356¤		228¤
62¤		58¤
¤		¤

1 Position the insertion point in the empty cell next to **Total** in the **Sept.** column.

2 Choose *Formula* from the *Table* menu.

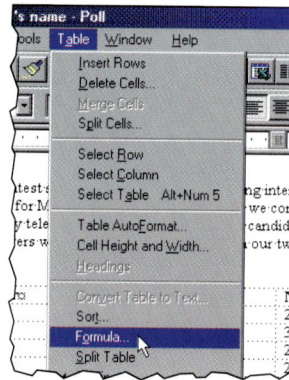

3 The *Formula* dialog box appears. The *Formula* box contains the formula =*SUM(ABOVE)*. Click on *OK*.

Formula

Formula:
=SUM(ABOVE)

Number Format:

Paste Function: Paste Bookmark:

OK   Cancel

4 You'll see the total of the column displayed in the bottom cell of the column. Repeat the procedure for the **Oct.** and **Nov.** columns. The total for each column should be 835.

Sept.¤		Oct.¤
267¤		287¤
150¤		262¤
356¤		228¤
62¤		58¤
835¤		¤

HOW TO SORT DATA IN A TABLE

You may want to reorganize the rows of your table so that the contents of cells in a specific column are listed in a particular order — alphabetically, for instance, or by size. To do so, you use the *Sort* command.

	Sept.¤
John·Red¤	267¤
Edith·Blue¤	150¤
Matt·Yellow¤	356¤
Undecided¤	62¤
Total¤	835¤

1 Select the four rows containing the polling data, as shown. Don't include the top or bottom row.

2 Choose *Sort* from the *Table* menu to open the *Sort* dialog box.

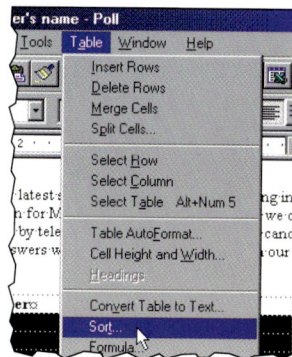

Sort

Sort By
Column 4   Type: Number   Ascending / Descending

Then By
Type: Text   Ascending / Descending

Then By
Type: Text   Ascending / Descending

My List Has
Header Row   No Header Row

OK   Cancel   Options...

3 Under *Sort By,* click on the down arrow next to the first drop-down list box and set it to *Column 4* so that the table is sorted according to the candidates' popularity in November. The *Type* list box, under *Sort By*, should then display *Number*. Select the *Descending* option to put the most popular candidate first. Then click on *OK.*

Be Calculating

You can direct Word to perform simple calculations and paste the result where you've placed the insertion point. Choose *Field* from the *Insert* menu. Type the numbers with the relevant mathematical symbol (- for minus, + for add, / for divide, * for multiply, % for percentage) after the equal sign in the *Field Codes* box. When you click on *OK,* the results appear in your document.

Lost in the *Sort* Box?

Some of the options in the *Sort* dialog box may need explaining. *Sort By* identifies the column by which to sort the data. Under *Type* you choose to sort data alphabetically, numerically, or by date. *Ascending* means sorts go from A to Z, or from 1 to larger numbers, *Descending* is the other way around.

Charts

ADDING CHARTS TO YOUR DOCUMENTS gives them a more professional look and greater visual impact. Studies suggest that people take in visual information far more quickly than written information. Illustrating data using the Graph feature that comes with Word not only makes your document look professional, it is the best way to get your message home.

Creating Charts

It's easy to convert the data within a table into a chart. You select all or part of the table and launch Microsoft Graph, an application included with Word. Two windows will appear within the *Graph* window — a *Datasheet* window that contains the data generating the chart, and a *Chart* window in which the chart's current appearance is displayed. Let's create a chart from the table you made in the last section. First, place the insertion point immediately below the foot of the table, press Enter, and add the text shown below right. Then follow the steps that begin at left.

How to Create a Column Chart

	Sept.
Edith Blue	267
John Red	150
Matt Yellow	356
Undecided	62
Total	835

1 Click the pointer in the selection bar at the top left of your table and drag the pointer down to select the first five rows.

2 Click on *Object* in the *Insert* menu to display the *Object* dialog box. Click on *Microsoft Graph 5.0* and then click on *OK*.

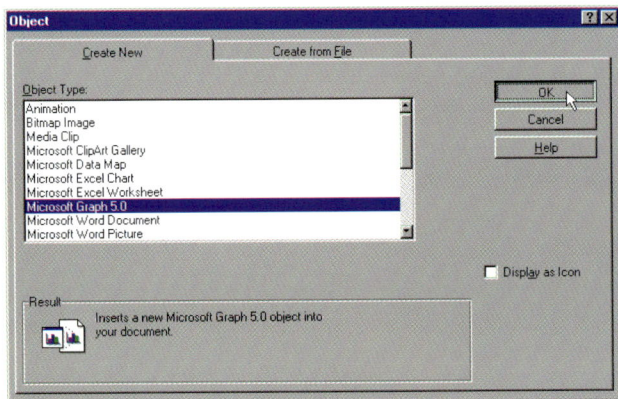

As you can see from the column chart, there appears to have been a late switch to Ms. Blue, mainly from previously undecided voters.

3 The table data appears in the *Datasheet* window and, underneath this, a chart appears in the *Chart* window. The first of four *ChartWizard* dialog boxes is superimposed over these two displays. The four *ChartWizard* dialog boxes take you through all the steps necessary to design your graph. The first box lets you choose the type of chart that you want to display your information. Click on *Column* in the center of the top row, then click on *Next*.

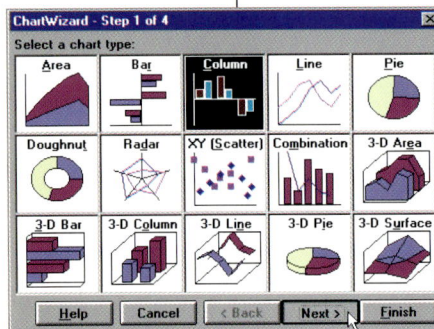

4 The second *ChartWizard* dialog box lets you choose the format for columns. Overlapping columns will allow easy comparison of the data in the table, so click on *4,* and click on *Next.* You can always click on *Back* if you change your mind and want to choose another type of chart or format.

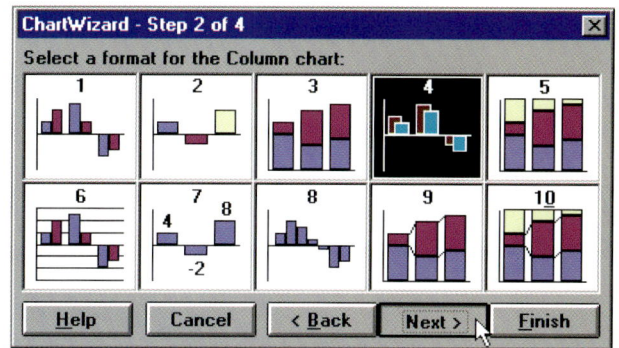

ChartWizard - Step 2 of 4

Select a format for the Column chart:

5 The third *ChartWizard* dialog box is where you can change the layout of the data in your chart. The first pair of option buttons, *Rows* and *Columns,* determines which set of labels appears along the bottom of your graph. It can be either the months, which are arranged along a row, or the candidates names, which are listed in a column.

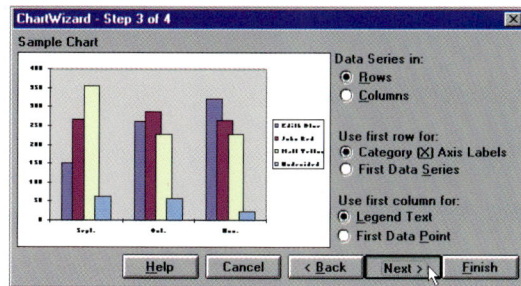

ChartWizard - Step 3 of 4

Sample Chart

Data Series in:
● Rows
○ Columns

Use first row for:
● Category (X) Axis Labels
○ First Data Series

Use first column for:
● Legend Text
○ First Data Point

6 The *Use first row for* buttons are used depending on whether the first row contains labels or data. If you have labels in the first row, then check *Category (X) Axis Labels.* If you have data, then check *First Data Series.*

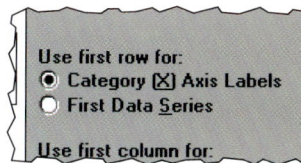

Use first row for:
● Category (X) Axis Labels
○ First Data Series

Use first column for:

7 The *Use first column for* buttons are checked according to whether you have labels or data in the first column. Make sure the three sets of buttons are checked as shown in these examples, and click on *Next.*

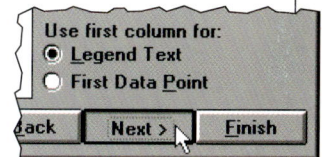

Use first column for:
● Legend Text
○ First Data Point

8 The final *ChartWizard* dialog box lets you add a legend and titles to your graph. Legends and titles are vital keys to your chart. The legend explains what the chart is illustrating — in this example, the colors of the columns are connected to the candidates' names in the legend. The axis titles define the data plotted in the chart. Type **Precision Poll Results** in the Chart Title textbox, then click on *Finish.*

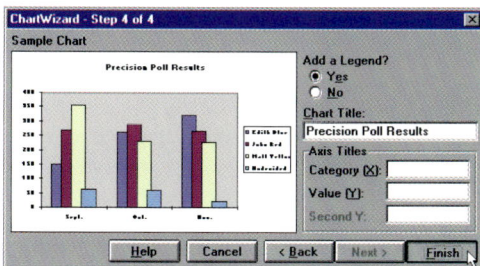

ChartWizard - Step 4 of 4

Sample Chart

Precision Poll Results

Add a Legend?
● Yes
○ No

Chart Title:
Precision Poll Results

Axis Titles
Category (X):
Value (Y):
Second Y:

9 Now click on the Close button of the Datasheet to close it and click outside the chart to close Microsoft Graph. The finished chart appears immediately below your table.

As you can see from the column chart, there appears to have bee previously undecided voters.

Precision Poll Results

- Edith Blue
- John Red
- Matt Yellow
- Undecided

Sept. Oct. Nov.

10 To move the chart, first click inside the chart to select it if the frame and handles aren't visible, then cut it. Move the insertion point to the end of the document and paste the chart to this location.

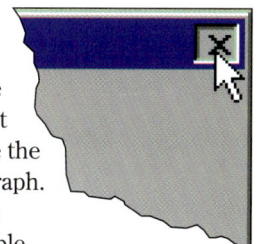

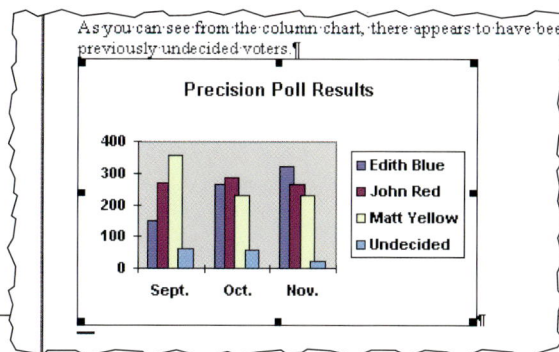

HOW TO CREATE A PIE CHART

Now let's add a second chart — a pie chart — to your document to show how voting intentions in the Smalltown election are distributed according to the latest (November) survey. Before creating the pie chart, add the text at right so that it follows the sentence you added on the previous page (it ends: **...previously undecided voters.**). Then follow the steps described below.

The pie chart shows how voting intentions are split by percentage according to our latest survey. <Enter>

1 Move the pointer into the selection bar and drag it down to select the first five rows in your opinion poll table. (Again, the **Total** row is not needed for this chart.)

sample of 835 Smalltown residents by telephone and asked them "Which candidate do you expect to vote for on December 10?" The answers were as follows (the results from our two previous surveys also appear).¶

	Sept.	Oct.	Nov.
Edith Blue	150	262	321
John Red	267	287	265
Matt Yellow	356	228	227
Undecided	62	58	22
Total	835	835	835

ChartWizard - Step 1 of 4

Select a chart type:

Area | Bar | Column | Line | Pie
Doughnut | Radar | XY (Scatter) | Combination | 3-D Area
3-D Bar | 3-D Column | 3-D Line | 3-D Pie | 3-D Surface

Help | Cancel | < Back | Next > | Finish

2 Click on *Object* in the *Insert* menu, click on *Microsoft Graph 5.0* in the *Object* dialog box, and click on *OK* (see page 82). In the first *ChartWizard* dialog box, click on *3-D Pie* and click on *Finish*.

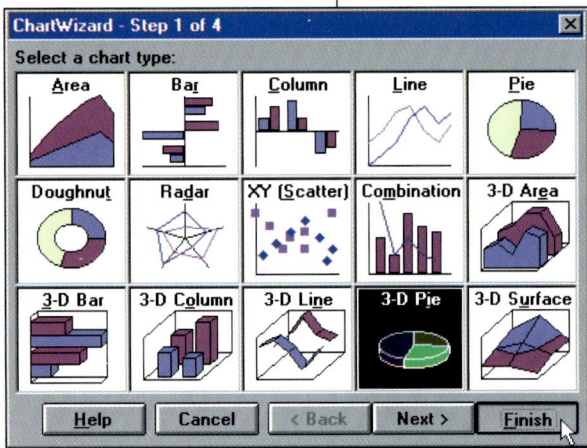

Datasheet

	A	B	No
	Sept.	Oct.	
Blue	150	262	
Red	267	287	
Yellow	356	228	
dec	62	58	
	Oct.		

3 As you want to chart only the November data, you need to exclude the September and October data. First, click once on the bar labeled *A* above **Sept.** in the *Datasheet* window. Now hold down the mouse button and drag the large "plus" pointer over to the bar labeled *B* above **Oct.**

name - Poll

Data | Window | Help

✓ Series in Rows
Series in Columns

Include Row/Col
Exclude Row/Col

Plot on X Axis

4 Choose *Exclude Row/Col* from the *Data* menu. You will see that these columns have been grayed out.

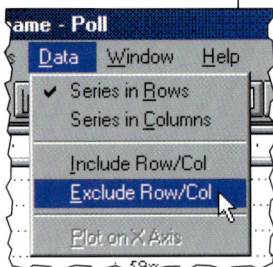

name - Poll

Data | Window | Help

✓ Series in Rows
Series in Columns

Include Row/Col
Exclude Row/Col

Plot on X Axis

5 Choose *Series in Columns* from the *Data* menu. You have now created your chart, so click on the Close button of the *Datasheet* window to close it.

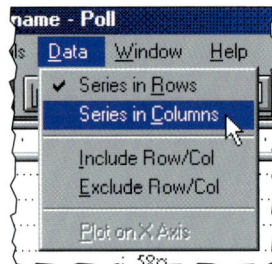

Get Chart Smart! Take care when choosing the type of chart to use when plotting data. Column charts and line graphs are especially suitable for indicating trends over time. Pie charts are best used to show how something breaks down into its parts — for example, how much income a company derives from various product lines.

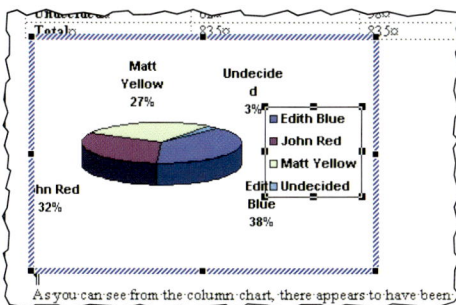

THE FINISHING TOUCH

You have now created an attractive pie chart. Let's add a few finishing touches to the chart and finalize your **Poll** document:

1 In the *Chart* window, click on the legend to select it. As the legend is redundant in this case, press Delete to remove it from the chart.

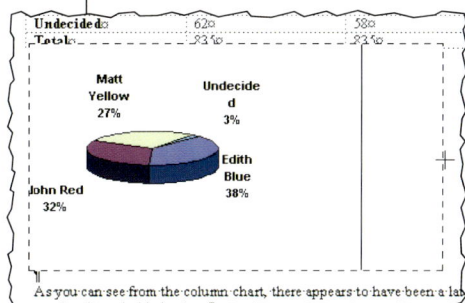

2 Enlarge the chart a little by dragging the handle in the middle of the right-hand border of the *Chart* window so that **Undecided** sits on one line and John Red's name is brought fully into the chart.

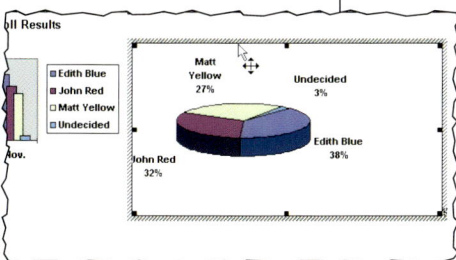

3 Click outside the chart to close Microsoft Graph. The pie chart appears immediately beneath the table. Click on the chart to select it, and then click on *Frame* in the *Insert* menu (see page 70). Now you can drag the frame containing the chart and place it at right of the column chart.

Looks like the final results could be close! <Enter> <Enter>
Sincerely yours, <Enter> <Enter>

Melvin T. Pollster

Chart Charter

To create effective charts, you must stick to a few basic rules:

■ Don't make charts too complicated — they should be easily understood.

■ Don't put too much data into a chart. For example, five series of data per column in a column chart is a sensible maximum.

■ Remember to specify the units and categories that are in your chart. Charts without labels mean nothing to people reading them.

■ Bear in mind that charts may lose some impact when printed in black and white.

4 Click below the chart to deselect it and place the insertion point at the end of the document. Press Enter and type the text above to finish your **Poll** document.

5 Finally, save your letter and print it. The finished document should look like the example shown here.

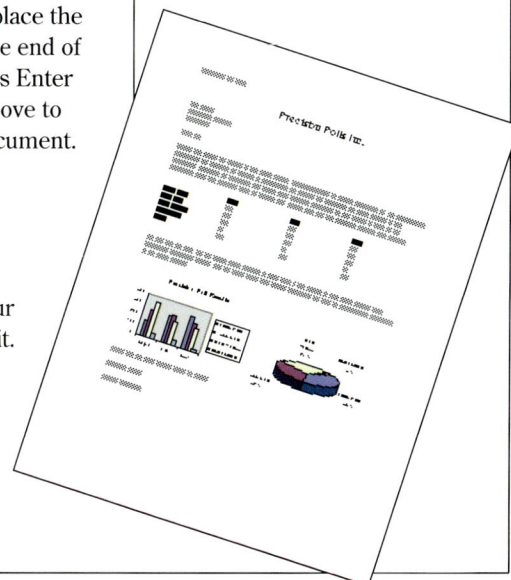

Be Creative

I N THIS SECTION, you'll find some more ideas for the different types of documents you can create using Word. Here we show you four different examples, but with lots of practice and plenty of imagination, you'll see just how easy it is to create virtually any type of document to suit your personal or business needs — or even just for fun.

Helpful Hints

You can create the example documents on these pages using the skills you've learned earlier in this book. The labels provide formatting information to help you along the way. Of course, these are just a few ideas; you can modify the documents in any way you wish using your newly-acquired skills, or you can create your own documents from scratch. So go ahead — be creative, and see how many different things you can do using Word.

Want to Crop?
With Word, it's easy to crop an image so that only part of it appears in your document. Simply select the image by clicking on it, then hold down Shift and drag one of the handles inward or outward, depending on how much of the image you want to see.

Travel Brochure Cover

Drawing Toolbar: Ellipse and Arc tools

Century Gothic, 34 point, bold, italic, centered

Drawing toolbar: Arc tool used for palms, Rectangle tool used for trunk

Century Gothic, 12 point, centered

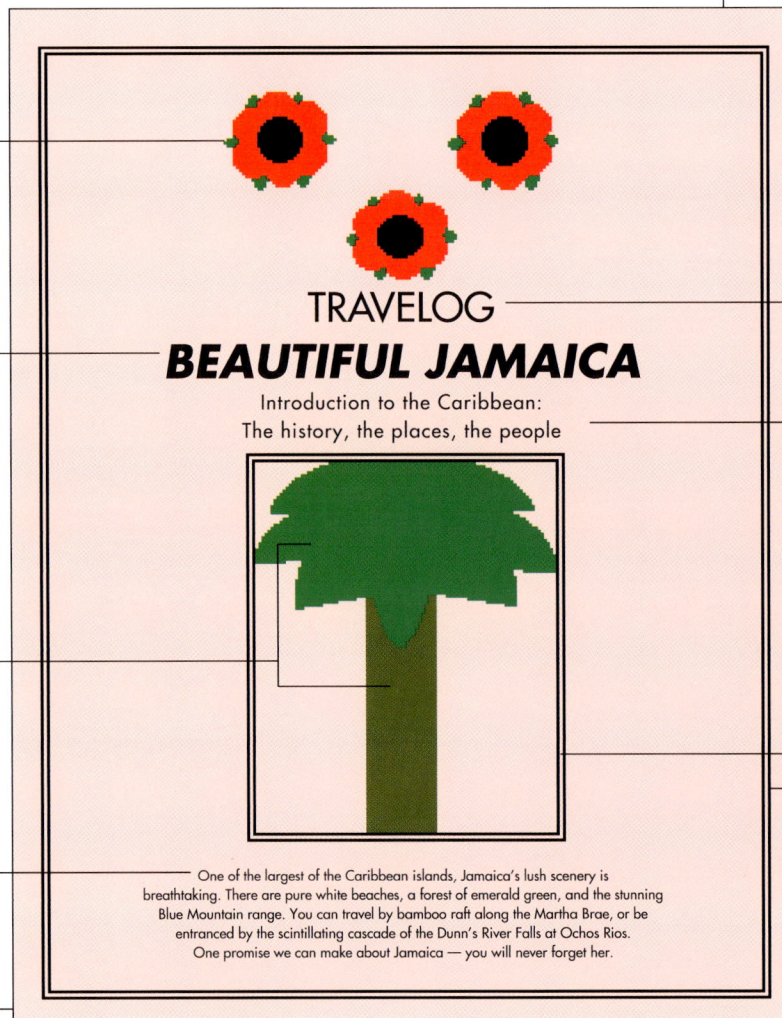

TRAVELOG
BEAUTIFUL JAMAICA
Introduction to the Caribbean:
The history, the places, the people

One of the largest of the Caribbean islands, Jamaica's lush scenery is breathtaking. There are pure white beaches, a forest of emerald green, and the stunning Blue Mountain range. You can travel by bamboo raft along the Martha Brae, or be entranced by the scintillating cascade of the Dunn's River Falls at Ochos Rios. One promise we can make about Jamaica — you will never forget her.

Century Gothic, 30 point, centered

Century Gothic, 18 point, centered

Double-line border

86

Promotional Leaflet

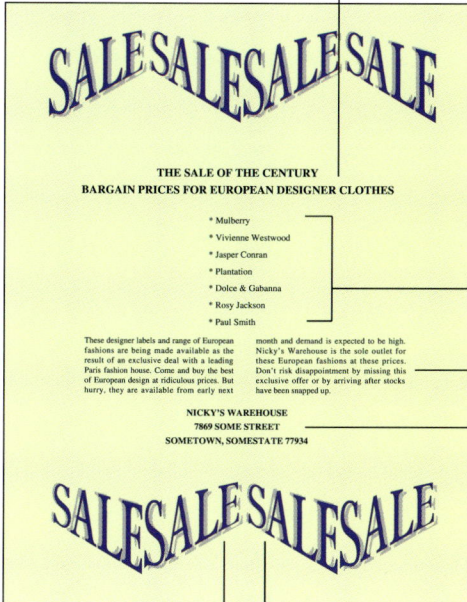

Times New Roman, 20 point, bold, small caps, centered

SALE SALE SALE SALE

THE SALE OF THE CENTURY
BARGAIN PRICES FOR EUROPEAN DESIGNER CLOTHES

* Mulberry
* Vivienne Westwood
* Jasper Conran
* Plantation
* Dolce & Gabanna
* Rosy Jackson
* Paul Smith

These designer labels and range of European fashions are being made available as the result of an exclusive deal with a leading Paris fashion house. Come and buy the best of European design at ridiculous prices. But hurry, they are available from early next month and demand is expected to be high. Nicky's Warehouse is the sole outlet for these European fashions at these prices. Don't risk disappointment by missing this exclusive offer or by arriving after stocks have been snapped up.

NICKY'S WAREHOUSE
7869 SOME STREET
SOMETOWN, SOMESTATE 77934

SALE SALE SALE SALE

Bulleted list

Times New Roman, 14 point, justified in two columns

Times New Roman, small caps, 16 point, bold, centered

WordArt: Cascade Up, Footlight MT Light, 64 point, Shading, Shadow

WordArt: Cascade Down, Footlight MT Light, 64 point, Shading, Shadow

Party Invitation

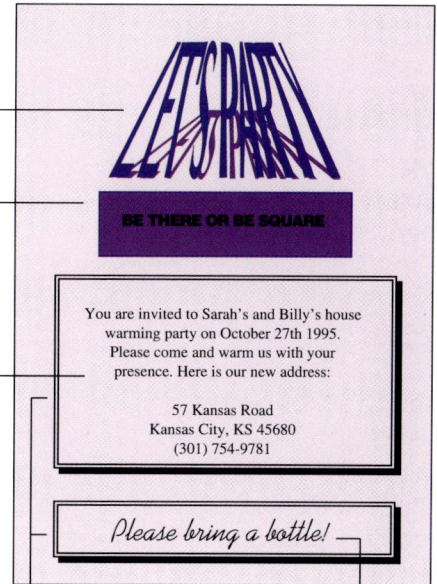

WordArt: Fade Up, Britannic bold, 40 point, centered, Shading, Shadow

LET'S PARTY

BE THERE OR BE SQUARE

You are invited to Sarah's and Billy's house warming party on October 27th 1995. Please come and warm us with your presence. Here is our new address:

57 Kansas Road
Kansas City, KS 45680
(301) 754-9781

Please bring a bottle!

Drawing Toolbar: Rectangle and text created using the Text Box tool

Times New Roman, 24 point, centered

Double-line border with shadow

Script, 38 point, centered

Order Form

Twinkle Toys
P.O. BOX 155 - SUMMERTOWN, WEST VIRGINIA
Tel: (285) 525-4445
Fax: (285) 525-4555

ORDER FORM

BILL TO:
Name
Address
City
State/Zip

PAYMENT BY:
Check (US funds only)
Visa
Card no.
MasterCard
Expiry
American Express
Signature

SEND TO:
Name
Address
City
State/Zip

PRODUCT DETAILS

Quantity	Size/Color	Description	Unit Price	Total

SUB TOTAL
CA residents tax
IN residents sales tax
Canadian residents add GST tax
Shipping
TOTAL

Please allow three weeks for delivery
Thank you

Times New Roman, 36 point, bold, italic, centered

Arial, uppercase, 14 point, bold, centered

Arial, uppercase, 10 point, tabbed

8x5 table; column widths altered

Arial, 22 point, bold, italic, centered

Arial, uppercase, 12 point, centered

Arial, uppercase, 14 point, tabbed

Arial, 12 point, tabbed as above; lines drawn using Shift and hyphen keys together

Arial, 12 point, tabbed; lines drawn as above

4

CHAPTER FOUR

Perfect Printing

*In this chapter, you'll learn how to print
your documents quickly and efficiently by making
the best use of Word's print options and features. You'll
see how Print Preview can give you an accurate picture
of what a document will look like before you print it and
how the Print dialog box can help you print exactly
what you want. You'll also learn how to use a
special timesaving feature called Mail Merge
to produce personalized form letters
and print mailing labels.*

PRINTING DOCUMENTS AND ENVELOPES
MAIL MERGE • PRINTING MAILING LABELS

Printing Documents and Envelopes

WITH WORD, PRINTING IS SIMPLE — if you want to print using Word's standard settings, you simply click on the Print button on the Standard toolbar. If you want to specify certain options, you choose *Print* from the *File* menu to access the *Print* dialog box. This section shows you how to print all or part of a document and how to use options in the *Print* dialog box to control how your document is printed.

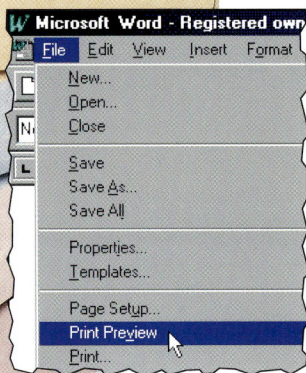

Print Preview Button

How to Use Print Preview

The Print Preview feature reveals all elements of your document, some of which you can't see in Normal or Page Layout View, so you can make sure your document looks just right before you print. You can also edit in this view if you want to edit something at the last minute.

In the Print Preview window, the document is reduced in size, so that you can see one or more pages on the screen. Let's display a document in Print Preview. Open **Poll** and choose *Print Preview* from the *File* menu or click on the Print Preview button on the Standard toolbar. An example document is shown in Print Preview on the opposite page, along with a description of the functions of the various buttons on the Print Preview toolbar.

Making Moves!

In the Print Preview window, you can easily change the margins of a document. If you can't see the rulers, click on the View Rulers button on the Print Preview toolbar. Move the pointer to the relevant margin boundary on the vertical or horizontal Ruler, where the pointer changes to a double-headed arrow (see opposite page), and then drag it to the new position.

Moving Through Your Document

There are a number of ways to display different pages of your Word document in the Print Preview window:

■ Press PgDn to see the next page of the document. Continue to press PgDn to move forward through your document one page at a time.

■ To move to the next page, click on the bottom single arrow in the vertical scroll bar. To scroll several pages forward, drag the box in the vertical scroll bar downward.

■ Press PgUp to see the previous page. Continue to press PgUp to move backward through the document one page at a time.

■ Click on the top single arrow in the vertical scroll bar to move to the previous page. To scroll several pages backward, drag the vertical scroll bar box upward.

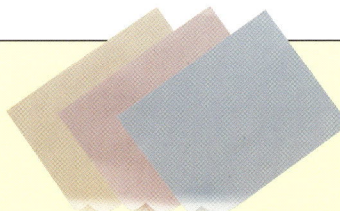

Preview Unavailable?

If the *Print Preview* command is unavailable, it may be because no printer has been installed, no default printer has been selected in the Printer folder, or the default printer isn't connected to a port. See page 118 for information on how to install a printer.

The Print Preview Window

Print
If you're satisfied with the way your document looks in the Print Preview window, click on the Print button to print your document.

Magnifier
Click on this button to edit your document. The pointer changes to a magnifying glass when moved onto the document. Click on the area you want to edit, and when the document is magnified, click on the Magnifier button to restore the normal I-beam pointer. Once you've finished with your changes, click on the Magnifier button again and then click on the document to return to the original view.

One Page
Click on this button to view only one page at a time.

Multiple Pages
Click here and drag the pointer over the grid to select the number of pages you want to view.

Zoom Control
Type a number in the text box or click on the down arrow to change the scale of your document's view.

View Rulers
Click to hide or show rulers. With the rulers displayed, you can adjust a document's margins (see "Making Moves!" opposite).

Shrink to Fit
If only a little text remains on the last page of a document, Word will try to fit it onto the previous page when you click on this button.

Full Screen
Click to maximize the Print Preview window. Click again to return to the original view.

Close
Click to close the Print Preview window and return to the previous view of your document.

Help
Click to get help on a specific command or screen item, or information on text formatting.

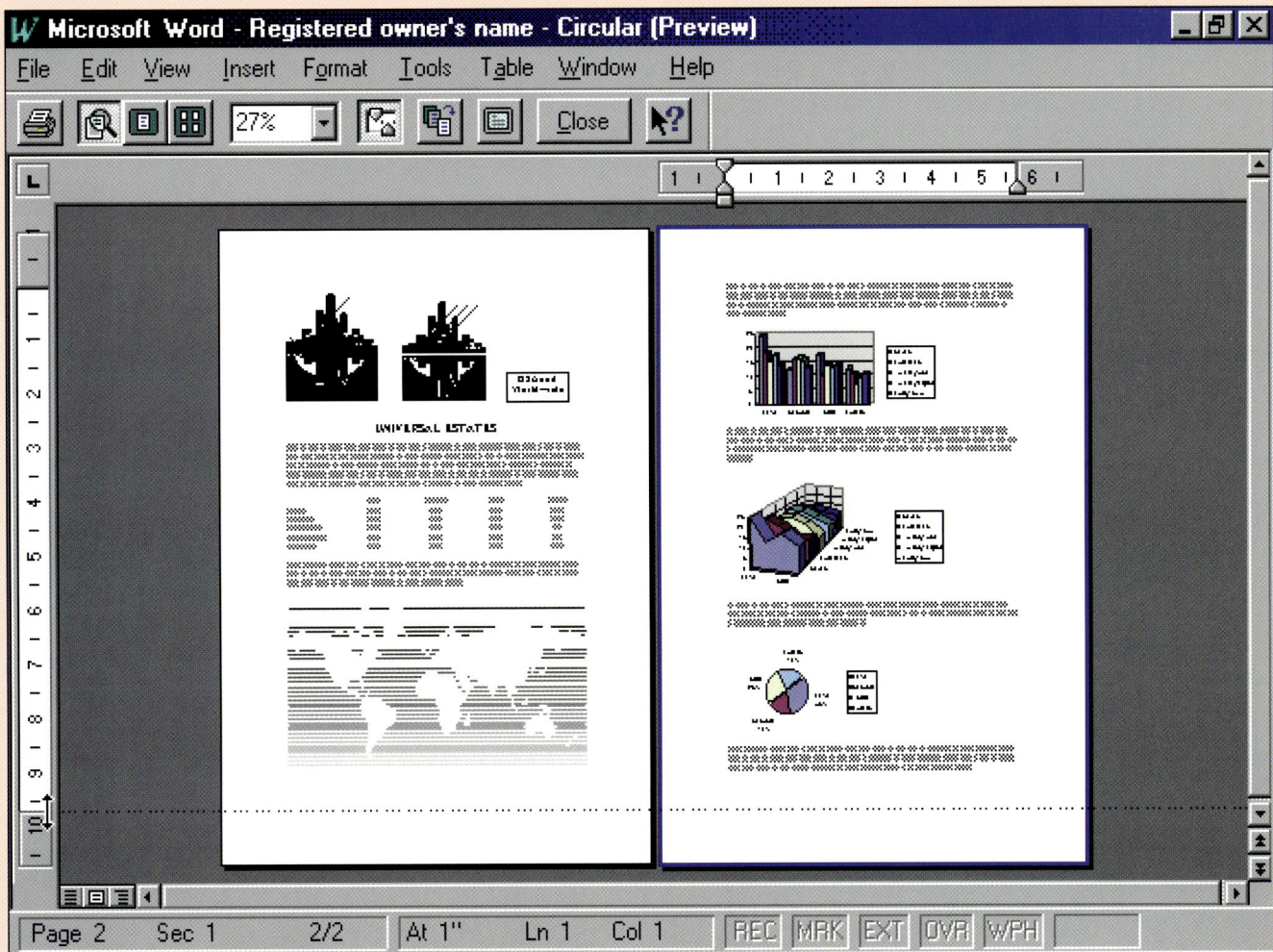

Microsoft Word - Registered owner's name - Circular (Preview)

File   Edit   View   Insert   Format   Tools   Table   Window   Help

27%   Close

UNIVERSAL ESTATES

Page 2   Sec 1   2/2   At 1"   Ln 1   Col 1   REC MRK EXT OVR WPH

The Print Dialog Box

When you're ready to print the document you're currently working on, you can click on the Print button on the Standard toolbar to print one copy of the whole document or, if you want to specify certain print options, you can choose *Print* from the *File* menu. Word displays the *Print* dialog box (see below). Remember to save your document before you print to make sure that no work is lost if a printer problem occurs.

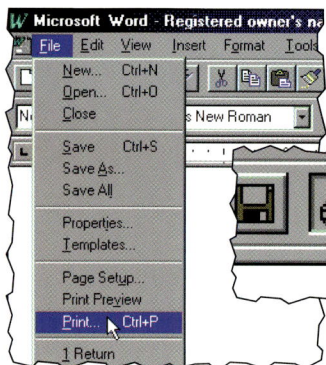

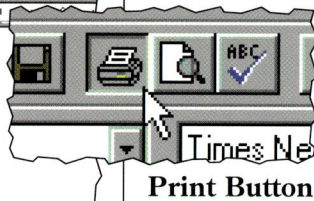

Print Button

Your Printing Options

Using the *Print* dialog box, you can specify a number of different options that allow you to control the way your document is printed. Once you have chosen your options, you simply click on *OK* to print. Here are a few examples of the print options that are available:

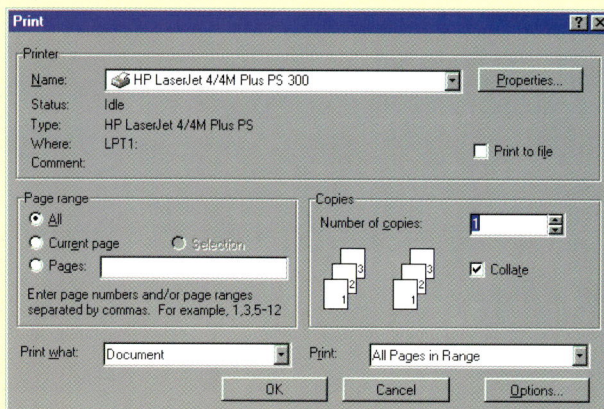

■ To print items related to your document, such as *Styles* (see page 108), choose the relevant item from the *Print What* drop-down list.

■ For more than one copy, select the desired number in the *Copies* box.

■ To print the page containing the insertion point, click on the *Current Page* option button under *Page Range*. (See also *Be Selective!* at right.)

■ To print a consecutive range of pages, click on the *Pages* option button under *Page Range*, and then type the page numbers, separated by a hyphen, in the *Pages*

box. To print discontinuous pages, type the page numbers separated by commas.

■ To print a section of a document, type in the letter **s** followed by the section number in the *Pages* box. For example, **s4** prints section four of a document. For information on sections, see page 69.

■ To print only odd or even pages, choose *Odd Pages* or *Even Pages* from the *Print* drop-down list.

■ If you print more than one copy, make sure the *Collate* box is checked so that Word prints a complete copy of a document before printing the next copy.

Be Selective!
To print just a selected part of your document, select the text or graphics you want to print, open the *Print* dialog box, click on *Selection* under *Page Range* (if text isn't selected, the *Selection* option is dimmed), and then click on *OK* to print the selection. This technique is useful for printing a selection that spans a soft page break (a break created automatically by the program) because you don't have to print both pages.

Don't Be a Loser!
Get into the habit of saving your document before you print it — if a printer error or other problem occurs while printing, Word may shut down. If you've saved your document, you won't lose any work.

The Options Dialog Box

For additional printing options, you can access the *Options* dialog box by clicking on the *Options* button in the *Print* dialog box. You can also display this dialog box by choosing *Options* from the *Tools* menu and then clicking on the *Print* tab. Once you set a print option in the *Options* dialog box, it remains in effect for all your documents, until you change it again. Some of the print options you may find most useful are explained here:

Summary Info

Summary Info *stores information about a document such as the author's name, subject, and keywords. If you check this box, Word will print any information you've stored in the* Summary Info *dialog box on a separate page.*

A Landscape View?
Most pages are printed in portrait (vertical) orientation. If your document is wider than it is long, you can print it in landscape (horizontal) orientation. Choose *Page Setup* from the *File* menu, and then click on the *Paper Size* tab. Under *Orientation*, choose *Landscape*, and then click on *OK*.

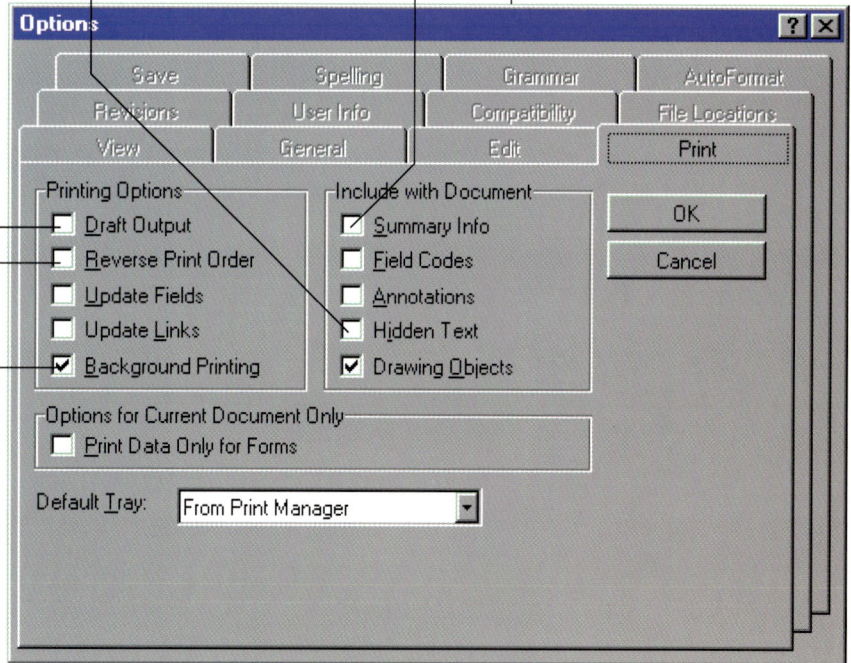

Hidden Text

Hidden text *is an option you can choose in the* Font *dialog box. It allows you to add text that appears on the screen (as underlined text), but doesn't get printed. Only by checking this box can you print any hidden text in a document.*

Draft Output

Prints the document with minimal formatting. By reducing a document's complexity — for example, by not printing graphics — the printing process can be speeded up.

Reverse Print Order

Prints the pages from last to first. This is useful for printers that stack pages face up.

Background Printing

Allows you to continue working while you are printing a document. However, the printing process speeds up if this box is not checked.

Options

Save	Spelling	Grammar	AutoFormat
Revisions	User Info	Compatibility	File Locations
View	General	Edit	Print

Printing Options
- ☐ Draft Output
- ☐ Reverse Print Order
- ☐ Update Fields
- ☐ Update Links
- ☑ Background Printing

Include with Document
- ☑ Summary Info
- ☐ Field Codes
- ☐ Annotations
- ☐ Hidden Text
- ☑ Drawing Objects

Options for Current Document Only
- ☐ Print Data Only for Forms

Default Tray: From Print Manager

OK   Cancel

The Nonprinting Area

Most printers are unable to print all the way to the outside edges of the paper. Any text or graphic that extends into the nonprinting area will not be printed. However, the exact dimensions of the nonprinting area depend on the printer you're using. In general, the size of the nonprinting area increases as the paper size increases. If you find you are missing parts of your document, you may have to reset the document's margins.

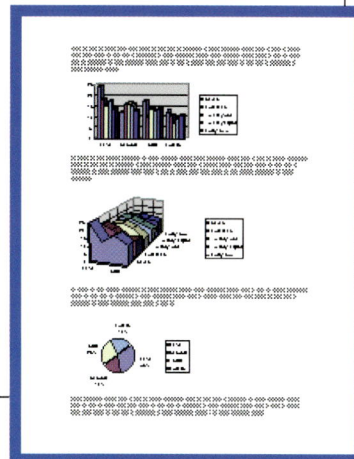

The Non-Printing Area

How to Set Up a Printer

It is possible to connect more than one printer or different types of printers to your PC. For example, you may have two printers in your office and want to swap printers, using the one that is least busy or that provides better printing quality. To change the printer you're printing from, you simply click on the down arrow to the right of the current printer's name in the *Print* dialog box and select another printer from the drop-down list that appears. If no other printers are listed, there are no other printers installed. For more information on installing a printer, see page 118.

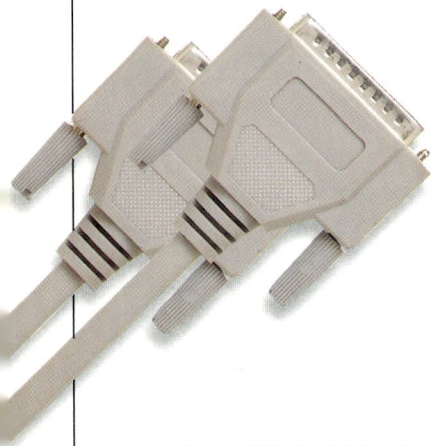

SETUP OPTIONS

Each type of printer comes with different printing capabilities, so you should check your printer manual for specific information. Most printers can accommodate different paper sizes, orientations, and paper sources, and you can change the settings for these in a special dialog box that varies depending on the printer that is selected. To change printer settings, click on the *Properties* button in the *Print* dialog box. The options for one printer model are described below. Don't change a printer's settings unless you know exactly what you want to achieve with the new setting.

Feeling Disoriented?
You should use the *Page Setup* command from the *File* menu to set the paper size, orientation, and paper source for your documents. In fact, these settings take precedence. For example, if you have specified landscape orientation for part of a document in the *Page Setup* dialog box, that part will print in landscape, even though the printer options dialog box remains set to portrait.

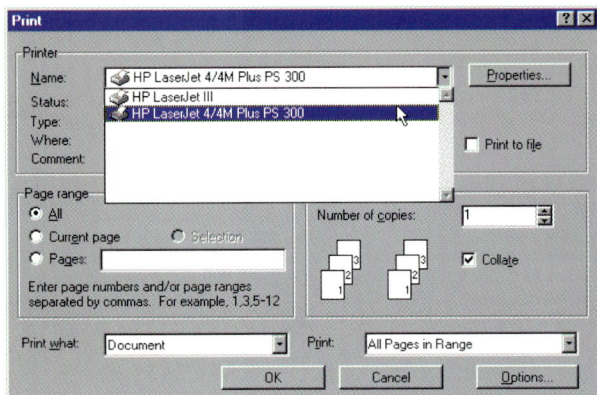

Paper Size
The paper sizes provided by your printer appear when you scroll across this display.

Paper Orientation
Portrait: *Document prints with short edge at the top.*
Landscape: *Document prints sideways with long edge at the top.*

Paper Source
Depending on your printer, you may be able to select different trays and manual feed from this drop-down list.

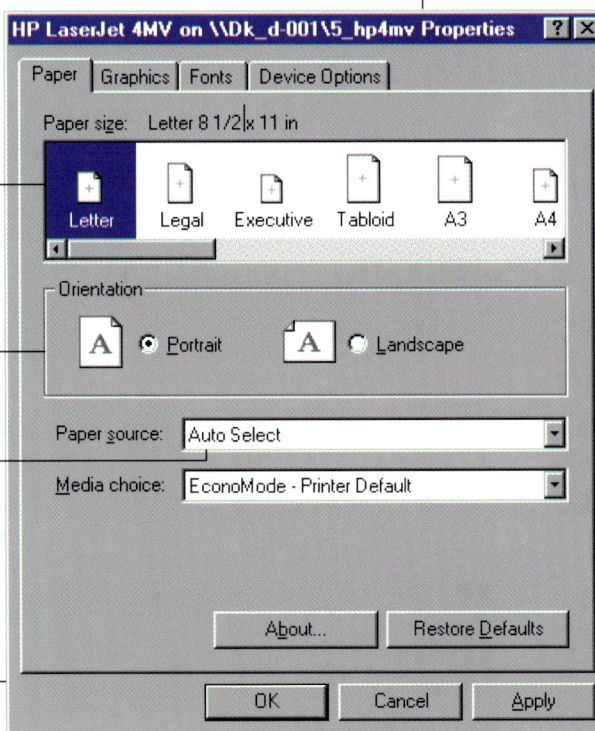

Printer Fonts

The fonts available for the documents you print in Word depend on your printer's make and model. Through Windows 95, however, you also have access to a number of other fonts called "TrueType." TrueType fonts can be printed on any type of printer. To check which fonts are installed on your PC, click on the Start button, select *Control Panel* from the *Settings* menu, then double-click on the *Fonts* icon. When the *Fonts* window appears, scroll through the list to see the fonts available to you. See page 119 for more information on the different types of fonts that you can use in your Word documents.

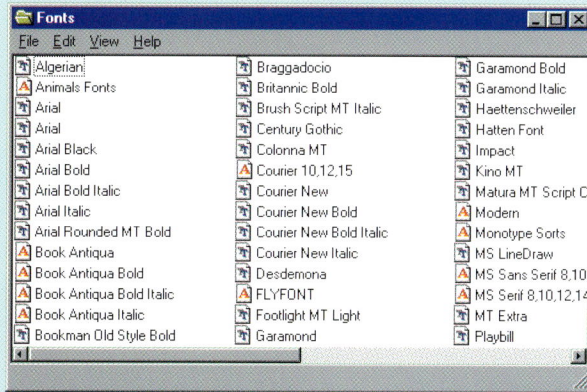

Fonts
File Edit View Help

Algerian	Braggadocio	Garamond Bold
Animals Fonts	Britannic Bold	Garamond Italic
Arial	Brush Script MT Italic	Haettenschweiler
Arial	Century Gothic	Hatten Font
Arial Black	Colonna MT	Impact
Arial Bold	Courier 10,12,15	Kino MT
Arial Bold Italic	Courier New	Matura MT Script C
Arial Italic	Courier New Bold	Modern
Arial Rounded MT Bold	Courier New Bold Italic	Monotype Sorts
Book Antiqua	Courier New Italic	MS LineDraw
Book Antiqua Bold	Desdemona	MS Sans Serif 8,10
Book Antiqua Bold Italic	FLYFONT	MS Serif 8,10,12,14
Book Antiqua Italic	Footlight MT Light	MT Extra
Bookman Old Style Bold	Garamond	Playbill

Font Samples
When you select a font by double-clicking on it in the Fonts window, a sample of the font appears in another window.

Meltdown!
If you're printing envelopes with a laser printer, make sure the envelopes are specifically designed for use with one. Be particularly careful with self-sealing envelopes. If envelopes are not designed for use with a laser printer, which uses very high temperatures inside as part of the printing process, the gum could melt and cause internal damage to your printer.

HOW TO PRINT AN ENVELOPE
Word can print an envelope using an address stored in a document or one that you type in. Follow these steps to practice printing an envelope:

owner's name - Poll

Tools Table Window Help

Spelling...   F7
Grammar...
Thesaurus...   Shift+F7
Hyphenation...
Language...
Word Count...

AutoCorrect...

Mail Merge...

Envelopes and Labels...

Protect Document...

2 Choose *Envelopes and Labels* from the *Tools* menu to open the *Envelopes* and *Labels* dialog box.

1 Open the **Poll** document and select the address.

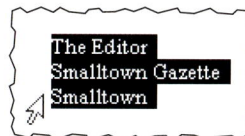

The Editor
Smalltown Gazette
Smalltown

3 On the *Envelopes* flipcard, the selected address appears in the *Delivery Address* text box. Under *Return Address,* either accept the proposed address, type in a new one, or check the *Omit* box. Now click on *Options* to open the *Envelope Options* dialog box.

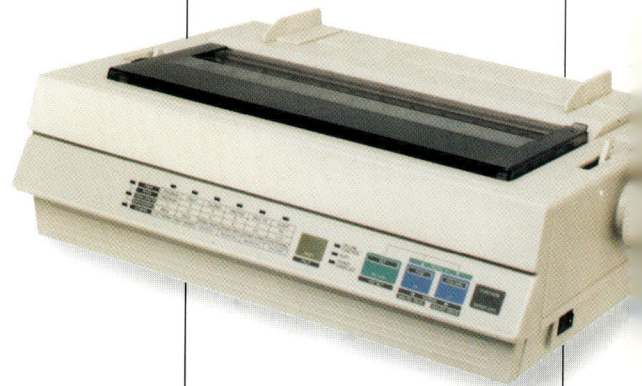

Envelopes and Labels

Envelopes | Labels

Delivery Address:
The Editor
Smalltown Gazette
Smalltown

Print
Add to Document
Cancel
Options

Return Address: Omit
Melvin T. Pollster
Precision Polls Inc.
Bigtown

Preview   Feed

When prompted by the printer, insert an envelope in your printer's manual feeder.

4 Make sure that the *Envelope Size* box is set to *Size 10 ($4\frac{1}{8}$ x $9\frac{1}{2}$in)*. Click on *OK* to close the *Envelope Options* dialog box.

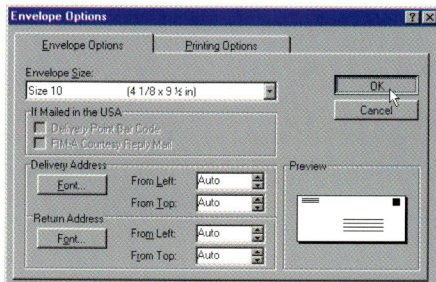

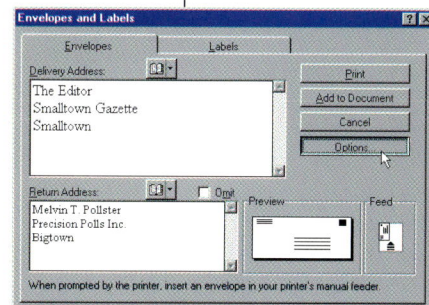

Envelope Options

Envelope Options | Printing Options

Envelope Size:
Size 10   (4 1/8 x 9 ½ in)

OK
Cancel

If Mailed in the USA
Delivery Point Bar Code
FIM-A Courtesy Reply Mail

Delivery Address
Font...   From Left: Auto
           From Top: Auto

Return Address
Font...   From Left: Auto
           From Top: Auto

Preview

5 Insert a size 10 (standard business size) envelope into your printer's envelope feeder or manual feed slot, placing the envelope according to the *Feed* diagram in the *Envelopes and Labels* dialog box. Then click on the *Print* button in the *Envelopes and Labels* dialog box.

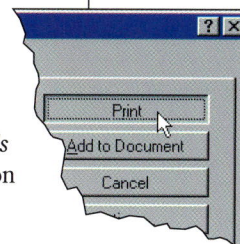

Print...
Add to Document
Cancel

Mail Merge

WORD's Mail Merge feature allows you to combine a standard form document with a list of data in another document to produce a set of individualized documents. For example, if you want to send the same basic letter to a number of different people but you want each letter to be customized for each individual, you can use Mail Merge.

A Clever Combination

To carry out a mail merge, you have to create two separate documents. The main document contains the basic text that you want to include in each letter. At specific points in this document, you place reference points called *merge field names*; these represent the variable information that Word will insert into each copy of the document during the mail merge. You then create a data source containing the specific information to be inserted at the reference points in each personalized letter. Creating the two documents is easy — a dialog box called the *Mail Merge Helper* guides you through the whole process. When you have created the documents, you then instruct Word to combine them.

Create Main Document

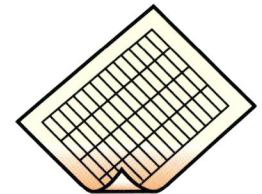

Create Data Source

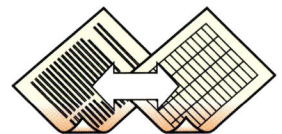

Merge Information in Both Documents

Print Individualized Documents

The Grunge Band Fan Club <Enter>
18 Main Street <Enter>
Seattle, WA 98473 <Enter>
<Enter> <Enter>

A B <Enter>
C <Enter>
D <Enter>
E <Enter> <Enter> <Enter>

Dear A, <Enter> <Enter>

Thank you for your recent communication by F. Please find enclosed the G that you ordered.
<Enter> <Enter>

We hope you'll be in touch with us again soon. <Enter> <Enter>

Sincerely, <Enter> <Enter> <Enter>

Tom Rogers <Enter>
Fan Club Secretary

THE MAIN DOCUMENT

Your main document will typically be a letter, invoice, or circular, although you can use any type of document. You format the document as you would any other; the only difference is that you must insert merge field names where you want the data items to be inserted. In this example, the main document is a letter from a fan club in the United States that mails orders to people all over the world. The example uses seven items of data, represented by the merge field names FirstName, LastName, Address1, Address2, Address3, Communication, and Order. In your letter you'll type the letters **A, B, C, D, E, F,** and **G** to represent each of these merge field names. To create your letter, open a new document and save it to the **My Documents** folder with the name **Fanclub**. Then enter the text to the left, pressing Enter only where you see <Enter> in the text. Then follow the steps on the next page.

Creating the Main Document

1 Choose *Mail Merge* from the *Tools* menu.

2 The *Mail Merge Helper* dialog box appears. Click on the *Create* button under *Main Document* and choose *Form Letters* in the drop-down list that appears. Choose *Active Window* in the message that follows.

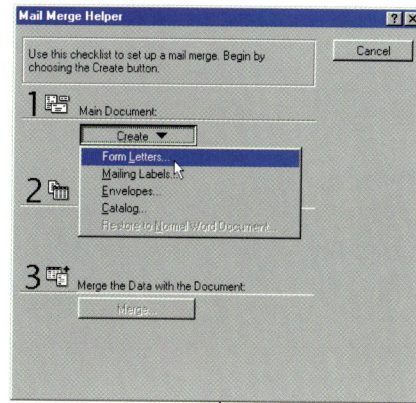

THE DATA SOURCE
Now you need to create your data source — the names, addresses, and other information that differs in each personalized letter.

1 In the *Mail Merge Helper* dialog box, click on the *Get Data* button under *Data Source* and choose *Create Data Source* in the drop-down list.

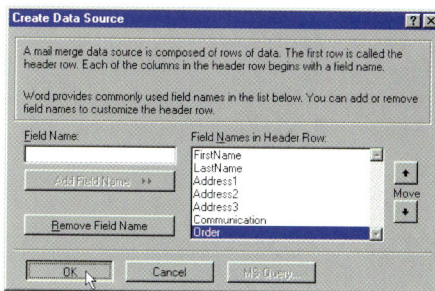

2 The *Create Data Source* dialog box appears, showing a list of commonly used merge field names. You can add a field name to the list by typing the name in the *Field Name* box and then clicking on the *Add Field Name* button. To remove a merge field name, highlight it and then click on the *Remove Field Name* button. Use these buttons to create the list shown in the dialog box at left. Then click on *OK*. The *Save As* dialog box appears. Save your data source to the **My Documents** folder with the name **Orders**.

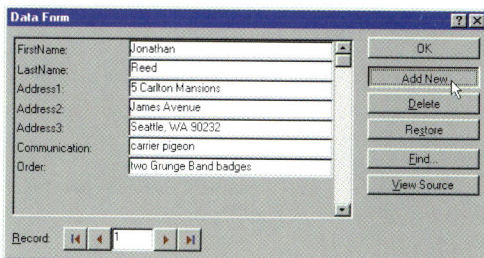

3 Click on *Edit Data Source* in the message that follows. The *Data Form* dialog box then appears, in which you enter the information for each addressee. Enter the information shown in the dialog box above, and then click on *Add New* to display a blank form for the next data record. Continue adding information so that you have the three entries shown at right. Then click on *OK* to return to the main document.

> ⚠️ **Spaced Out!**
> The field names you choose for the header list in your data source can contain up to 40 characters. Each name must start with a letter, and the following characters must be letters, numbers, or underscore characters. You must not use spaces in a merge field name.

Separate Entries
Because you cannot use paragraph marks in the Data Form *dialog box, you have to enter each line of the address as a separate entry. This ensures that each address is formatted correctly in the final letter.*

First Name	Last Name	Address	Communication	Order
Jonathan	Reed	5 Carlton Mansions James Avenue Seattle, WA 90232	carrier pigeon	two Grunge Band badges
Marie	Blanc	33 Rue de Gaulle Paris 7500 France	telephone	signed photograph of Eddie Grunge
Bruce	Davis	63 Golden Square Sydney Australia	letter	Greatest Hits Collection cassette

The Mail Merge Toolbar

When you return to the main document after completing your data source, you'll see a new toolbar just above the Ruler called the Mail Merge toolbar (below). You use the buttons on this toolbar to control and perform your mail merge. To discover a button's function, move the mouse pointer over the button — an explanation of its action will then appear in the status bar.

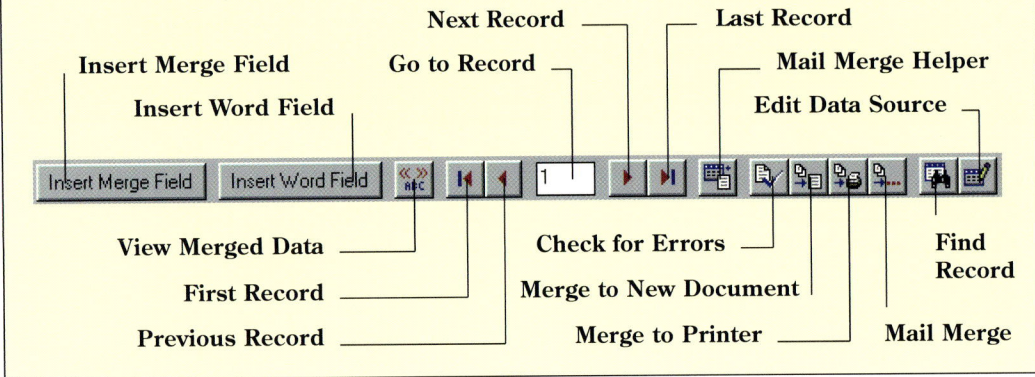

Insert Merge Field
Insert Word Field
Next Record
Go to Record
Last Record
Mail Merge Helper
Edit Data Source

| Insert Merge Field | Insert Word Field | «» ABC | |◀ | ◀ | 1 | ▶ | ▶| | | | | | | | | |

View Merged Data
First Record
Previous Record
Check for Errors
Merge to New Document
Merge to Printer
Find Record
Mail Merge

Changing Your Data?
You can add or change information in your data source at any time during a mail merge. Click on the Edit Data Source button on the Mail Merge toolbar. Then make the changes you want in the *Data Form* dialog box. When you have completed your changes, click on *OK* to return to your main document.

INSERTING MERGE FIELDS

You're now ready to complete your main document. Use the Mail Merge toolbar to insert the merge field names from your data source.

1 Highlight the first occurrence of *A* in your **Fanclub** document. Then click on the Insert Merge Field button on the Mail Merge toolbar, and choose the merge field name that you want to insert from the list that drops down. In this case, choose *FirstName*.

2 In **Fanclub**, the merge field name appears inside double angle brackets.

The·Grunge·Band·Fan·Club¶
18·Main·Street¶
Seattle,·WA·98473¶
¶
¶
«FirstName»·B¶

3 Go through the rest of the document using the procedure described in steps 1 and 2 to insert the remaining merge field names in place of the letters representing them. Make sure that you type any spaces or punctuation that you want between the merge field names. When you have finished, your main document will look like the example shown at right.

«FirstName»·«LastName»¶
«Address1»¶
«Address2»¶
«Address3»¶
¶
¶
Dear·«FirstName»,¶
¶
Thank·you·for·your·recent·communication·by·«Communication».·Please·find·enclosed·the·«Order»·that·you·ordered.¶
¶

4 Click on the Save button on the Standard toolbar. **Fanclub** is now saved as a Mail Merge document, attached to the data source called **Orders**.

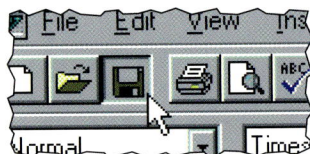

TIME TO MERGE AND PRINT

Now you're ready to merge the information contained in your two documents, and print the resulting personalized letters. Word prints a different version of the letter for each record in the data source. So you'll get three letters, each with the merge field names replaced by the specific information contained in the data source. Follow the steps below to merge the data source and print the letters.

1 Click on the Merge to Printer button on the Mail Merge toolbar. Then click on *OK* in the *Print* dialog box.

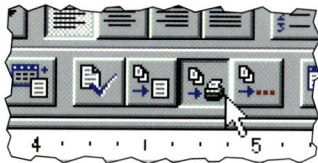

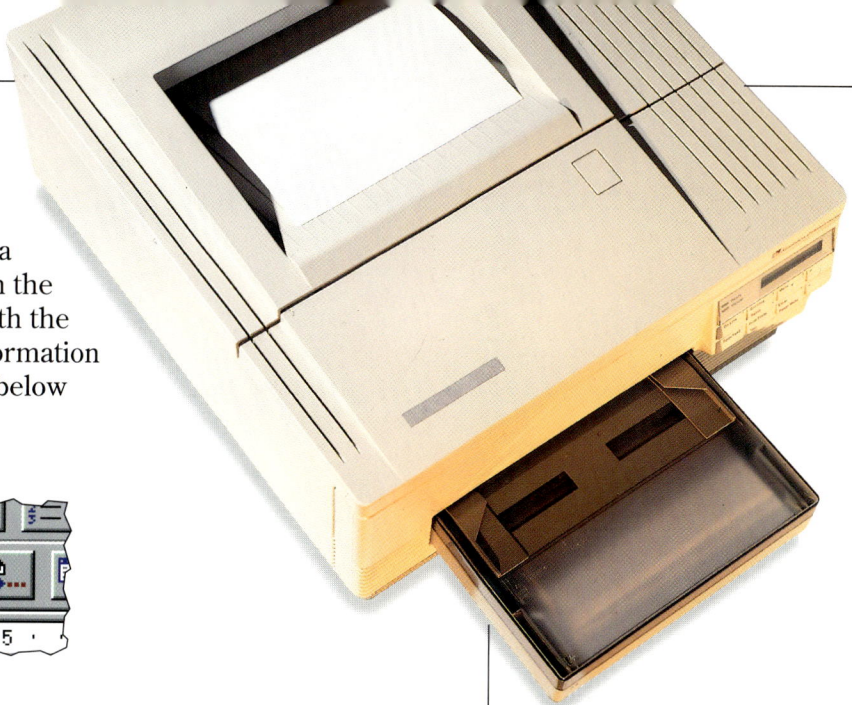

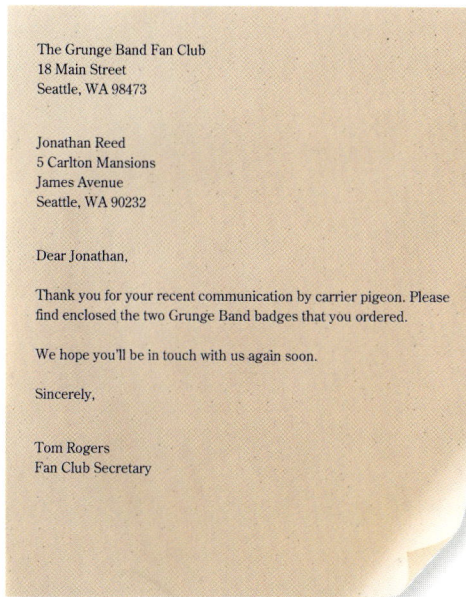

The Grunge Band Fan Club
18 Main Street
Seattle, WA 98473

Jonathan Reed
5 Carlton Mansions
James Avenue
Seattle, WA 90232

Dear Jonathan,

Thank you for your recent communication by carrier pigeon. Please find enclosed the two Grunge Band badges that you ordered.

We hope you'll be in touch with us again soon.

Sincerely,

Tom Rogers
Fan Club Secretary

2 Word prints one copy of your Mail Merge document for each record in your data source. The example shown here shows the information contained in the first personalized letter. At the positions of the seven merge field names, you can see the data from the first record in the data source. When you have finished printing, simply close your merged **Fanclub** document. Also save and close the data source **Orders**.

Want More Choice?
Before you merge your document, you can click on the Mail Merge button on the Mail Merge toolbar to open the *Merge* dialog box. This provides you with more options to control the way you merge your document. For example, you can choose to merge only certain data records.

Personal Preview

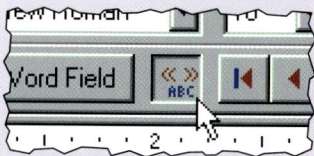

View Merged Data Button

If you want, you can see your personalized letters on screen before you print them. This allows you to check and further change each version of the letter. There are two ways of previewing your letters. If you click on the View Merged Data button on the Mail Merge toolbar, Word displays the information from the first data record in place of the merge field names in the main document text. To view the information from the other data records, you click on one of the arrow buttons next to the Go to Record box on the Mail Merge toolbar, or type the number of the data record you want to see in the Go to Record box.

If you click on the Merge to New Document button on the Mail Merge toolbar, Word merges the information in the main document and the data source and displays the merged documents as a single, new document, temporarily named *Form Letters1*. To view the different personalized letters, you scroll through the document using the vertical scroll bar.

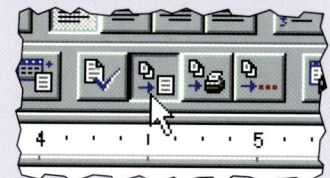

Merge to New Document Button

Printing Mailing Labels

WITH WORD, you can use Mail Merge to print names and addresses on many types of commonly used mailing labels. Word creates the main document for you; you simply attach the necessary data source. You can use information from an existing data source, or you can create a new data source (see page 97).

A Guided Tour

To print mailing labels, you must create a main document formatted for mailing labels. If you choose the *Mailing Labels* option in the *Mail Merge Helper* dialog box, Word will create the main document for you and will guide you through the process of producing your mailing labels. Using this method, you can set up a document for most types of Avery brand labels.

Before you can set up your mailing labels, you have to know what type of printer you're using. There are two kinds of mailing labels for the two main types of printers — continuous-feed labels for dot-matrix printers and label sheets for laser printers. Make sure you feed your printer with the correct type of label.

SETTING UP
Let's produce some mailing labels using information from the **Orders** file you created in the previous section. Load your printer with the correct labels, open a new document, and then choose *Mail Merge* from the *Tools* menu so that the *Mail Merge Helper* dialog box appears. Then follow the steps below:

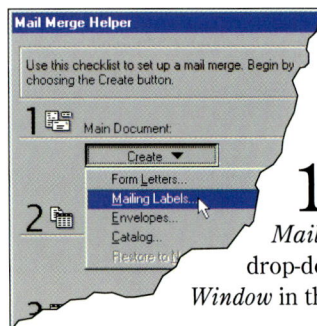

1 Click on the *Create* button and choose *Mailing Labels* from the drop-down list. Choose *Active Window* in the message that follows.

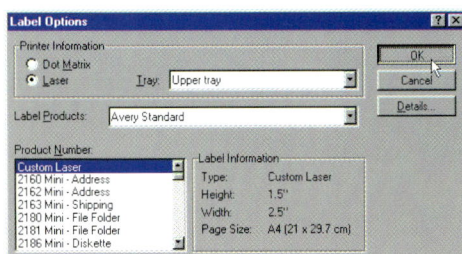

2 Click on the *Get Data* button, and then choose *Open Data Source* from the drop-down list. In the *Open Data Source* dialog box, choose **Orders** from the main window, and then click on *Open*. Click on the *Set Up Main Document* button in the message that follows.

3 The *Label Options* dialog box appears. Under *Printer Information*, select the type of printer you're using and the feed source. Then choose the type of label you want. For now, just click on *OK* to use *Custom Laser*.

Size Problem?
If you want to use a brand of labels other than Avery, select an Avery Standard label of the same size in the *Label Options* dialog box and then click on the *Details* button to open the relevant *Information* dialog box. If the labels you are using do not exactly match the dimensions of the Avery label, simply enter the exact dimensions in the relevant text boxes. Finally, click on *OK* to create a main document based on this new label size.

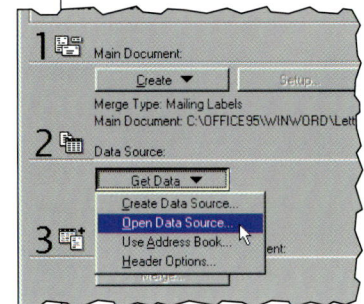

DESIGNER LABELS

Word now displays the *Create Labels* dialog box. In this dialog box, you insert the merge field names from your data source in a sample label. Word then automatically duplicates the set of merge field names from the sample label onto each label. Follow these steps to design your labels:

Creating Your Label Layout

1 In the *Create Labels* dialog box, the insertion point should be positioned inside the *Sample Label* box. Click on the *Insert Merge Field* button and choose *FirstName* from the drop-down list.

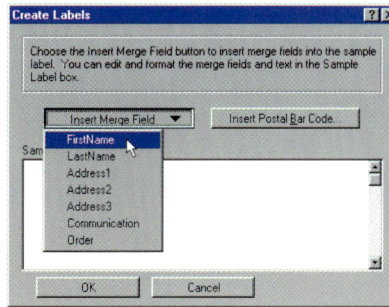

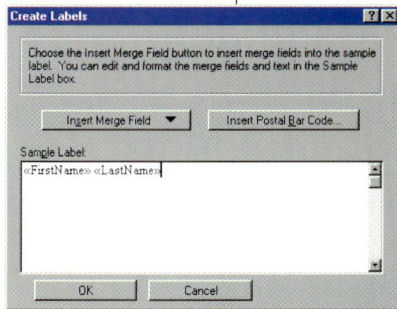

2 In the *Sample Label* box, you'll see the field you have just added. Press the Spacebar to insert a space after the first name and then choose *LastName* from the *Insert Merge Field* list to insert this merge field name into the *Sample Label* box.

3 To start a new line, press the Enter key, and then add the three lines of the address in the same way. When you have inserted these merge fields, click on *OK* to close the *Create Labels* dialog box.

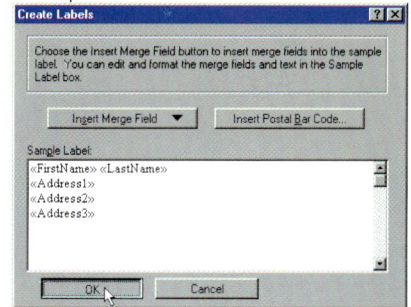

4 The *Mail Merge Helper* dialog box appears. Under *Merge the Data with the Document*, click on the *Merge* button.

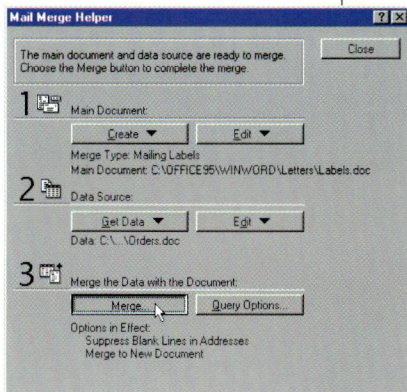

5 The *Merge* dialog box appears. Under *Merge To*, click on the down arrow next to the text box and select *Printer*. Then click on the *Merge* button to merge the information from your data source and print the finished mailing labels. Click on *OK* in the *Print* dialog box.

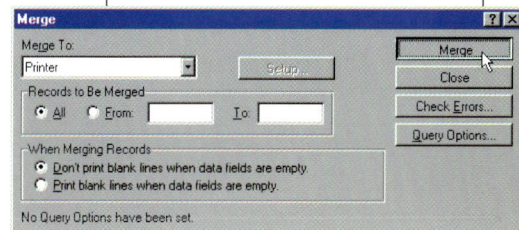

⚠ A Sticky Ending!
Your labels must be specifically designed for use with the printer you're using. If they are not, the labels may peel off the backing sheet and get stuck inside the printer, causing extensive internal damage. If you are using a laser printer, use labels sheets specifically designed for a laser printer, as indicated by the manufacturer. If you have a dot-matrix printer, use continuous feed labels and set your printer to use a straight-through paper path, if it has one, to reduce the chance of labels getting stuck.

5

Timesavers

With features such as templates,
styles, AutoCorrect, AutoText, and macros,
Word allows you to automate or speed up tasks that
you perform frequently. Through just a little extra effort
in understanding and setting up these features, you can
save yourself a great deal of time in the long run. In this
chapter, you'll see how to use these features to create
your own Word tools designed to suit your specific
needs. The chapter also introduces you to some
Word Wizards that show you step by
step how to create various
types of documents.

TEMPLATES AND WIZARDS • STYLES
AUTOCORRECT AND AUTOTEXT
MACROS

TEMPLATES AND WIZARDS *104*

Every document you create is based on a template. Find out all about templates — what they are, how to use them, and how to create your own custom templates. Then discover how using a wizard is often the fastest way to create an agenda, letter, resume, or other common type of document — Word does most of the thinking for you!

STYLES *108*

Learn to format with styles. Styles are easy to use, they save time, and they help ensure a consistent format within or between documents. Discover how to use them to format your documents quickly and efficiently.

AUTOCORRECT AND AUTOTEXT *110*

With Word's AutoCorrect and AutoText features, you can store text, graphics, and other items that you use frequently and quickly insert them into documents whenever they are needed. Find out how to use these time-saving features.

MACROS *112*

Macros are little programs you can create yourself for accomplishing everyday tasks in Word. Find out how easy it is to create a macro that will save you valuable time.

Templates and Wizards

A TEMPLATE PROVIDES A READY-MADE pattern for documents. A template can contain formatting, text, and graphics; it provides styles (see page 108) and stores AutoText entries and macros (see pages 110 and 112), which the documents based on that template will inherit. Using templates helps you avoid certain routine tasks that occur when you create documents from scratch. You can also use a wizard to facilitate the process of creating a new document. Wizards take you step by step through the creation of certain common types of documents.

Document Blueprints

Every Word document is based on a template. A template not only helps you create a particular type of document, it also ensures an overall consistency among documents created from the same template. So far in this book, you have used only the Blank Document template to create your documents. But a number of other templates come with more specific features. Word offers templates for letters, invoices, and fax cover sheets, among others. You can use any template as it is or you can modify it to suit your individual needs.

THE BLANK DOCUMENT TEMPLATE

You select a template on which to base your document when you create a new document. Word opens a copy of the template as a new document — the new document contains all the information from that template.

Unless you select another template in the *New* dialog box, Word will automatically base any new document on the Blank Document template — a general-purpose template for any document. When you start Word and begin typing in the empty document window, the Blank Document template is used, just as it is for the documents created by clicking on the New button on the Standard toolbar.

The Blank Document template provides more than just an empty document — it also stores the AutoText entries and macros and the toolbar, menu, and keyboard settings that you routinely use in Word. Items stored in the Blank Document template are global — which means they are available to all Word documents. If you were to delete the Blank Document template, you would lose all of these items. Items stored in any other template are available only to documents based on that template.

Choosing the Blank Document Template

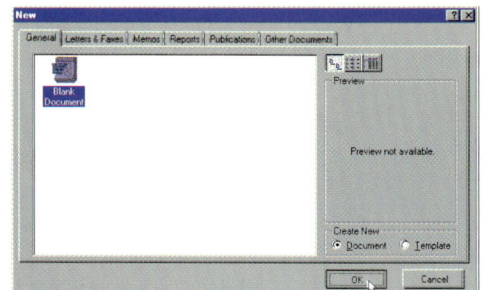

USING A TEMPLATE

If you want to create new documents such as memos, letters, and fax cover sheets, you can save time by basing the document on one of the templates that come with Word. To demonstrate how useful and easy to use templates are, let's create a fax cover sheet. When you choose the template from the list, Word opens a document copy of the template on the screen. All you have to do is insert your own text. Choose *New* from the *File* menu, and then follow the steps below.

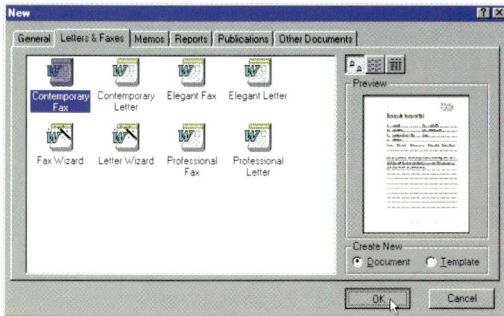

Creating a Fax Cover Sheet

1 In the *New* dialog box, make sure the *Document* option is selected at bottom right, and click on the *Letters & Faxes* tab. Click on *Contemporary Fax* and click on *OK*.

2 A document copy of the template appears on the screen in Page Layout View. Simply click in the areas of text that you want to change and insert your own text. Then save your fax cover sheet with a name before printing it.

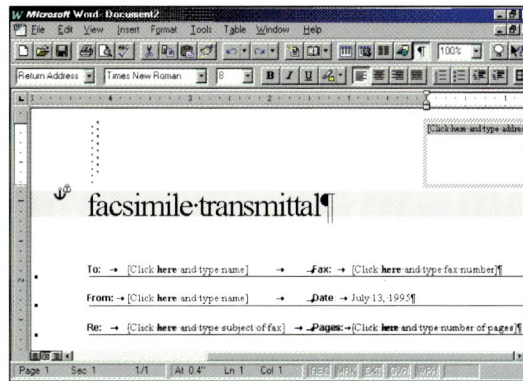

Modifying and Creating Templates

You can produce professional-looking documents just by using the templates that Word provides. But if you prefer, you can modify a template to suit your needs. You modify a template just as you would a document; you simply open the template, edit and format the text and graphics, and then save the changes you have made. You must bear in mind, however, that any changes you make will apply to any new documents based on that template. If you want to maintain the original features of the template, you should create a new template based on that template. On the following page, you'll learn how to create a new template. In the "Styles" section (see page 108), you'll practice modifying this template by adding new styles.

CREATING A NEW TEMPLATE

Word lets you create your own document templates. The easiest way to create a template is to open the Blank Document template, rename it, and then adapt it in any way you choose. The scope for customizing templates is limited only by your imagination! For now, let's adapt the Blank Document template to begin the process of creating a template for a bulletin board notice; you'll finish the template in the "Styles" section on page 108. Choose *New* from the *File* menu, and then follow these steps.

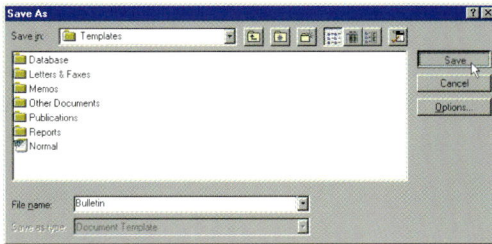

2 Word creates a template called *Template1*. Choose *Save As* from the *File* menu. In the *Save As* dialog box that opens, you'll see that *Document Template* appears in the *Save as type* box, and that the **Templates** folder appears in the *Save in* box. Replace **Dot1** by typing **Bulletin** in the *File name* box, and then click on *Save*.

Creating a Bulletin Template

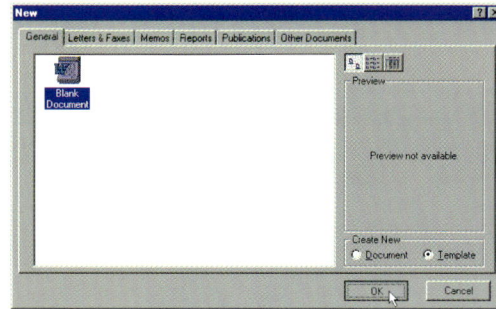

1 In the *New* dialog box, choose *Blank Document* in the *General* flipcard. Click on the *Template* option button and click on *OK*.

3 Choose *Page Setup* from the *File* menu. In the *Margins* flipcard of the *Page Setup* dialog box, change the margin settings as shown here and click on *OK*. Then save and close your **Bulletin** template.

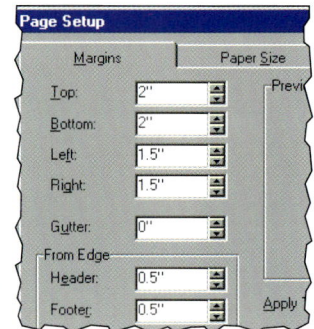

Wonderful Wizards

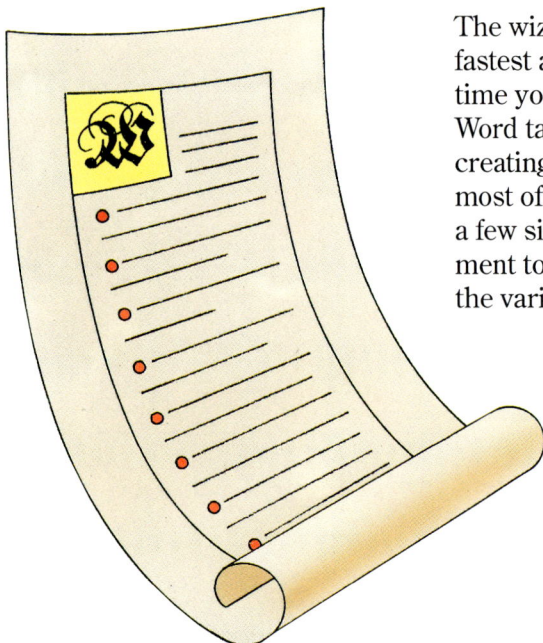

The wizards supplied with Word provide probably the fastest and easiest way to create new documents. Each time you choose a specific wizard to create a document, Word takes you step by step through the process of creating that type of document. In fact, the wizard does most of the work for you — all you have to do is answer a few simple questions about how you want the document to look (and even then Word provides you with the various choices) and then type in your text.

STEP BY STEP

Word provides ten wizards to help create the following commonly used documents: agenda, award, calendar, fax, legal plead, letter, memo, newsletter, resume, and table. Whichever wizard you choose, the process is the same — you simply follow the on-screen instructions, selecting options along the way. To see how easy it is to use a wizard, let's create a letter. Choose *New* from the *File* menu, and then follow these steps:

Using the Letter Wizard

1 In the *New* dialog box, click on the *Letters & Faxes* tab, click on *Letter Wizard,* and click on *OK.* This begins the Letter Wizard.

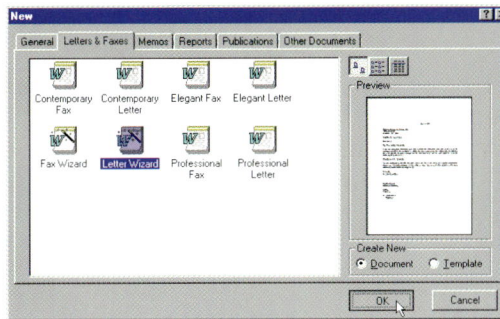

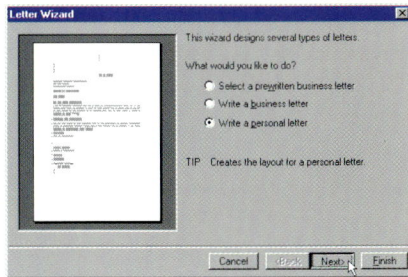

2 In the first box that appears, you can choose between two types of business letter and a personal letter. Click on the *Write a personal letter* option button, then click on *Next.*

3 In a short personal letter, page numbers won't be needed, so click on that option button to deselect them and click on *Next* to open the next box.

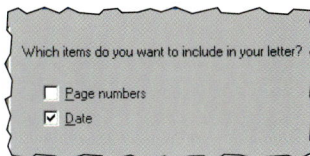

4 If you have letterhead stationery, then click that option button. Otherwise, simply click on *Next* to accept the plain paper option.

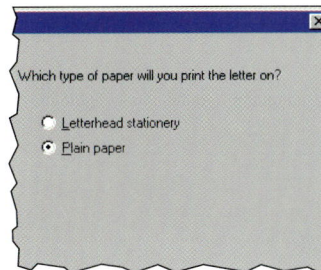

5 Select *Contemporary* as a choice of style and click on *Next.*

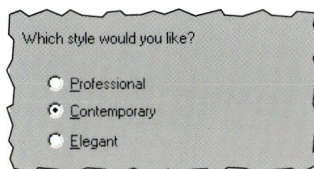

6 Word tells you that you have answered all the necessary questions. Choose whether you want Word to produce either a letter, a mailing label, or simply display the document, then click on *Finish.*

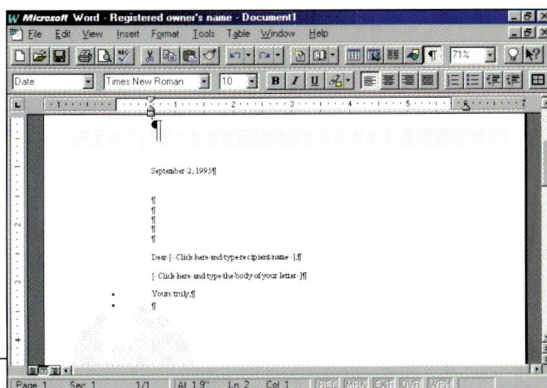

7 The letter appears in Page Layout View for you to enter your text. When you have finished the letter, save it and print it in the usual way.

Finished Business
Each time you use a wizard, Word saves the settings you have selected. The next time you use the wizard, you don't have to go through the whole process again if you want to use the options you previously set. Simply click on the *Finish* button in the first box that appears.

Styles

I N WORD, A STYLE is a specific set of character and paragraph formats identified by a name. Word has several built-in styles designed for specific uses, such as a variety of headings styles and the Normal style, which is the standard style you'll probably use most often. You can also create your own styles to suit your particular formatting requirements.

Choosing a Style

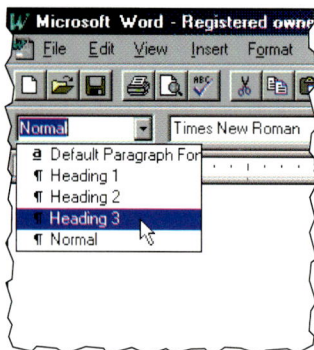

The Function of Styles

Styles help ensure a consistent format within a long document or among documents of a certain type. Styles also make global formatting changes simple because any changes to the style will automatically apply to all the paragraphs assigned to that style.

Styles are applied at paragraph level — to apply one of Word's built-in styles, for example, you select the paragraph(s) you want to style and choose a style from the Style drop-down list on the Formatting toolbar (see left). The selected text will be formatted accordingly.

?

Changed Your Mind?
It's easy to change the attributes of a specific style. Choose *Style* from the *Format* menu to open the *Style* dialog box. Under *Styles*, choose the name of the style you want to change, click on *Modify*, and then make your changes. Once you have modified the style, click on *OK* in the *Modify Style* box, and then close the *Style* dialog box. Word then automatically reformats any text assigned to this style.

HOW TO DEFINE A NEW STYLE

You can define styles for documents or templates. If you define a style for a document, the only way to make that style available in other documents is to add it to the document template (see step 7 on page 109). If you define a style for a template, however, it is automatically available in any new document based on that template. The easiest way to define a new style is to adapt an existing style. Let's create a new style for your **Bulletin** template. Choose *Open* from the *File* menu. In the *Open* dialog box, choose *Templates* from the MSOffice folder. Select *All files* in the *Files of type* box, select **Bulletin** and click on *Open*.

1 Choose *Style* from the *Format* menu.

2 The *Style* dialog box opens, with *Normal* highlighted under *Styles*. To adapt the Normal style to create a new style, click on *New*.

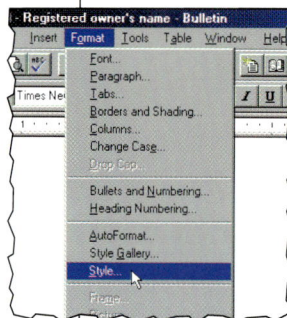

3 The *New Style* dialog box appears, revealing more options. Under *Name,* choose a name for the new style you want to create; in this case type **Banner**. Click on the *Format* button to display a drop-down list, and then choose *Font*.

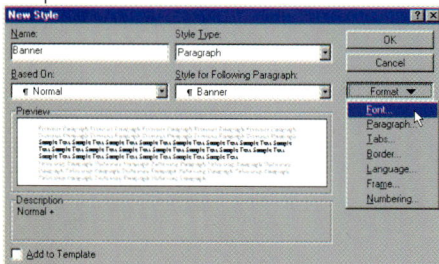

4 The *Font* dialog box appears. Choose *Arial* in the *Font* list box, click on *Bold* in the *Font Style* box, set the *Size* at *24* pt, and then check *All Caps* under *Effects*. Click on *OK* to return to the *New Style* dialog box.

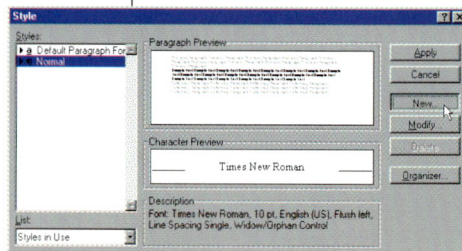

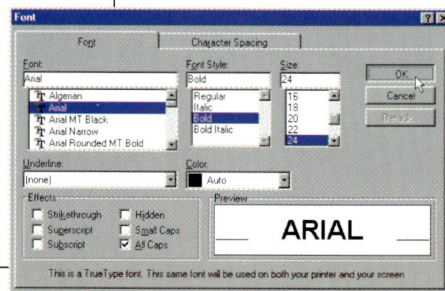

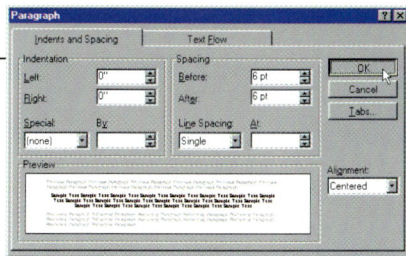

5 In the *New Style* dialog box, choose *Paragraph* from the *Format* drop-down list. In the *Paragraph* dialog box, choose *Centered* from the *Alignment* drop-down list. Under *Spacing,* set both *Before* and *After* to *6 pt.* Click on *OK* to return to the *New Style* dialog box.

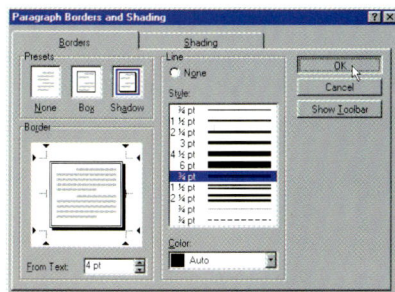

6 In the *New Style* dialog box, choose *Border* from the *Format* drop-down list. In the *Paragraph Borders and Shading* dialog box, click on *Shadow* under *Presets.* Increase the value in the *From Text* box under *Border* to *4 pt.* Under *Line* choose the ¾ *pt* double-line border. Then click on *OK* to return to the *New Style* dialog box.

7 You've now defined your **Banner** style, and its details are listed in the *Description* box. Click on *OK* to add the style to your template. If you had defined a style for a document, you could add it to the template on which the document was based by checking the *Add to Template* box. Click on the Close button in the *Style* dialog box.

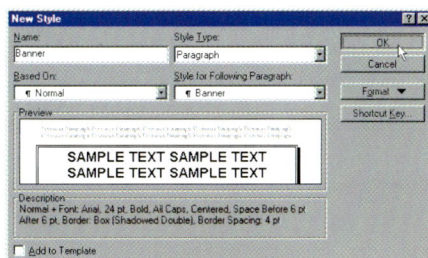

In a Hurry?
After you've typed a document, you can save time by letting Word format the text for you. If you click on the AutoFormat button on the Standard toolbar, Word will analyze each paragraph and determine how it is used — for example, as a heading — and will then apply an appropriate style to that paragraph. Word also makes small changes to improve the document's appearance, such as indenting paragraphs.

Selling Out

Now let's add another style to your template and then apply both of the new styles you've created to complete the template. Follow the procedure described in steps 1 and 2 on page 108. When the *New Style* dialog box opens, make sure that the *Based On* list box is set on *Normal,* call the new style **Contact**, and then do the following:

■ Access the *Font* dialog box via the *Format* drop-down list, and select *Bold* under *Font Style*. Click on *OK*.

■ Access the *Paragraph* dialog box, and choose *Centered* from the *Alignment* drop-down list. Click on *OK*.

You have now defined your **Contact** style. Click on *OK* in the *New Style* dialog box to add this style to your template and then close the *Style* dialog box to return to your **Bulletin** template. If you drop down the Style list on the Formatting toolbar, you'll see both of your new styles in the list. Now enter the text of your template:

■ Click at the top of the text area, type **For Sale**, and then press Enter twice.

■ Choose *Date and Time* from the *Insert* menu, select an option and click on *OK*. Then press Enter three times.

■ Type **Main text here** and press Enter five times.

■ Type **Contact:** and type your name and address.

Now apply the new styles you have created:

■ Select **For Sale** and choose *Banner* from the Style drop-down list on the Formatting toolbar.

■ Select the last part, from **Contact** through to your address, and choose *Contact* from the Style drop-down list. Finally, save and close **Bulletin**.

Now whenever you want to use the template at a later date, you simply choose *New* from the *File* menu, and then choose *Bulletin* in the *New* dialog box to open a new document with your "boilerplate" text in place. You then replace the line **Main text here** with your new text.

Your New Template
When you have finished the **Bulletin** *template, it should look like the example at right.*

FOR·SALE¶

¶
11·November·95¶
¶
¶
Main·text·here¶
¶
¶
¶
¶
Contact:·Sammy·Lewis¶
16·Park·Road¶
Blackwood,·WA·34100¶

AutoCorrect and AutoText

AUTOCORRECT AND AUTOTEXT ARE TWO of Word's most useful timesavers. Using AutoCorrect, you can quickly store and retrieve graphics and text that you use frequently in your documents. You store the item with a short code — then whenever you type this code, AutoCorrect automatically inserts the stored item in its place as you type. AutoText is a similar feature that will insert a stored item when you choose a specific command.

Speed Up Your Typing

AutoCorrect is especially useful for phrases that are repetitive or difficult to type. Let's suppose your company's name is All Nations Exports. Because you use this name regularly, you can save time by storing it as an AutoCorrect entry called **ANE** (a sort of code-name). From now on, if you type **ANE** followed by a punctuation mark or space, AutoCorrect will automatically replace it, as you type, with **All Nations Exports**.

Let's create an AutoCorrect entry. First open a new document based on the Blank Document template and call it **Nature**. Then follow these steps:

Creating an AutoCorrect Entry

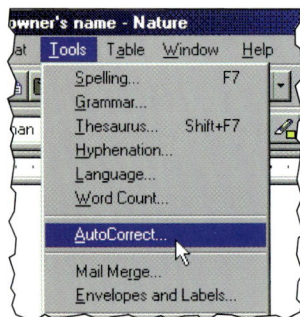

1 Choose *AutoCorrect* from the *Tools* menu. The *AutoCorrect* dialog box appears, with a set of predefined AutoCorrect entries listed by default.

2 Type **Ys** in the *Replace* box. Then type **Yours sincerely** in the *With* box and click on *OK*. If you wanted to add more than one entry at a time, you would click on *Add* after each entry, and then click on *OK* when you had finished.

Now whenever you want to include the words **Yours sincerely** in a document, you simply type **Ys** followed by a space or punctuation mark.

STORING COMPLEX TEXT AND GRAPHICS

To store a graphic, a long piece of text, or formatted text, select the item before you open the *AutoCorrect* dialog box. The item will appear in the *With* box. To save the entry with its original formatting, select the *Formatted Text* option. To save it as plain text, in which Word matches the formatting of the surrounding text, select the *Plain Text* option — but bear in mind that a plain text entry can only contain up to 255 characters. Then type a name for the entry in the *Replace* box.

Check That Name!
An AutoCorrect name can have up to a maximum of 31 characters. Don't give an AutoCorrect entry a name that is a real word because you might type the word as part of your text and have it inadvertently replaced! To cancel an AutoCorrect entry, click on the Undo button on the Standard toolbar.

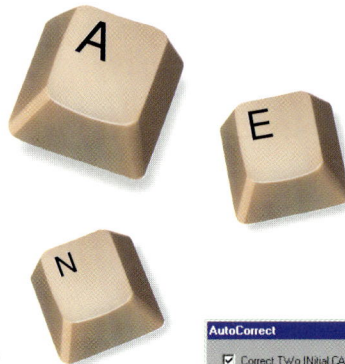

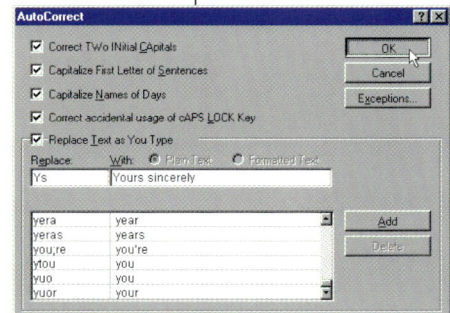

Habitual Misspeller?
You can set up AutoCorrect to correct any word that you habitually misspell. (Make sure the misspelling is not itself a proper word!) To do so, open the *AutoCorrect* dialog box, type the misspelling in the *Replace* box, and then type the correct spelling in the *With* box. Click on *OK*.

Controlled Entry

You can create AutoText entries for text and graphics that you don't want Word to insert automatically. Unlike AutoCorrect, AutoText allows you to insert a particular entry only by typing the name of the entry and pressing a combination of keys or by choosing *AutoText* from the *Edit* menu and then choosing the entry's name.

CREATING AN AUTOTEXT ENTRY

To practice creating an AutoText entry, let's use procedures you learned in Chapter 3 to prepare a letterhead consisting of a graphic and some text. Open the file **Nature** if it's not already open, and insert the graphic **Butterfly.wmf** from the Clipart library (see page 77). Type the name and address for the **Nature Society** beneath the butterfly graphic, as shown at right. Change the type size to 16 point and the type style to bold. You're now ready to store this letterhead as an AutoText entry:

Example Letterhead

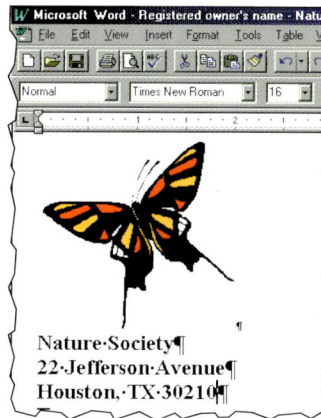

Nature·Society¶
22·Jefferson·Avenue¶
Houston,·TX·30210¶

Magic Touch
A quick way to insert an AutoText entry is simply to type the name of the entry into your document wherever you want the entry to appear, and then press F3.

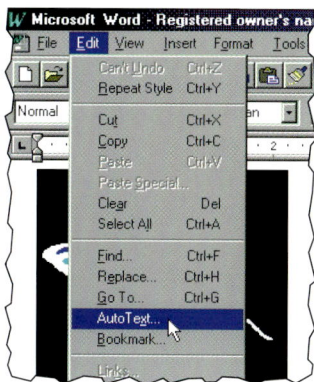

1 Select the graphic and text you've just entered, including the paragraph mark at the end of the text. This retains the paragraph formatting in the AutoText entry. Then choose *AutoText* from the *Edit* menu.

2 The *AutoText* dialog box appears with the letterhead displayed in the *Selection* box. Under *Name*, type **NS logo**, and then click on *Add*. (An AutoText name can have up to 32 characters, including spaces.) The letterhead is now stored as an AutoText entry.

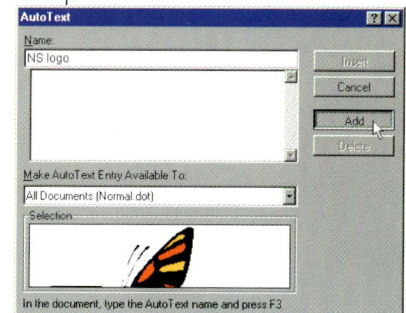

INSERTING AN AUTOTEXT ENTRY

Once you've saved an AutoText entry, adding it to a document is easy. You simply call up the entry and insert it wherever you want it to appear. Delete the graphic and name from your **Nature** document and follow these steps:

1 Choose *AutoText* from the *Edit* menu. The *AutoText* dialog box appears.

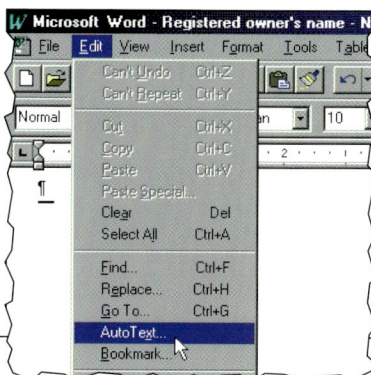

2 Choose **NS logo** from the *Name* list. Word displays the letterhead with its original formatting in the *Preview* window. You'll see the *Formatted Text* option selected under *Insert As*. Click on *Insert* to enter the logo into your document. Then save and close **Nature**.

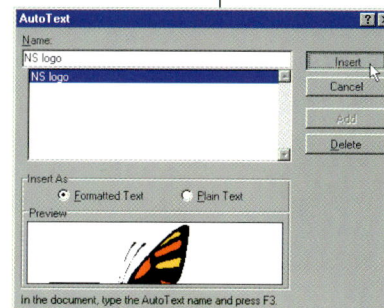

Macros

A MACRO IS A SERIES OF COMMANDS that are grouped together in one single command, which is then assigned to a menu, toolbar button, or key combination. Macros provide shortcuts for accomplishing certain routine tasks. For example, you can create a macro that hides the Standard toolbar, Formatting toolbar, and Ruler all at once or one that opens a document with an address and the date already inserted. You can then assign this macro to a toolbar button and run the macro by clicking on that button.

Using Macros

To produce a macro, you must record the commands you want the macro to perform. Before you start recording, decide which commands you'll use and in which order. Let's create a macro that opens a new document with a company logo, an address, the date, and the opening sentence already inserted. The commands you'll need to record are shown in the box at right.

How to Record a Macro

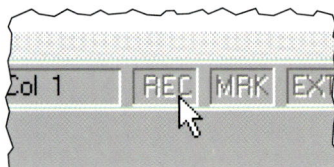

1 Open a new document and double-click on *REC* on the status bar. The *Record Macro* dialog box opens.

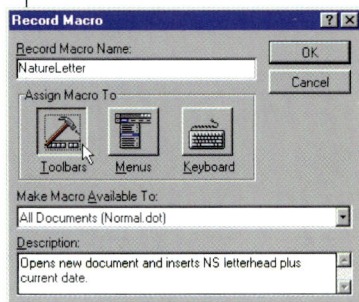

2 In the *Record Macro Name* text box, type the name **NatureLetter**. Make sure that the *Make Macro Available To* box is set on *All Documents (Normal.dot)*. This makes your macro available in any document you are working on. Then, in the *Description* text box, type **Opens new document and inserts NS letterhead plus current date**. Now click on the *Toolbars* icon to assign the macro to a toolbar button.

3 The *Customize* dialog box appears, with the *Toolbars* flipcard displayed. Select **NatureLetter** from the list of macros, and then drag it to a position on a toolbar — you'll see the outline of a square accompanied by a plus sign move on screen as you move the mouse. For now, position this square between the Highlighter button and the Align Left button on the Formatting toolbar.

- Choose *New* from the *File* menu.

- Choose the *Blank Document* template in the *New* dialog box and click on *OK*.

- Choose *AutoText* from the *Edit* menu.

- Choose a logo in the *AutoText* dialog box and click on *Insert*.

- Choose the *Date and Time* command from the *Insert* menu.

- Choose a Date format in the *Date and Time* dialog box and click on *OK*.

- Type the opening to your letter.

Cast a Macro Spell
To use a set of ready-made macros, choose *Open* from the *File* menu and double-click on the **Macros** folder in the **Winword** folder, which itself is in the **MSOffice** folder. Make sure that *Document Templates* is displayed in the *Files of type* box, choose **Macros7** from the main window, and then click on *Open*. Choose *Macro* from the *Tools* menu and select a macro in the *Macro* dialog box. If you don't have the Macros folder, you will need to install **Macro Templates** from your original disks.

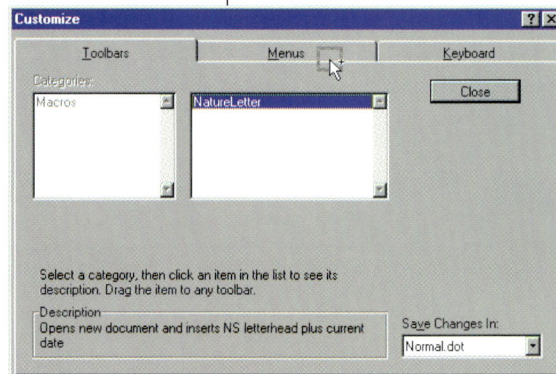

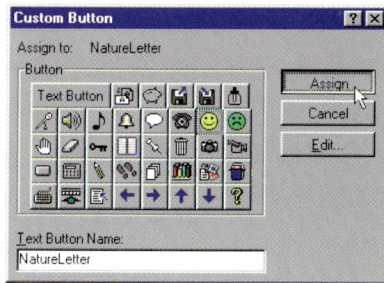

4 As soon as you release the mouse button, the *Custom Button* dialog box opens. Choose a symbol for your new toolbar button by clicking on the symbol — for example, the smiley — and then click on *Assign*. The smiley appears on the new button on the Formatting toolbar. Click on *Close* in the *Customize* dialog box.

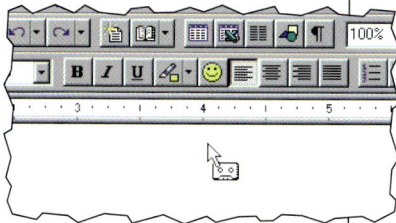

5 Any command you choose now will be recorded. To indicate this, the mouse pointer is accompanied by a small recorder graphic (see left). You'll also see two buttons appear on your screen — one to stop and one to pause the macro recording (see right).

Stop Button

Pause Button

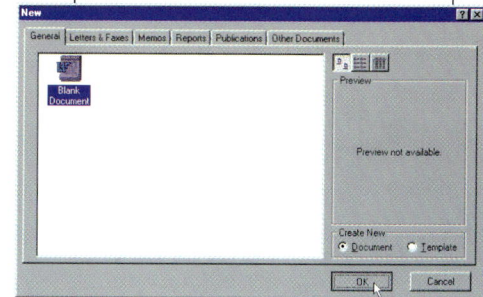

6 Start by choosing *New* from the *File* menu to access the *New* dialog box. In this box, click on *OK* to base your document on the *Blank Document* template.

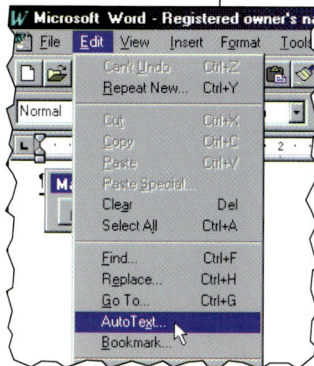

7 Now choose *AutoText* from the *Edit* menu.

8 In the *AutoText* dialog box, choose *NS logo* from the *Name* list, and then click on *Insert*.

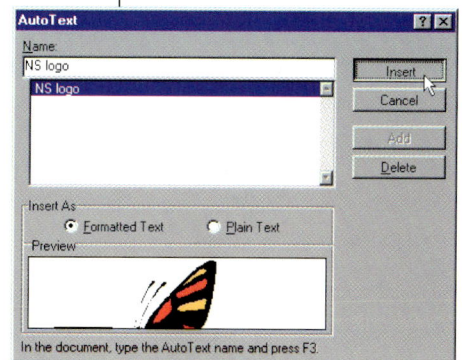

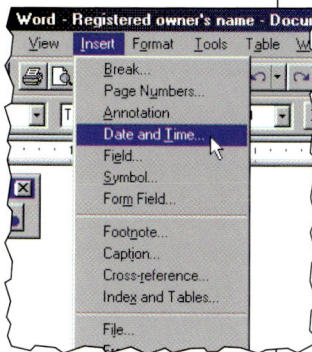

9 Press Enter twice, and then choose *Date and Time* from the *Insert* menu. When the *Date and Time* dialog box appears, choose a date format, and then click on *OK*.

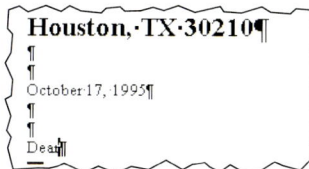

10 Press Enter three times, and then type **Dear**.

The Finished Product
This is the letter heading that the macro you've created will produce each time you run the macro.

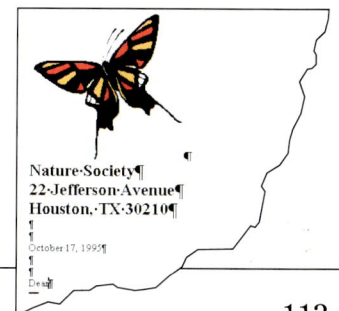

11 To stop recording your macro, click on the Stop Macro Recording button. Your macro has now been recorded.

113

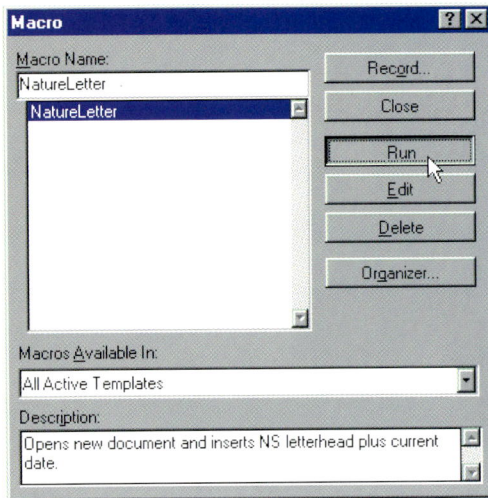

Macro Dialog Box

RUNNING A MACRO

When you run a macro, Word "plays back" all the actions you performed when you recorded that macro, but at a much higher speed. Because you have assigned your NatureLetter macro to a toolbar button, you simply have to click on that button to begin running the macro. If you do not assign the macro to a toolbar button, a menu command, or a combination of keys when you record the macro, you have to access the *Macro* dialog box to run the macro. To do this, choose *Macro* from the *Tools* menu. When the *Macro* dialog box opens, choose the name of the macro and click on *Run* to use the macro.

Bear in mind that you can also use the *Macro* command when you want to record a macro. You choose *Macro* from the *Tools* menu, and then click on *Record* to access the *Record Macro* dialog box — but this method is not as quick and easy as double-clicking on *REC* on the status bar.

Give Me a Break!
When you're recording a macro, you may need to pause, for example, if there are actions you want to perform that you don't want recorded. To pause while recording a macro, click on the Pause Macro Recording button. When you're ready to resume, simply click again on the button.

Managing Macros

If you want to copy a macro to a different template, delete a macro, or rename a macro, you can do so in the *Organizer* dialog box. First choose *Macro* from the *Tools* menu to open the *Macro* dialog box, and then click on the *Organizer* button; the *Organizer* dialog box appears on the screen with the *Macros* flipcard displayed (see at right).

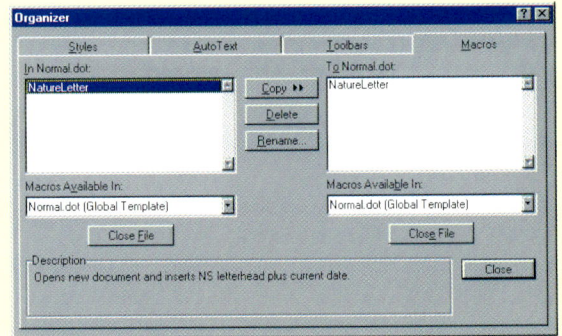

■ To copy a macro to another template: In the *Macros Available In* box on the left-hand side of the *Organizer* dialog box, choose the template in which the macro you want to copy is stored. Then select your destination template in the *Macros Available In* box on the right-hand side. Finally, click on the *Copy* button.

■ To delete a macro: Choose the relevant template from the *Macros Available In* box on the left side of the dialog box, select the macro you want to delete, and then click on *Delete*.

■ To rename a macro: Choose the relevant template from the *Macros Available In* box on the left side of the dialog box, select the name of the macro you want to rename, and then click on the *Rename* button. When the *Rename* box appears, simply type in the new name, and then click on *OK*. Don't use spaces, commas, or periods in your macro name.

Reference Section

*The first few pages of this section
list some useful keyboard and mouse shortcuts
and also describe how to outline a document. The
next several pages show you how to install a printer
and discuss the different types of fonts. You'll also find
some additional help on managing your files, converting files, and linking files with those created
in other applications. You'll then learn how
to customize Word to suit your methods
of working. Finally, you'll find an
index to the whole volume.*

TOP TEN SHORTCUTS
OUTLINING • INSTALLING A PRINTER • FONTS
CONVERTING FILES • MANIPULATING YOUR FILES • OLE
CUSTOMIZING WORD FOR WINDOWS 95 • INDEX

Top Ten Shortcuts

I N THIS SECTION, we provide a list of "top ten" shortcuts, for both the keyboard and the mouse. As you become proficient in Word, you'll find you may prefer to carry out some commands with the keyboard and others with the mouse — and you'll gradually build up a repertoire of shortcuts. Below we've listed some of our own favorites.

Keyboard Shortcuts

Command	Keyboard Keys
Move to the beginning of a document.	Ctrl and Home
Move to the end of a document.	Ctrl and End
Obtain context-sensitive help.	F1
Switch between Overtype mode and normal mode.	Insert
Save new document (Save As).	F12
Close the application window.	Alt and F4
Delete a single word (after the insertion point).	Ctrl and Delete
Insert a page break into a document.	Ctrl and Enter
Repeat previous command.	F4
Switch between applications on the screen.	Alt and Tab

Mouse Shortcuts

Command	Mouse Action
Select an entire document.	Triple-click anywhere in the selection bar.
Open the *Help for WordPerfect Users* dialog box.	Double-click on *WPH* on the status bar.
Make the toolbar "floating."	Double-click on an empty area on any toolbar.
Return a "floating" toolbar to its original position.	Double-click on an empty area on the toolbar.
Open the *Go To* dialog box.	Double-click anywhere on the status bar.
Open the *Margins* flipcard in the *Page Setup* dialog box.	In Page Layout View, double-click on the top left corner of the page, outside the margins.
Open the *Symbol* dialog box.	Double-click on any inserted symbol.
Open the *Layout* flipcard in the *Page Setup* dialog box.	Double-click on any section break.
Open the *Tabs* dialog box.	Double-click on any tab stop.
Restore or maximize a window.	Double-click on the title bar of the window.

Outlining

O UTLINING IS A USEFUL PROCESS for structuring a document and organizing your ideas in relation to each other. In an outline you view headings rather than text, making it easy to reorganize the document's structure, scroll through the document, and get a quick overview.

Promotes a selection up one level	←
Demotes a selection down one level	→
Demotes a heading to body text	⇒
Moves a selection above the preceding text	↑
Moves a selection below the following text	↓
Displays the next level beneath a heading	+
Collapses the next level beneath a heading	−
Expands or collapses an outline to show only the heading levels you want to view	1 2 3 4 5 6 7 8
Expands the entire outline to display all heading levels and body text	All
Displays all body text or only the first line of body text	=
Shows or hides all character formatting	AA
Switches between Outline and Master Document view	▣

Using the Outline Toolbar

Whether you want to create a document from scratch using outlining, or apply outlining to an existing document, you must put the document into Outline View by clicking on the Outline button above the status bar, or choose *Outline* from the *View* menu.

In Outline View, a new toolbar — the Outline toolbar — appears. The Outline feature gives you eight heading levels (heading 1 for the top level, heading 8 for the lowest level). Each heading level comes with its own predefined style that you assign to your headings. If you assign a level to a heading but then change your mind about its significance within the document, you can easily "promote" the heading to a higher level or "demote" it to a lower level.

When outlining has been applied, you can collapse an outline so that only the main headings show while the supporting text gets hidden. You can then quickly scroll through the headings, and rearrange them by selecting a heading and clicking on the up- or down-arrow button. This moves the heading a paragraph up or down, taking any supporting text automatically with it.

Once you've finished rearranging your document, you can expand the outline again to work on the details. The buttons on the Outline toolbar and the actions they perform are explained at left.

CREATING AN OUTLINE

The steps below show you how to assign levels to headings and how to move them around. If you want to create an outline, make sure you are in Outline view first.

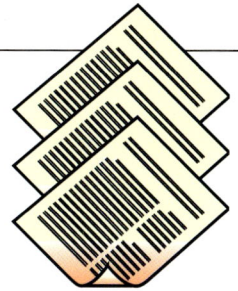

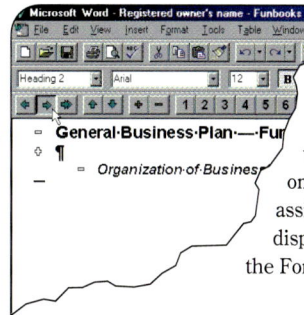

1 When you first start typing, Word automatically assigns heading 1 level to the text. To assign a lower level to a heading, move your insertion point anywhere within that heading and click on the Demote button. The level assigned to a selected heading is displayed in the Style box on the Formatting toolbar.

2 To turn a paragraph into body text, move the insertion point anywhere within that paragraph and click on the Demote to Body Text button. Outline view indents headings and body text to show how they relate to one another — in Normal view, however, they are not indented.

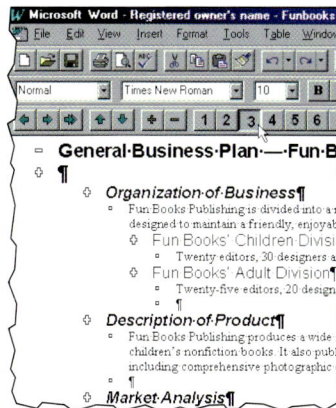

3 To collapse an outline, select the heading level that you want to display. In the example shown here, three heading levels were used to create the document. You would therefore click on the 3 button to collapse the outline so that the body text disappeared and only the headings were visible.

4 To move text to a new location further up the document, select the text you want to move — either a heading and/or text — and click on the Move Up button. To view the "normal" appearance of the document, click on the Normal button above the status bar.

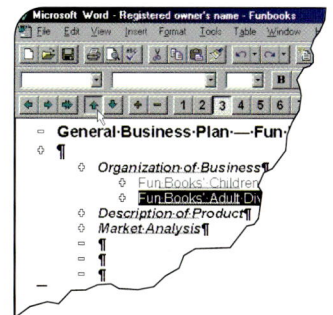

117

Installing a Printer

STRICTLY SPEAKING, INSTALLING A PRINTER isn't a feature of Word — it's something that is done within Windows 95 itself, which then serves all Windows 95 applications, including Word. As well as installing a printer, you'll also have to prepare the printer itself by plugging it in, adding paper and a ribbon or toner, and then connecting it to your computer before you can print any Word documents.

Printer-Driver Files

Every printer needs a printer-driver file to make it work. The printer-driver file processes data it receives from an application, such as Word, and then issues the commands to the printer.

It is possible to install more than one printer driver or different types of printer drivers on your PC. For example, you may be connected to a network on which you have access to more than one printer. Windows 95 is supplied with printer-driver files for the most commonly used printers. You need to know the name and model of your printer. If your printer is not supported by any of the printer-driver files that come with Windows 95, follow the instructions from the printer manufacturer. Let's install a printer on your PC for which Windows 95 provides a printer-driver file.

Installing a Printer-Driver File

1 Click on *Control Panel* in the Start menu.

2 In the Control Panel, double-click on the *Printers* icon.

3 The *Printers* window opens. As this is the first printer to be installed, no printers are listed. Click on *Add Printer* and click on *Next* in the introductory window of the *Add Printer Wizard*.

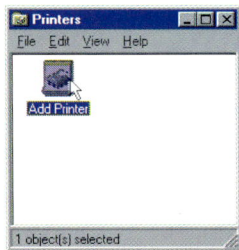

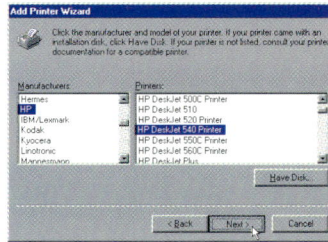

4 The next window of the *Add Printer Wizard* is where you select your printer. Let's suppose you want to install a Hewlett-Packard DeskJet 540. Select this option in the *Printers* list. Even though this printer comes with installation disks, simply click on *Next*. The following window asks you to select a socket, or *port*, for your printer. Click on *Next* after selecting one (it's usually called *LPT1*).

5 Either accept the Printer name that is suggested here, or type in your own choice. Choose *Yes* or *No* as to whether this will be the printer that is automatically selected for your documents, then click on *Next*.

6 Accept the offer to print a test page, and click on *Finish*.

7 You are now asked to insert your Windows 95 CD-ROM installation disk. If you installed Windows 95 from floppy disks, you will be asked to insert one of them. Insert the disk into the drive and click on *OK*. Windows 95 will copy the printer-driver file onto your hard disk.

8 When the printer-driver file has been copied onto your hard disk, the test page is printed to confirm that your printer has been installed. The *Printers* window reappears containing the new printer icon. The *File* menu shows you some of the options available when you need them. For now, click on *Close* in the File menu and close the Control Panel.

Fonts

A FONT IS ONE COMPLETE COLLECTION of letters, punctuation marks, numbers, and special characters that have a particular design. The fonts and font sizes you can use in your Word documents depend on the fonts available on your printer and the fonts installed on your PC.

Types of Fonts

Font List

If you click on the down arrow next to the Font list box on the Formatting toolbar or if you open the *Font* dialog box by choosing *Font* from the *Format* menu, you'll see a list of the fonts that are available to you in Word. You'll also see symbols beside many of them — these identify the type of font (see at left). There are three types of fonts — TrueType fonts (TT symbol), Windows (vectored) fonts (no symbol), and printer fonts (printer symbol).

TrueType fonts are stored in the **Fonts** folder in the **Windows** folder on your PC and are available to any application that is run on Windows 95. Some of these fonts may have been installed on your PC with Windows 95, others when you installed Word or another application. TrueType fonts are scaleable to any point size and look exactly the same on screen as they do when printed. They can be printed on any type of printer.

Windows (vectored) fonts also come with Windows 95, but they can be printed in only a few sizes and have limited use in practice. Printer fonts are built into your printer. Like TrueType fonts, these fonts print well in any size. If an exact match is not available on screen, a substitute TrueType font will be displayed. Printer fonts are specific to the make and model of the printer you are using.

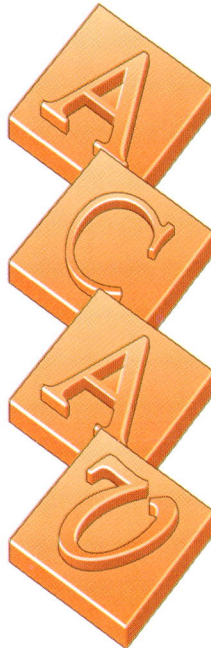

STICK TO TRUETYPE!
If possible, stick to TrueType fonts. This ensures that your fonts look exactly the same on screen as they do when printed. It also makes documents more portable because they will look the same when printed on different printers.

Want More Fonts?

If you want to add more fonts for use in your Word documents, you must access the *Add Fonts* dialog box. You can add fonts from folders other than **Windows\Fonts**, or you can buy fonts and install them on your system. To install extra fonts, follow these steps:

1 Double-click on the *Fonts* icon in the *Control Panel*.

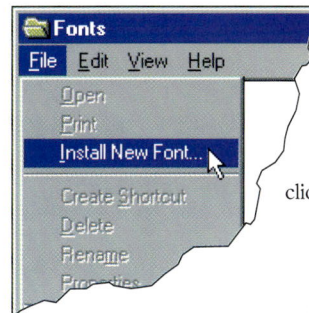

2 In the *Fonts* window, click on *File* and then click on *Install New Font*.

3 The *Add Fonts* dialog box appears. Click on the drive and folder where the fonts are located that you want to add.

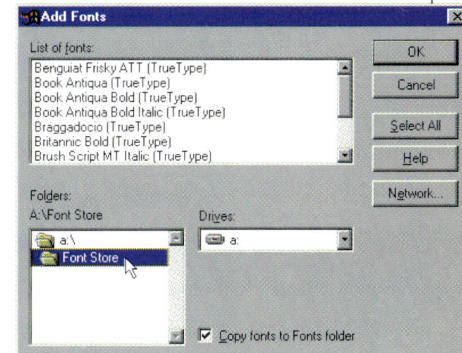

4 Double-click on the name of the font that you want to add. To select several fonts, hold down either Ctrl or the Shift key as you click on each one. If the fonts you want are grouped together, hold down either Ctrl or Shift as you drag the cursor over the fonts. If you want to add all the fonts, click on *Select All*. When you have chosen the fonts that you want to add, click on *OK*.

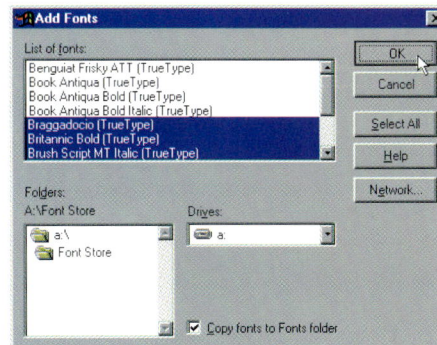

5 The *Fonts* window reappears with the new fonts listed. Click on the Close button of the *Fonts* window to close it.

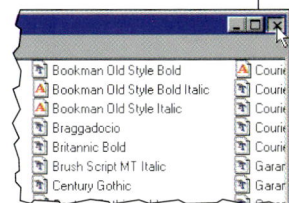

Converting Files

WITH WORD, you can open and work with documents created in other applications. Word recognizes the formats of many applications and can convert the documents to the Word format when you open them. Conversely, you can also save Word files in formats used by other applications.

Converters

To convert documents, you must have the appropriate converters. If there is no converter for the application you're using, you can still import the text, but you may lose some formatting elements.

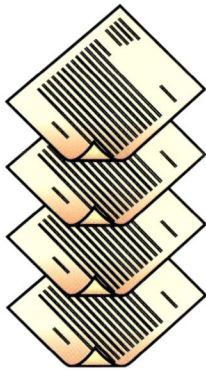

OPENING DOCUMENTS CREATED IN OTHER APPLICATIONS

To convert most types of documents created in other applications, you simply open the document. Word performs the conversion automatically once you have confirmed the format that the file should be converted from. But bear in mind that if the document contains fonts that are not available on your PC (see page 119), Word will use substitute fonts — you may need to alter the text to account for this.

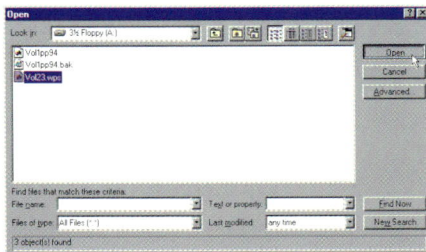

1 Click on the Open button to access the *Open* dialog box. In the *Files of type* list box, choose the type of file you want to open. If you're not sure of its format, choose *All Files*. Use the *Look in* box to locate the drive and folder containing the file. Finally, click on *Open*.

2 If you attempt to open a file that is not in Word format, the *Convert File* dialog box will appear. The current file format will be highlighted. Click on *OK* to convert it and open it. (If you can't find the appropriate converter for a particular application, you may have to install it.)

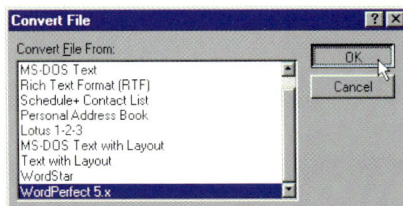

SAVING WORD FILES IN DIFFERENT FORMATS

You may need to save a Word document in another format — for example, if you want to share a file with someone who uses a different application. First choose *Save As* from the *File* menu. In the *Save As* dialog box, scroll through the *Save as type* list and choose the format in which you want to save the file. Specify a destination drive and folder, and name the file in the *File name* box. Then click on *Save* to store the file in the new format.

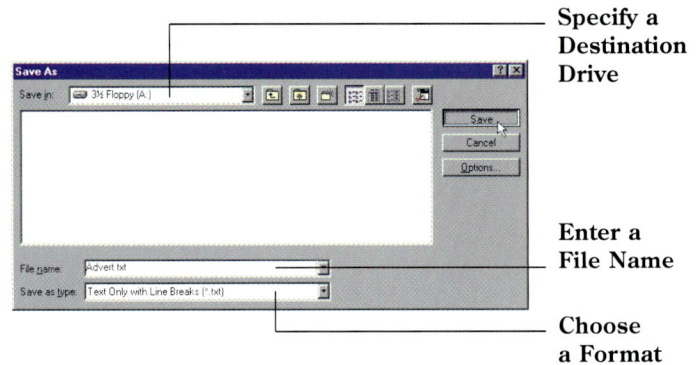

Specify a Destination Drive

Enter a File Name

Choose a Format

Importing Picture Files

You can also import and export pictures among different applications. You cannot convert a picture file, but you can embed the image into any Word document. With Word, you can import graphics with the following file formats (among others). The three-letter extension indicates the file format:

■ Windows bitmaps (BMP)

■ Windows metafile (WMF)

■ Computer Graphics Metafile (CGM)

■ PC Paintbrush (PCX)

■ Encapsulated Postscript (EPS)

■ Tagged Image File Format (TIF)

For example, you can import an image created in the Paint program into a Word document. To do this, you create your image in Paint, and save it to a specific folder as a BMP file. You then open a Word document and choose *Picture* from the *Insert* menu. Locate your image file in the relevant directory, and finally click on *OK* to import the image.

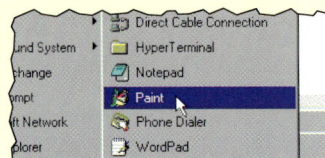

Paint
The Paint program is supplied with Windows 95; its icon is usually located in the Accessories *group menu.*

Manipulating Your Files

Earlier in this book, you learned all about the structure and organization of the files and folders on your PC's hard disk. Here we show you how to move and copy files from one folder to another, how to change the name of a file, and how to delete files you no longer need.

Making Changes

As your files and folders increase in number, you'll make more and more use of Windows Explorer to manipulate your data. In the *Explorer* window (see page 49), click on the plus sign next to the **My Documents** folder to display a list of the folders it contains. Now click on the **My Documents** icon itself to display its contents in the right-hand window, and practice the procedures described here.

Moving or Copying a File

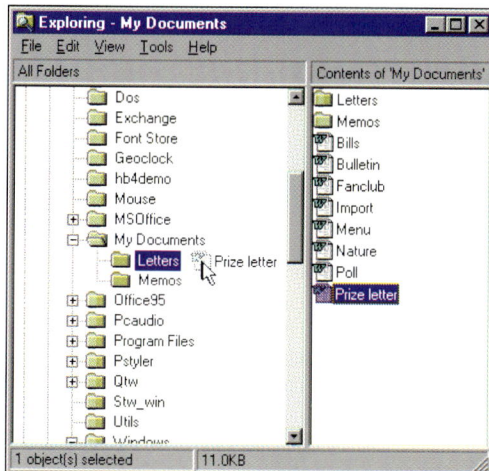

1 Place the mouse pointer over the file in the right-hand window that you want to move. Then hold down the mouse button and drag the file symbol into the left-hand window toward the target folder. If you want to copy the file instead of moving it, hold down Ctrl.

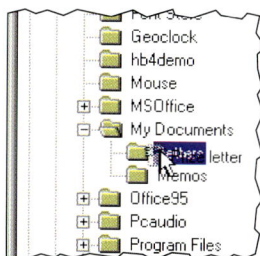

2 Position the file symbol over the target folder so that it's highlighted as shown here, and then release the mouse button. Click on *Yes* if the *Confirm Mouse Operation* box appears. The file has now been moved or copied to the target folder. If you want, click on the folder to check that the file is there.

Renaming a File

1 Select the file that you want to rename in the right-hand window.

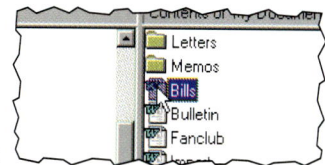

2 Choose *Rename* from the *File* menu, or click on the file name so that the name is highlighted within a rectangle. Type the new name in the rectangle, and then press Enter.

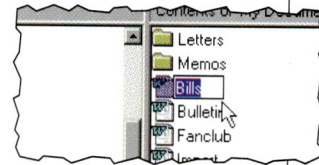

3 The next time you list the contents of the folder, the file, now renamed, will appear in the alphabetic sequence.

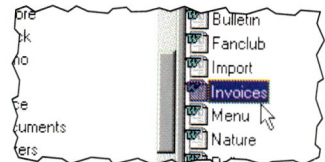

Deleting a File

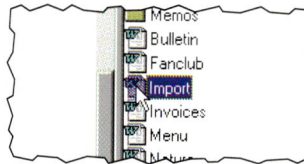

1 Choose the file you want to delete, and then choose *Delete* from the *File* menu, or drag it to the Recycle Bin.

2 When you empty the Recycle Bin, Windows 95 will ask you to confirm that you want to delete the file. Click on *Yes*.

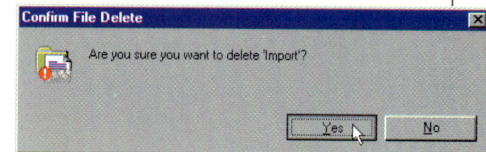

Multiple Actions

To move or copy several adjacent files at once, place the pointer next to the first or last file and hold down the mouse button. Now drag the mouse diagonally across the file names until all the files you want are highlighted. To move or copy several files that are not listed together, hold down Ctrl and click on each file in turn. Then drag all the highlighted files at once toward the new folder, making sure that the folder is highlighted before you release the mouse button.

To delete multiple files listed next to each other in one folder, highlight them by dragging the mouse across them while the mouse button is held down. If the files you want to delete are not adjacent, hold down Ctrl and click on each file individually. Then choose *Delete* from the *File* menu or drag them to the Recycle Bin. Click on *Yes to All* when you are asked to confirm the deletion. The files will remain in the Recycle Bin until you either empty the Bin or retrieve the files.

OLE

OLE PROVIDES WAYS of exchanging information, or "objects," between documents or applications. In Word, you can both link and embed information. The main difference between linking and embedding is where the linked or embedded data is stored. Linked objects remain in the original source file, whereas embedded objects become part of the Word document itself.

Linking

Creating a link is easy — you simply copy information, called an object, from one document (the source) and paste it into another document (the destination) using the *Paste Special* command. If you then change the information in the source file, Word updates the destination document. You can create links between two Word documents or between a Word document and a file in another application.

CREATING A LINK

A typical use of linkage might be a table in a Word document that is linked to a Microsoft Excel spreadsheet. Let's create a link between two documents in different applications. First open your Word document, then click on the Start button and click on Microsoft Excel in the *Programs* menu to open the application. If you don't have Microsoft Excel, open another Word document. Next, open the source file containing the information you want to link and follow these steps:

From the Source...

1 In the source file, highlight the information you want to paste as a linked object into your Word document.

2 Choose *Copy* from the *Edit* menu of the source application.

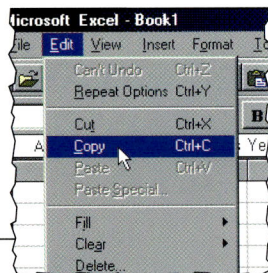

To the Destination

1 Switch to your Word document and position the insertion point where you want the linked information to appear. Then choose *Paste Special* from the *Edit* menu.

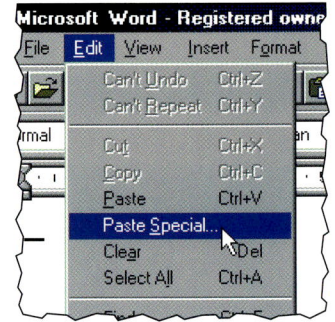

2 In the *Paste Special* dialog box, click on the *Paste Link* option, and then select the type of linked object in the *As* box, in this case *Microsoft Excel Worksheet Object*. Finally, click on *OK* to insert the information into your Word document.

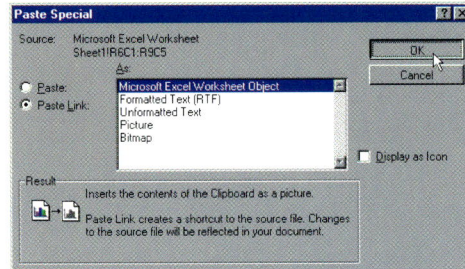

Updating or Breaking a Link

By default, Word automatically updates the information in a linked document whenever the original (source) document changes. But you can change a link to manual updating so that you can choose how frequently to update the information. To do this, select the linked information in your Word document, and then choose *Links* from the *Edit* menu. In the *Links* dialog box, click on the *Manual* option, and then click on *OK*. Now whenever you want to update your document, you select the linked information, open the *Links* dialog box, and click on *Update Now*. Alternatively, select the information to be updated and simply press F9.

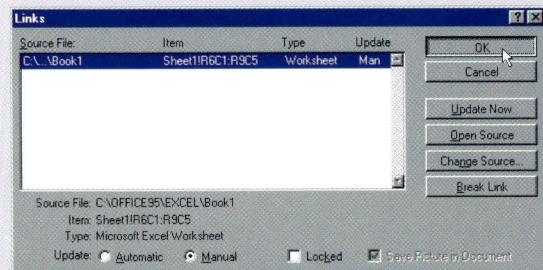

Links Dialog Box

If you don't want further changes to occur in a linked document, you can cancel the link to prevent it from updating. To do this, select the linked information, open the *Links* dialog box, and then click on *Break Link*. Click on *Yes* in the box asking you to confirm the action. Once a link is broken, it can't be reconnected unless you set it up from scratch again.

Embedding

Embedding also means inserting information such as a chart, image, or equation from another application into a Word document. Once you have embedded the information, called an object, it becomes part of the Word document.

You can embed objects created using WordArt, Graph, and Equation Editor, all of which are supplied with Word. You can also embed objects from other applications installed on your PC, including Paint, which is supplied with Microsoft Windows 95; you can even embed one Word document in another.

EMBEDDING A NEW OBJECT IN A WORD DOCUMENT

You use embedding instead of linking when you don't need to share the information with other documents, but you want to be able to edit and format the information quickly and easily within Word. An object to be embedded can either be newly created or copied from an existing file. To see how easy it is to embed an object in a Word document, let's embed an equation created in Equation Editor — a companion application that provides you with a range of symbols for technical documents.

In Microsoft Word

1 Position the insertion point in your Word document where you want to embed the equation, and then choose *Object* from the *Insert* menu.

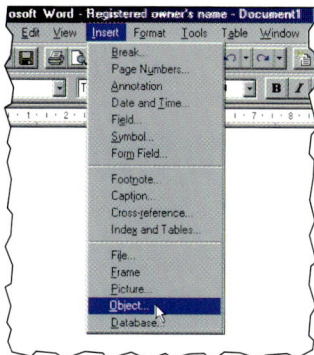

2 In the *Object* dialog box, choose the *Create New* tab. Under *Object Type,* you'll see a list of the types of objects you can create and embed. Choose *Microsoft Equation 2.0,* and then click on *OK.* If you don't have Microsoft Equation 2.0, you will need to install it from your original disks.

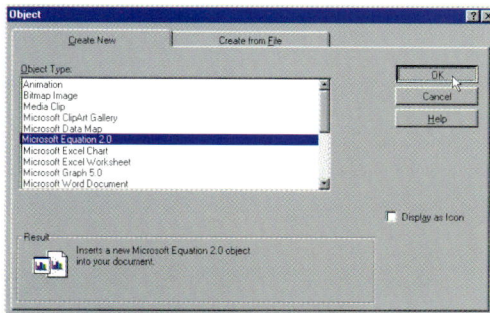

In Equation Editor

1 The Equation Editor toolbar and special menus appear in the document window together with a rectangular box with a shaded gray border where you enter your equation. Type the equation, choosing the relevant symbols from the Equation Editor toolbar.

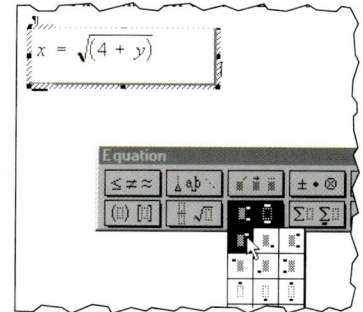

$$x = \sqrt{(4 + y)}$$

2 When you've finished creating the equation, click anywhere outside the gray-bordered rectangle. The equation is inserted into the document, and the regular Word menus and toolbars reappear.

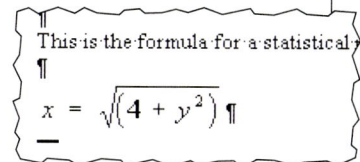

This is the formula for a statistical

$$x = \sqrt{(4 + y^2)}$$

OBJECT ALREADY EXISTS?

To embed an existing file, choose the *Create from File* tab in the *Object* dialog box. Use the Browse button to find file you want to embed. Click on *OK* to embed the file in your document.

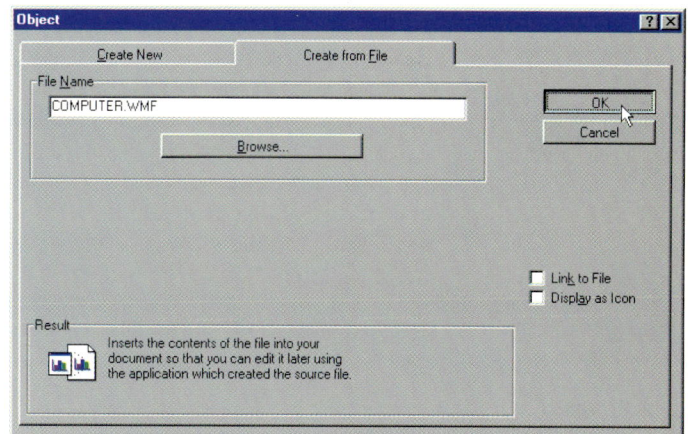

Making Changes

If you want to change an embedded object in any way, all you have to do is double-click on the object in your Word document. After a pause, the relevant toolbars and special menus appear or the application window in which the object was created opens, with the object displayed. You then make your changes and either just click outside the object in your Word document or choose *Exit* from the application's *File* menu to return to your Word document and insert the updated object.

Customizing Word for Windows 95

To SUIT YOUR INDIVIDUAL STYLE of working, you can customize Word in a number of ways. You can, for example, change the appearance of your Word application window. You can change some of the default settings; you can alter the appearance of a toolbar; or you can assign a command or macro to a toolbar, menu, or shortcut key so that you don't have to wade through layers of menus to carry out a specific action or series of actions.

Modifying Screen Items

If you want, you can easily customize your Word application window. You may, for example, want to hide screen items, such as the scroll bars, the status bar, the Ruler, and so on, in order to see more of the document that you are working on. You can also customize your toolbars — changing the buttons that appear on a particular toolbar, for example.

How to Hide Screen Elements

1 Choose *Options* from the *Tools* menu. In the *Options* dialog box, you'll find twelve tabs. When you click on a particular tab, the dialog box changes to show you the settings assigned to that flipcard.

2 In the *Options* dialog box, click on the *View* tab (if it isn't already selected) to reveal the *View* flipcard.

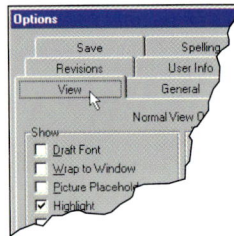

3 Here, you can modify a number of screen items. For example, you can hide the scroll bars and status bar by clearing the relevant check boxes under *Window*; or you can choose which nonprinting characters are displayed by checking the relevant boxes under *Nonprinting Characters*. To make your changes apply, simply click on *OK*.

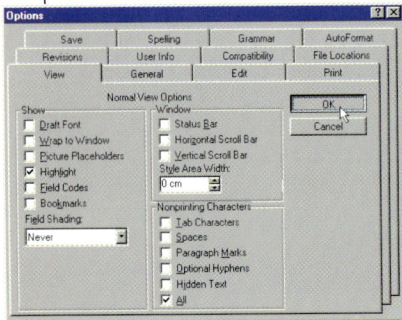

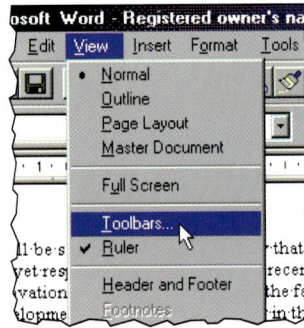

How to Change the Display of the Toolbars

1 Choose *Toolbars* from the *View* menu.

2 In the *Toolbars* dialog box, you can switch off the color of your toolbar buttons by clearing the *Color Buttons* check box; enlarge the toolbar buttons by clicking on the *Large Buttons* check box; or hide the brief descriptions of the toolbar buttons that appear when the mouse pointer pauses over a button by clearing the *Show ToolTips* box. Make your changes, and then click on *OK*.

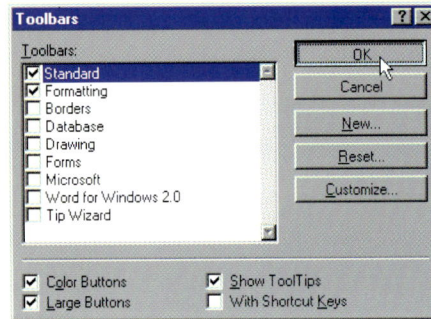

Changing Your Display and Command Settings

You can also change a number of default settings that come with Word. Make yourself familiar with the various options by choosing *Options* again from the *Tools* menu to open the *Options* dialog box. You are already familiar with the options available under *View*; now explore the other flipcards and their settings.

YOUR GENERAL OPTIONS

In the *General* flipcard, you can decide whether or not a sound is made to indicate an error; how many files appear in the *File* menu as recently opened files; the units of measurement that appear on the rulers; and so on.

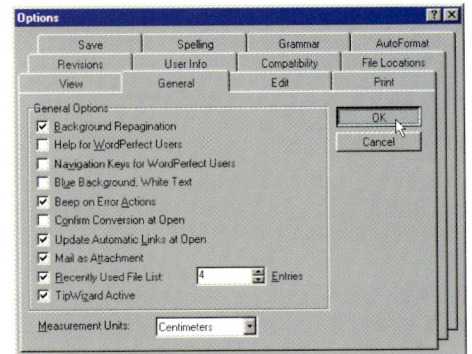

Customizing Toolbars, Menus, and Shortcut Keys

Word lets you customize your toolbars, menus, or shortcut keys to suit your personal needs. In Chapter 5, on page 112, you were shown how to assign a macro to a button on a toolbar. Using the same procedure you can also assign other items to a toolbar, such as a command, a style, a font, an AutoText entry, or a special character. You can further optimize your Word application by customizing your menus and shortcut keys in a similar fashion. Let's suppose you want to add a new command to your *File* menu that closes all the Word for Windows files that are currently open on the screen.

How to Assign a Command to a Menu

1 Choose *Customize* from the *Tools* menu.

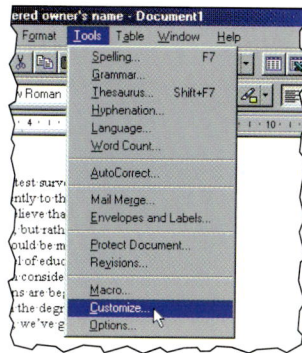

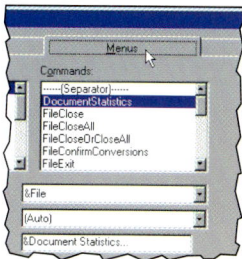

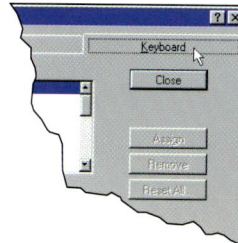

2 When the *Customize* dialog box appears, click on the *Menus* tab to display the *Menus* flipcard.

3 In the *Categories* box, choose the category into which the new command falls — because the new command has to do with files, leave *File* highlighted. In the *Commands* box, choose *FileCloseAll* as the command you want to assign to your menu. In the *Change What Menu* box, leave *&File* as the menu to which you want to assign the new command. In the *Position on Menu* box, leave *(Auto)*, which means similar menu items will automatically be grouped together.

In the *Save Changes In* box, leave *Normal* highlighted so the new command is stored as part of the Normal template. Click on *Add*, then click on *Close*. You'll find the new *Close All* command on your *File* menu.

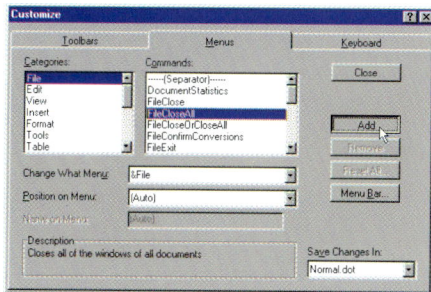

CUSTOMIZING SHORTCUT KEY ASSIGNMENTS

Let's assume that you use the copyright symbol regularly in your letters — perhaps because you work for the music industry. Currently, you have to choose *Symbol* from the *Insert* menu, and then click on the copyright symbol or remember the keyboard combination Alt+Ctrl+C. You can considerably speed up this routine task by assigning the copyright symbol to an easy-to-remember key combination. This is how you do it:

How to Assign a Keyboard Shortcut to a Common Symbol

1 Choose *Customize* from the *Tools* menu.

2 When the *Customize* dialog box appears, click on the *Keyboard* tab.

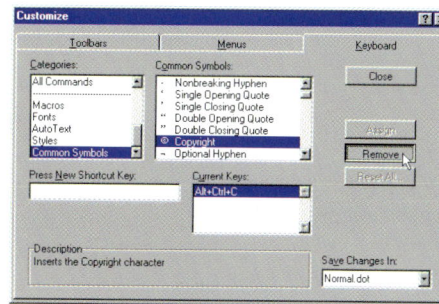

3 In the *Categories* box of the *Keyboard* flipcard, choose *Common Symbols*. Then choose © *Copyright* in the *Common Symbols* box. The *Current Keys* box reveals that a shortcut key for © already exists — *Alt+Ctrl+C* — too long for your taste. In the *Current Keys* box, highlight *Alt+Ctrl+C*, and then click on *Remove* as shown here. Click in the *Press New Shortcut Key* box, and press *Alt+C* on your keyboard — this is the combination to which you want the copyright symbol assigned. The *Currently Assigned To* box reveals whether the key combination you've designated is already assigned. In this case, it states that it is *unassigned*. Make sure the *Save Changes In* box is set to *Normal*. Click on *Assign*, and then on *Close*.

Now you simply press Alt and C together whenever you want the copyright symbol inserted in a Word document.

Equipment suppliers:

The facsimile machine on
page 105 was supplied by
Panasonic, UK; all other
computer equipment was
supplied by Mesh, London,
UK. The type blocks on pages
88-89 were loaned by James
Robinson, Covent Garden,
London, UK. The shoe
photographed on page 67 was
supplied by Hobbs, UK, and
the boot on page 67 is courtesy
of Shelleys Shoes, UK.